Thomas' Midwest Rail-Trails Travel Guide

By J. F. Thomas

THREE RIVERS PUBLIC LIBRARY
25207 W. CHANNON DRIVE
P.O. BOX 300
CHANNAHON, IL 60410-0300

###############

Geneva Publishers, Inc.

Copyright © 1998 by Geneva Publishers, Inc.

All rights reserved. No part of this book may be reproduced in any form or by any electronic or mechanical means, including storage and retrieval systems, without permission in writing from the publisher: Geneva Publishers, Inc., P. O. Box 926 Williams Bay, WI 53191

Interior design and layout by Mary Tomasello

Maps and cover by Dave Conant

ISBN 0-9633842-1-X

Printed in the United States of America

10 9 8 7 6 5 4 3 2 1

PLEASE NOTE:

This book has been designed to expose recreational travel enthusiasts to Midwest Railroad Corridors that have been converted for recreational use. The author has gone to great lengths to gather the most current and accurate information pertaining to the rail-trails listed in this book. Nonetheless, there may be some errors in content as well as typography, therefore this book is intended as a general guide. The publisher, author and designer shall have no liability or responsibility to any person or entity with respect to any damages caused by the information contained in this book.

DEDICATION

To Mary, who merely made this all possible.

CONTENTS

INTRODUCTION iv

HOW TO USE TRAVEL GUIDE vi

TRAIL SAFETY AND ETIQUETTE vii

ILLINOIS 1
Constitution Trail 6
Fox River Trail 9
Great Western Trail 12
Illinois Prairie Path 15
Long Prairie Trail 19
McHenry County Prairie Trail 22
Virgil Gilman Nature Trail 25

IOWA 28
Cedar Valley Nature Trail 33
Chichaqua Valley Trail 36
Heart of Iowa Nature Trail 39
Heritage Trail 42
Hoover Nature Trail 45
Kewash Nature Trail 48
Prairie Farmer Recreational Trail 51
Raccoon River Valley Trail 54
Sauk Trail 57
Wabash Trace Nature Trail 60

MICHIGAN 63
Bergland to Sidnaw Rail Trail 68
Bill Nicholls Trail 71
Hancock/Calumet Trail 74
Hart-Montague 77
Kal-Haven Trail 80
Paint Creek Trailway 83
Pere Marquette Rail-Trail of Mid-Michigan 86
Stateline Trail 89

CONTENTS

MINNESOTA 92
Cannon Valley Trail 97
Douglas State Trail 100
Heartland State Trail 103
Luce Line Trail 106
Paul Bunyan Trail 109
Root River State Trail 112
Sakatah Singing Hills State Trail 115
Soo Line Trail 118
Willard Munger State Trail 121

WISCONSIN 124
"400" State Trail, The 130
Ahnapee State Park Trail 133
Bearskin State Park Trail 136
Cheese Country Recreation Trail 139
Chippewa River State Trail 142
Elroy-Sparta State Park Trail 145
Gandy Dancer Trail 148
Glacial Drumlin State Park Trail 151
Great River State Park Trail 154
La Crosse River State Park Trail 157
Military Ridge State Park Trail 160
Mountain-Bay Trail 163
Omaha Trail 166
Pine Line 169
Red Cedar State Trail 172
Sugar River State Park Trail 175
Tuscobia State Trail 178
Wild Goose State Trail 181

OTHER TRAILS 184

ILLINOIS 184

IOWA 188

MICHIGAN 193

MINNESOTA 203

WISCONSIN 206

Introduction

The early 1900's marked the heyday of railroading in the United States. More than 300,000 miles of track crisscrossed this country. It was the most extensive railroad transportation system in the world, reaching from coast to coast and from border to border.

As the use of railroads waned and the use of automobiles increased, the need for such a network of tracks was in jeopardy. In fact, by the late 1950's, nearly two thirds of all railroad tracks were out of service. Today, only 50% of the original track system still exist. Cars, trucks, buses and airplanes continue to lead to the decline of the railroad industry, resulting in Railroad Lines continuing to abandon more than 2,000 miles of track every year.

Beginning in the Midwest in the late 1960's, this phenomenon set the stage for a new movement whose goal was to keep these abandoned railroad beds in the hands of the public for recreational paths. This movement became known as "rails to trails." The rail corridors, once removed of tracks, allowed local residents to use them for recreation. Competition for the abandoned corridors intensified, as developers and adjacent landowners immediately recognized their value.

The move to preserve the abandoned railroad corridor and convert them for public use spread from the Midwest to the entire country. In 1983 Congress passed the most significant piece of legislation, aiding agencies and local groups to acquire abandoned railroad corridors. It enacted an amendment to the National Trail Systems Act directing the Surface Transportation Board to allow "Railbanking." Simply put, this act allowed the rail corridor to be set aside for future transportation use while being used as recreational trails during the interim. This legislation greatly assisted agencies and local groups to acquire rail corridors for use as recreational trails.

In 1986, the Rails-to-Trails Conservancy (RTC) was formed, giving the rail-trail movement a national voice. While continually working to defend the new railbanking laws, RTC has simultaneously assisted public agencies and local rail-trail groups throughout this country in the conversion process. Currently, there are over 900 converted rail-trails in the U.S. totaling 10,000 miles.

Future Projected trail conversions total 1,200, which translates to over 18,000 miles of recreational rail-trails. The Conservancies ultimate vision of creating an interconnected network of trails across the United States is becoming a reality.

The rail-trails gentle grading and diverse scenery traverse through urban, suburban and rural areas across this country. The trails link homes to work, shopping, schools and recreation by providing a transportation corridor. Uses allowed on individual trails are based on their surfaces as established by the individual trail management.

There are a number of invaluable benefits of rail-trails. One main benefit of rail-trail use is recreational. They are used year round by recreational enthusiasts, bicyclists (mountain and road), snowmobilers, cross-country skiers, walkers, hikers, horseback riders and in-line skaters. Depending on the season and climate, the trail may be used by one or all of the recreational activities previously listed.

The trail experience is enhanced by the recognition of historic structures that line the trail. Historic structures such as, bridges, train stations tunnels, mills, canals and factories. Knowledge of the various railroad lines that traveled the corridor from its inception further enhances the users ability to enjoy this trail experience.

The final benefit of the rail-trail is the wildlife that can be viewed from the trail. Birds, plants, wetlands and in some cases, endangered animal species are located along the rail-trail. Many trails serve as plant and animal conservation corridors.

These are only some of the most obvious benefits of rail-trail usage. These benefits coupled to those that the trail user may discover, creates a "dream come true" rail-trail experience.

HOW TO USE THIS RAIL-TRAIL TRAVEL GUIDE

At the start of each state, you will find a map of the state depicting the approximate location of the rail-trails featured for that state. The rail-trail number listed in the state map corresponds to the rail-trail listed for that state. The following glossary of text headings appear in each chapter:

Trail Uses: Permitted recreational trail uses.
Trail Heads: The endpoints of the trail. Usually identified by the city or towns nearby.
Length of Trail: Indicates the length of the trail.
Surface: The materials that make up the rail-trail surface.
Grade: The slope or pitch of the rail-trail.
Date Established: Year trail was converted for recreational use.
Trail Name Origin: The source of the name.
Trail Highlights: Notable features of the trail.
Future Plans: Trail expansion or future links to other trails.
Suggested Auto Routes: Direct auto routes from metropolitan areas to trail heads.
Additional Information Sources: Names addresses and phone numbers of area contacts that have access to additional information about the trail: Trail Managers, Chambers of Commerce, Commerce, Tourism Offices and etc.
Internet Website: Trail website found on the World Wide Web.

Every rail-trail depicted in this travel guide has its own special features and characteristics; the above headings will assist in understanding the differences. The trail manager in light of the trail surface determines the uses permitted on each rail-trail. Trails permitting bicycle use may also be used for mountain bicycling. Trails that only list mountain bicycling are not suitable for road bicycling due to the rough terrain. Mountain bicycling use is limited to the trail and not permitted on adjacent areas.

TRAIL SAFETY AND ETIQUETTE

As we discussed earlier, a variety of recreational trail users utilize rail-trails. It is the responsibility of those who use the rail-trail to exercise caution. Only by constantly exercising caution while on the trail can trail users help prevent unforeseen accidents from occurring.

The most common trail courtesy rule is "Wheels yield to heels." This rule translates to Bicyclists and in-line skaters yield to the heel user: hiker, walker etc. Pedestrians always yield to the horseback rider. Warning users ahead of you of your presence and or passing intention could prevent an accident from occurring. Certainly, slowing down prior to passing and making verbal contact of your intentions is an absolute requirement. Also observe the following rail-trail safety and etiquette guidelines:

>Always look ahead and behind when passing.
>Be aware of traffic environment.
>Be aware of hills or bumps in the trail.
>Be alert for dogs or other animals along the trail.
>Descend downgrades slowly.
>Do not disturb wildlife or wild plants.
>Do not eat wild berries.
>Do not speed.
>Do not trespass on private property.
>Do not block traffic on bridges.
>Exercise caution on wet trail surfaces during heavy rains.
>Obey all posted trail rules.
>Observe the passing warning protocol: "Passing on your Left."
>Pull to the far right or off the trail when stopping.
>Put all litter in proper receptacles.
>Ride or walk on the right side of the trail.
>"STOP & LOOK" when crossing streets and roads.
>Use a pet leash of 8-feet or less.
>Wear bright colored clothing.
>Yield to other trail users when entering or crossing the trail.

Illinois

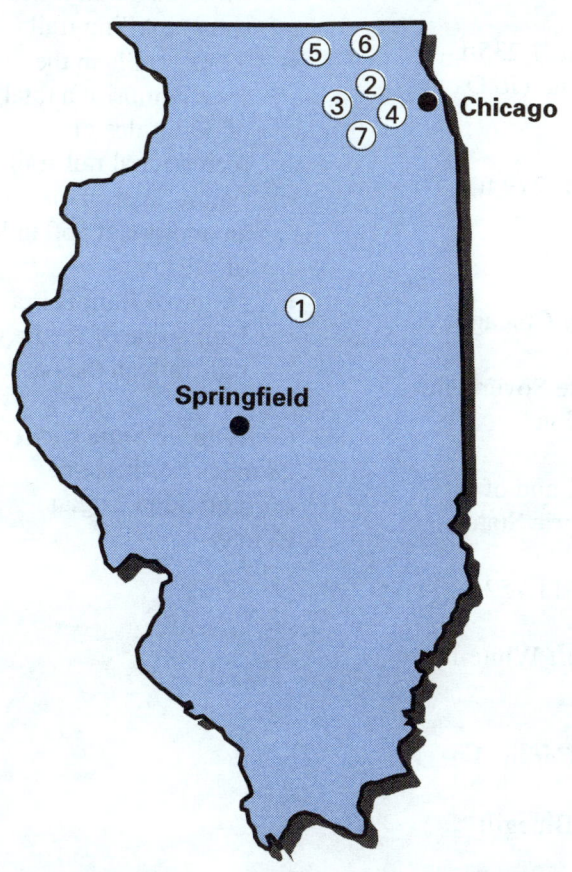

#1 Constitution
#2 Fox River
#3 Great Western
#4 Illinois Prairie Path
#5 Long Prairie
#6 McHenry County
#7 Virgil Gilman

FACTS ABOUT ILLINOIS

Capital: Springfield

Elevation:
Highest Point: 1,235ft.
Charles Mound (Jo Daviess Co.)

Lowest Point: 279 ft.
Mississippi River
(Alexander Co.)

Largest City: Chicago

Motto: "State Sovereignty, National Union"

Nickname: Land of Lincoln; Prairie State

Population: 11,752,000

State Animal: White-tailed Deer

State Bird: Cardinal

State Fish: Bluegill

State Flower: Native Violet

State Tree: White Oak

Statehood: December 3, 1818 (21st state)

Time Zone: Central DST

Boasting Rights:
- More than 300 miles of snowmobiling trails.
- 32 rail-trails in the state comprise a total of 357 miles of recreational rail-trails.
- Future plans to develop an additional 550 miles of rail-trails.
- Home to Illinois Prairie Path – one of the first rail-trails in the nation.

Geographic State Center:
28 miles northeast of Springfield in Logan County

PLACES OF INTEREST

Apple River Canyon State Park: Near Warren; trails.
Baha'i House of Worship: In Wilmette; noted architecture.
Cahokia Court House State Memorial: In Cahokia; possibly the oldest building in Midwest (1737).
Cahokia Mounds State Park: Near East St. Louis; Monk's Mound; possibly the largest prehistoric Indian site in nation.
Carlyle Lake: Near Carlyle; 20,000-acre (8,094-hectare) lake and recreation region.
Chain O' Lakes State Park: Near McHenry; lake and recreation region.
Chicago Historical Society: In Chicago; museum and reference library; Lincoln Collection.
Chicago Portage National Historic Site: Near Chicago; portion of the famous portage discovered by Marquette and Joliet and used by French and American pioneers.
Chicago Zoological Park (Brookfield Zoo): In Brookfield; animals in natural settings.
Crab Orchard National Wildlife Refuge: Near Carbondale and Marion; lake and recreation region.
Dickson Mounds State Memorial: Near Havana; archaeology museum of American Indian.
Douglas Tomb State Memorial: In Chicago; honors Stephen A. Douglas.
Early American Museum and Botanical Garden: Near Mahomet; collection of pioneer life; waterfall.
Elijah Lovejoy Monument: In Alton; honors abolitionist editor.
Fort de Chartres State Park: Near Prairie du Rocher; restored early fort.
Fort Kaskaskia State Park: Near Chester; fort built by French during French and Indian War.
Galena: Old Market House State Memorial; Ulysses S. Grant Home; noted local architecture.
Giant City State Park: Near Makanda; huge blocks of stone in Illinois Ozarks.
Illinois State Museum: In Springfield; exhibits on natural and social sciences.
John G. Shedd Aquarium: In Chicago; exhibits of fresh- and saltwater fishes, mammals, reptiles, and invertebrates.
Kankakee River State Park: Near Kankakee; woodlands and canyons.
Lake Shelbyville: Near Shelbyville; lake and recreation region.

Lincoln Home National Historic Site: In Springfield; Abraham Lincoln's residence from 1844 to 1861.
Lincoln Park: In Chicago; conservatory and zoo.
Lincoln Trail State Memorial: Near Lawrenceville; figure of Lincoln stands on the site where he and family entered state in 1830.
Lincoln's New Salem State Park: Near Petersburg; restored village; Lincoln's home from 1831 to 1837.
Lowden Memorial State Park: Near Oregon; Chief Black Hawk statue on Rock River.
Metamora Court House State Memorial: In Metamora; here Lincoln practiced law.
Mississippi Palisades State Park: Near Savanna; scenic riverside cliffs.
Nauvoo State Park: In Nauvoo; Mormon settlement from 1839 to 1846; Joseph Smith home.
Oak Park: Residential suburb of Chicago; birthplace of author Ernest Hemingway; works of architect Frank Lloyd Wright.
Pere Marquette State Park: Near Grafton; here Marquette and Joliet entered the Illinois River in 1673.
Pierre Menard Home State Memorial: Near Chester; home of first lieutenant governor, friend of Indian and pioneer.
Pullman: Chicago historic district; railroad car company built by George M. Pullman in 1890's.
Rend Lake: Near Benton and Mount Vernon; lake and recreation region.
Shawnee National Forest: In southern Illinois; 240,000-acre (97,000-hectare) preserve with lakes and recreation sites.
Shawneetown State Memorial: In Shawneetown; early gateway to Illinois.
Starved Rock State Park: Near Utica; rock formations and canyons.
Vandalia State House State Memorial: In Vandalia; capitol building built in 1836.
Woodstock: In McHenry County; Old McHenry Courthouse (1857-58); Opera House (1889-90); Spring house, built over a mineral spring in 1873.

Additional information sources:
Road Conditions Hotline
(312) 368-4636
(217) 782-5730
(800) 452-4368 (Nov-Apr)

Road Construction Hotline
(800) 452-4368 (May-Oct)

Illinois Bureau of Tourism
100 West Randolph Street,
Suite 3-400
Chicago, IL 60601
(800) 226-6632
(312) 814-4732

Web Page
http://www.state.il.us/

TRAIL COUNTIES

***Constitution*:** McLean

•

***Fox River*:** Kane, McHenry

•

***Great Western*:** DeKalb, Kane

•

***Illinois Prairie Path*:** Cook, DuPage, Kane

•

***Long Prairie*:** Boone

•

***McHenry County Prairie*:** McHenry

•

***Virgil Gilman*:** Kane

WEATHER CONDITIONS

	Temperature				Precipitation (inches)	
	Chicago		Springfield			
	High	Low	High	Low	*Chgo	Sprng
JAN	31	17	35	19	10S	6S
FEB	34	20	39	22	7S	6S
MAR	45	29	49	30	7S	5S
APR	59	40	64	43	3	4
MAY	70	50	74	53	3	4
JUNE	79	60	83	62	4	4
JULY	83	65	87	66	4	4
AUG	82	64	85	64	3	3
SEPT	75	56	79	56	3	3
OCT	65	46	68	45	3	3
NOV	48	33	51	33	2	2
DEC	35	22	38	23	10S	5S

*Chgo – Chicago; Sprng – Springfield; S - Snow

CONSTITUTION TRAIL

Trail Uses: Bicycling, Hiking, In-line Skating and Cross-country Skiing

Trail Heads:
North - Normal
South - Bloomington

Surface: Asphalt

Grade: 2 %

Length of Trail: 13 miles

Date Established: 1987

Trail Name Origin:
Name was chosen to commemorate the two hundredth anniversary of the signing of the Constitution.

Trail Highlights:
- Former Illinois Central Gulf Railroad line.
- South access begins a short distance from Illinois State University campus.
- Trail provides scenic views of neighborhoods, parks and prairie landscape. Also offers access to nearby shops.
- Portions of the trail are adjacent to Sugar Creek.

Future Plan:
Extend trail to encircle the city of Bloomington and extend from Normal City Hall to Lake Bloomington.

Suggested Auto Routes

Chicago to Normal		
Road	Direction	Miles
I-90 to I-55	S	2.3
I-55 to US51	SW	128.1
US51	S	1.8
TOTAL: 132.2 miles; 2 hours 10 minutes		

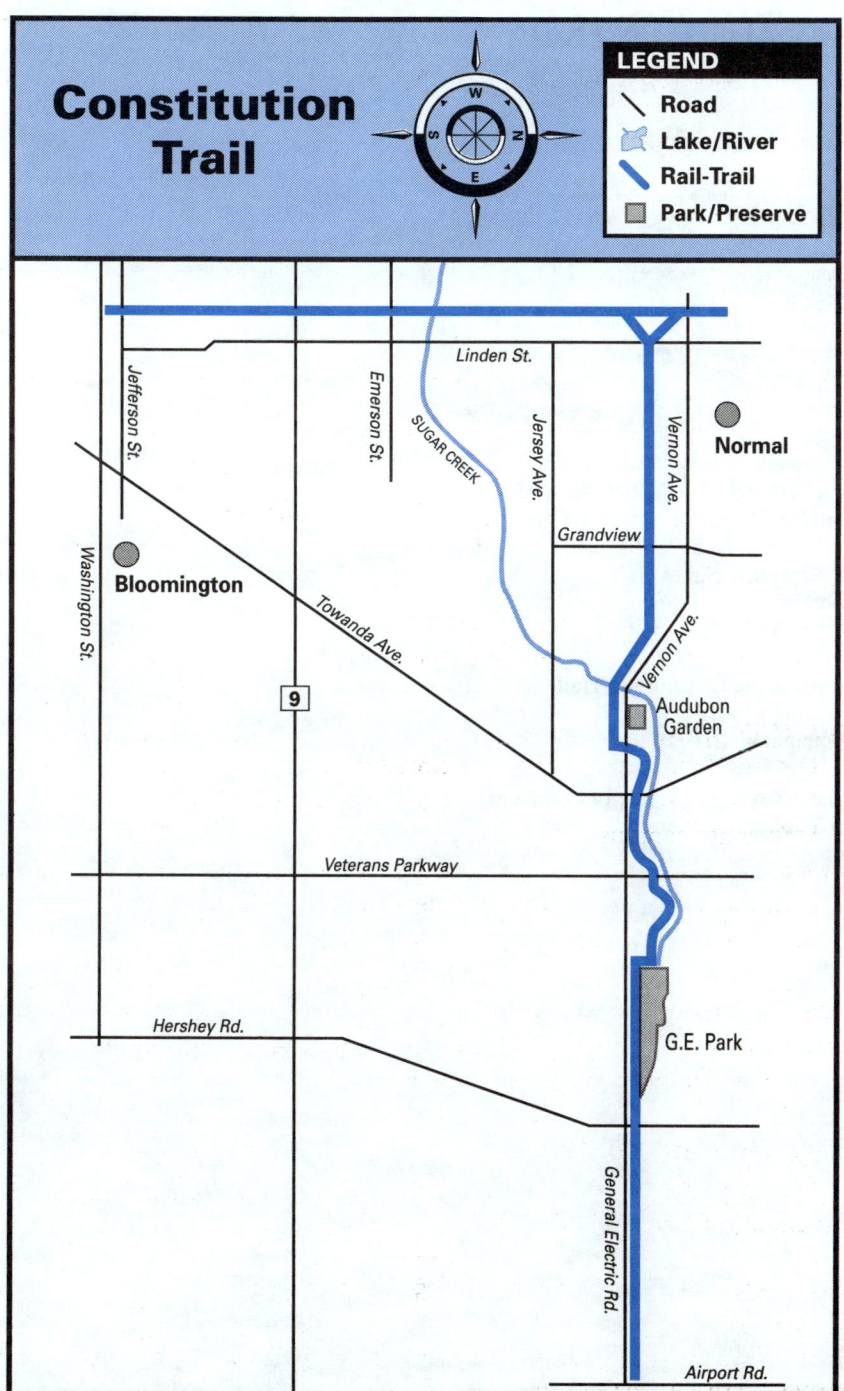

CONSTITUTION TRAIL

Auto Routes (cont.)

Springfield to Normal		
Road	Direction	Miles
9th St to Peoria	N	2
Peoria to I-55	NE	5.8
I-55 to US51	NE	53
US51	N	3.9
TOTAL: 64.7 miles; 1 hour 3 minutes		

Additional information sources:

Keith Rich, Director
Bloomington Parks & Recreation Department
109 East Olive Street
Bloomington, IL 61701
(309) 823-4260

Friends of the Constitution Trail
P. O. Box 4494
Bloomington, IL 61702

McLean County Chamber of Commerce
210 South East Street
Bloomington, IL 61702
(309) 829-6344

# FOX RIVER TRAIL

Trail Uses: Bicycling, Hiking, Horseback Riding, In-line Skating and Cross-country Skiing

Trail Heads:
North - Crystal Lake
South - Aurora

Surface: Asphalt

Grade: Level

Length of Trail: 41 miles

Date Established: 1978

Trail Name Origin:
Derived from the Fox River, which parallels most of the trail.

Trail Highlights:
- Former Chicago Northwestern and Aurora & Elgin Railroad lines.
- Trail provides the users with a scenic blend of historic towns, parks, forest preserves, original railroad structures, antique shops and access to the tourist center.
- A unique Trail bridge crosses over the Fox River and under Interstate 90.
- Links with Illinois Prairie Path, Great Western Trail and Virgil Gilman Trail.

Suggested Auto Routes

Chicago to Crystal Lake		
Road	Direction	Miles
I-90 to ST53	NW	25
ST53 to US14	NE	3.1
US14	NW	16.3
TOTAL: 44.4 miles; 1hour 12 minutes		

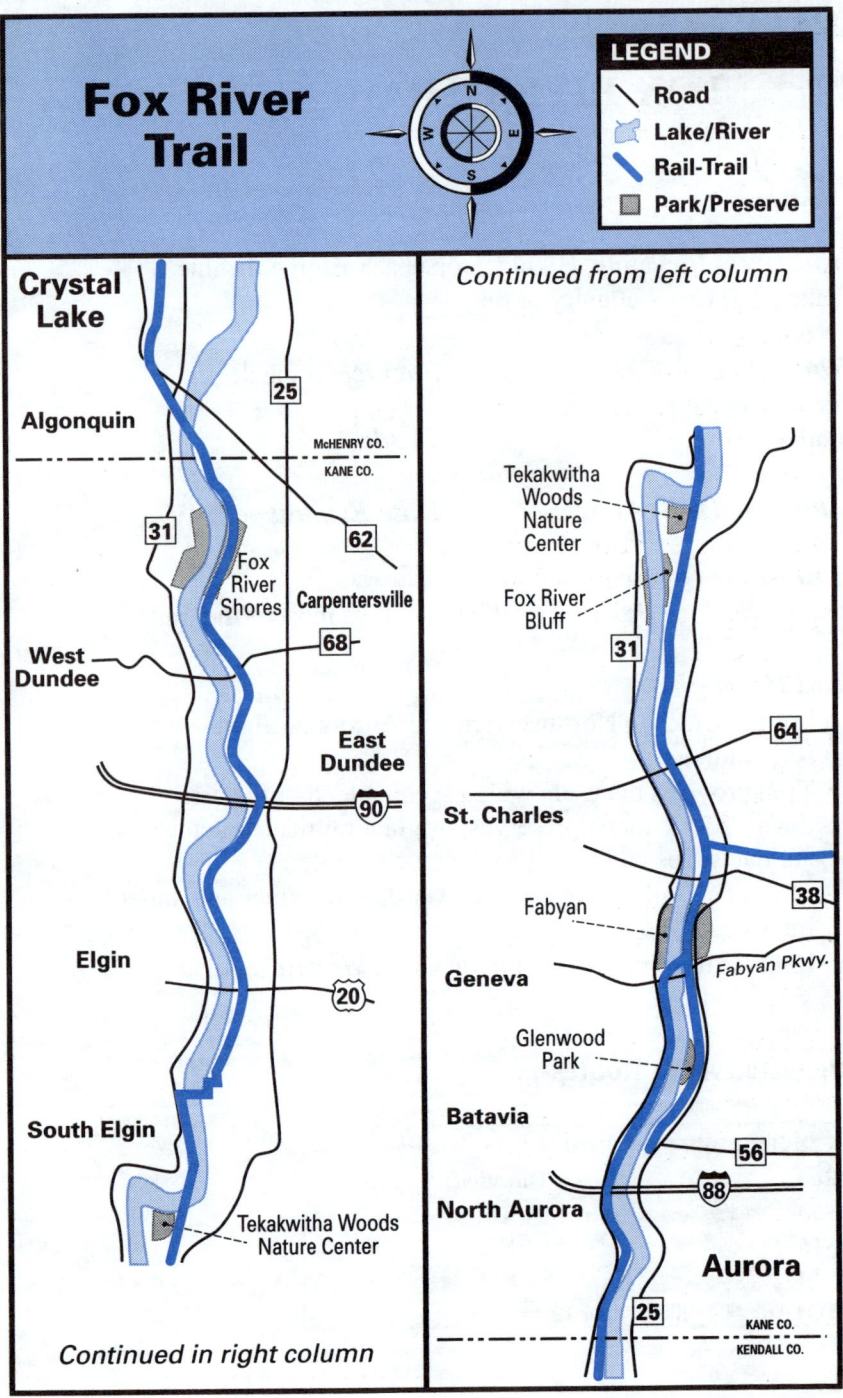

FOX RIVER TRAIL

Auto Routes (cont.)

Springfield to Aurora		
Road	Direction	Miles
9th St to Peoria	N	2
Peoria to I-55	NE	5.8
I-55 to US30	NE	150.6
US30 to Hill Ave	NW	11
Hill Ave to Aurora Ave	N	2.5
Aurora Ave	W	2.3
TOTAL: 174.2 miles; 3 hours, 19 minutes		

Additional information sources:
Jon J. Duerr, Director of Field Services
Kane County Forest Preserve
719 Batavia Avenue
Geneva, IL 60134
(630) 232-5981

Bill Donnell, Landscape Architect
Fox Valley Park District
712 South River Street
Aurora, IL 60507
(630) 897-0516

Greater Aurora Chamber of Commerce
40 West Downer Place
Aurora, IL 60507
(630) 897-9214

Crystal Lake Chamber of Commerce
427 Virginia
Crystal Lake, IL 60014
(815) 459-1300
(815) 459-0243 FAX

 # GREAT WESTERN TRAIL

Trail Uses: Bicycling, Horseback Riding, Cross-country Skiing and Snowmobiling

Trail Heads:
West - Sycamore
East - St. Charles

Length of Trail: 18 miles
Adjacent Equestrian trail

Surface: Asphalt & Crushed Limestone

Grade: Flat

Date Established: 1979

Trail Name Origin:
Trail was named after the former railroad.

Trail Highlights:
- Former Chicago Great Western Railroad
- Wooded trail winds through farmlands, residences, wetlands and crosses small streams.
- Considered one of the most rural rail-trails in the suburban Chicago area.
- Trail links with the fox River Trail.

Suggested Auto Routes

Springfield to St Charles		
Road	Direction	Miles
9th St. to Peoria	N	2
Peoria to I-55	NE	5.8
I-55 to US30	NE	150.6
US30 to Hill Ave.	NW	11
Hill Ave. to Aurora Ave.	N	2.5
Aurora Ave. to ST31	W	2.3
ST31	N	10.3
Total: 184.5 miles; 3 hours, 44 minutes		

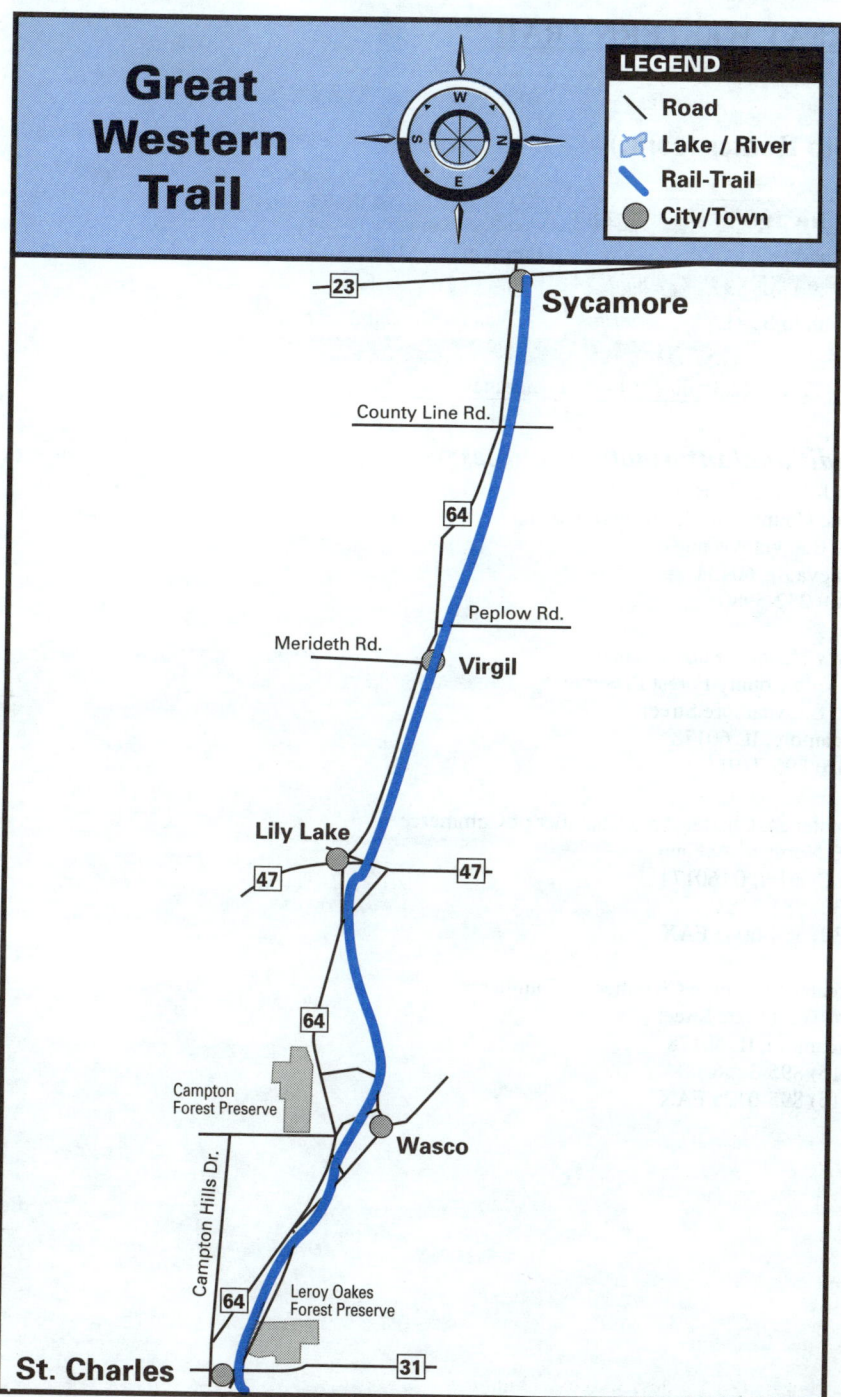

GREAT WESTERN TRAIL

Auto Routes (cont.)

Chicago to St. Charles

Road	Direction	Miles
I-290 to I-88	W	14.1
I-88 to ST31	W	20.2
ST31	N	8
TOTAL: 42.3 miles, 1 hour, 11 minutes		

Additional information sources:

Jon J. Duerr, Superintendent
Kane County Forest Preserve District
719 Batavia Avenue
Geneva, IL 60134
(630) 232-5980

Terry Hannan, Superintendent
DeKalb County Forest Preserve
110 E. Sycamore Street
Sycamore, IL 60178
(815) 895-7191

Greater St. Charles Area Chamber of Commerce
103 North 1st Avenue
St. Charles, IL 60174
(630) 584-8384
(630) 584-6065 FAX

Greater Sycamore Chamber of Commerce
206 West State Street
Sycamore, IL 60178
(815) 895-3456
(815) 895-0125 FAX

ILLINOIS PRAIRIE PATH

Trail Uses: Bicycling, Hiking, Horseback Riding and Cross-country Skiing

Trail Heads:
West - Wheaton
East - Maywood

Length of Trail: 55 miles

Surface: Crushed Stone & Asphalt

Grade: 2%

Date Established: 1965

Trail Name Origin:
May Theilgaard Watts, a distinguished naturalist, teacher and author sent a letter to the Chicago Tribune in 1963 outlining a proposal to convert abandoned railroad areas to "Prairie Paths" established for recreational use. The letter inspired a small group of advocates to make the idea a reality.

Trail Highlights:
- Former Chicago Aurora & Elgin Railroad Electric line.
- The trail winds through the suburbs, scenic prairie areas and two county forest preserves.
- Spurs to Aurora, Batavia, Elgin and Geneva.
- Trail users may visit the restored Clintonville Station in South Elgin (a model railroad club) and the R.E.L.I.C. Trolley Museum.
- Designated as a National Recreation Trail.
- Nation's first rail-trail conversion.
- Links with the Great Western and Fox River Trails.

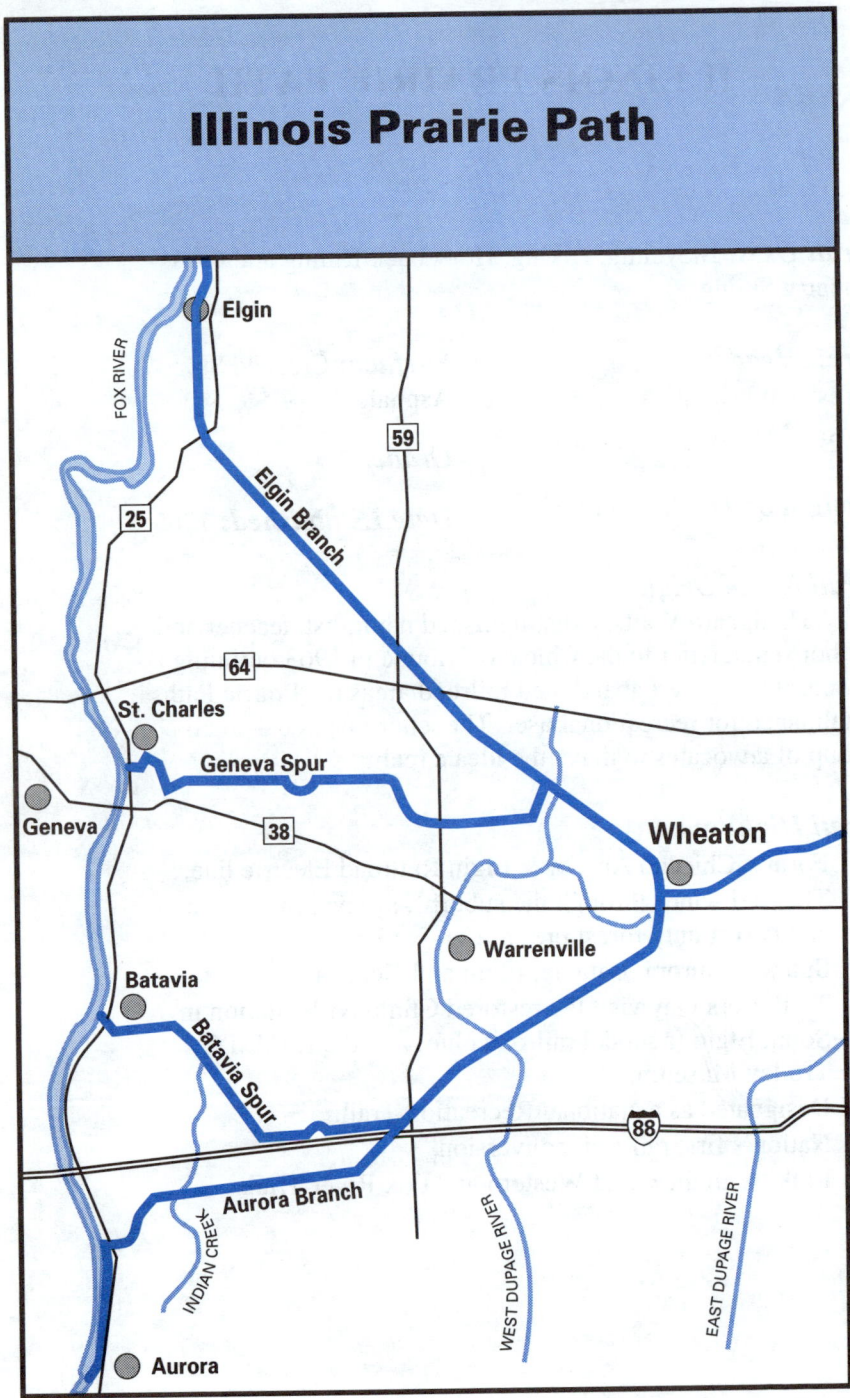

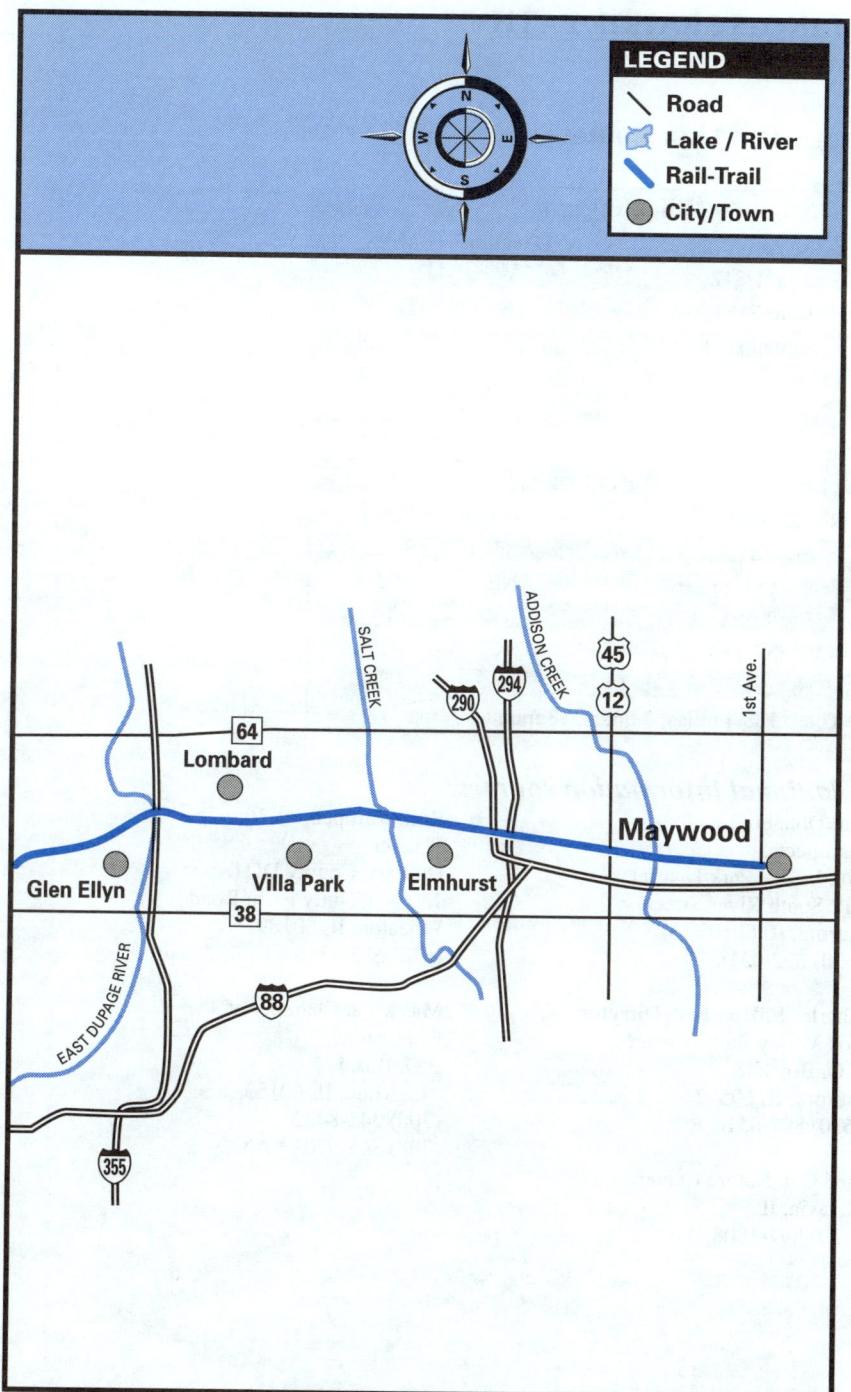

ILLINOIS PRAIRIE PATH

Suggested Auto Routes

Chicago to Wheaton

Road	Direction	Miles
I-290 to US12	W	12.8
US12 to Roosevelt Hwy	S	.5
Roosevelt Hwy to ST38	W	3.9
ST38	W	8.8
Total: 26 miles, 30 minutes		

Springfield to Wheaton

Road	Direction	Miles
9th St. to Peoria	N	2
Peoria to I-55	NE	5.8
I-55 to I-355	NE	160.6
I-355 to ST38	N	12.6
ST38	W	7.4
Total: 188.4 miles, 3 hours, 18 minutes		

Additional information sources:

Bill Donnell, Landscape
Architect
Fox Valley Park District
712 South River Street
Aurora, IL 60507
(630) 897-0516

Charles E. Hoscheit, Director
Fox Valley Park District
P.O. Box 818
Aurora, IL 60507
(630) 897-0516

Red Oak Nature Center
Batavia, IL
(630) 897-1808

Ruth Karupensky, Principal
Planner
Du Page County DOT
130 N. County Farm Road
Wheaton, IL 60189
(630) 682-7318

Maywood Chamber of
Commerce
P.O. Box 172
Maywood, IL 60153
(708) 345-8422
(708) 345-9701 FAX

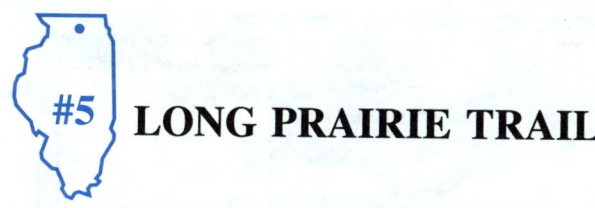

#5 LONG PRAIRIE TRAIL

Trail Uses: Bicycling, Hiking, In-line Skating and Cross-country Skiing

Trail Heads:
West - Poplar Grove
East - County Line Road, Capron

Length of Trail: 14.2 miles

Surface: Asphalt

Grade: 1-2% Grade

Date Established: 1989

Trail Name Origin:
Trail passes through the town of Capron, formerly called Long Prairie

Trail Highlights:
- Chicago Northwestern Railroad
- Trail offers users scenic views of peat bogs, fens, prairies and rolling terrain

Future Plan:
Extend trail west through Boone County to link with Stone Bridge Trail, which will continue to the Wisconsin border.

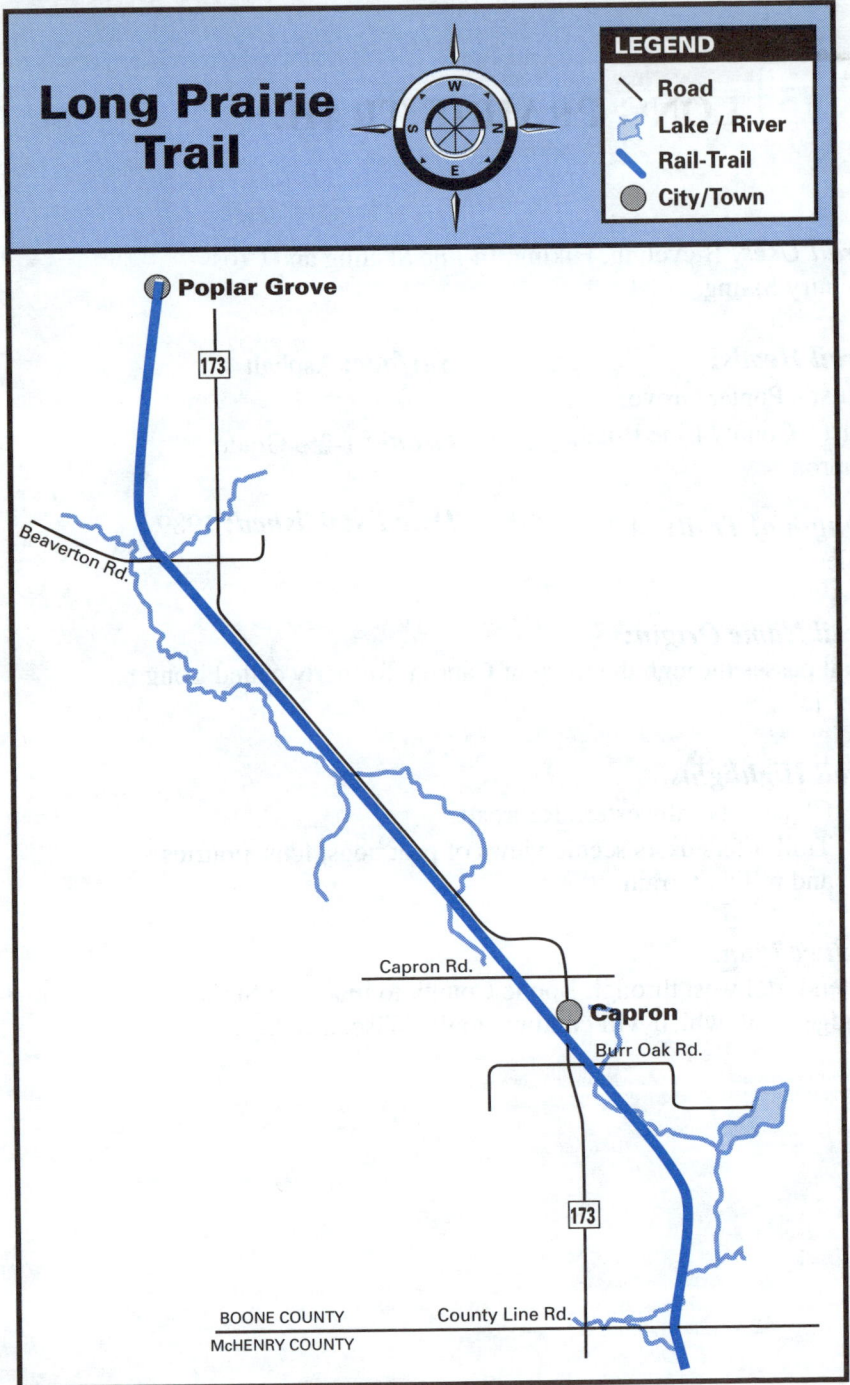

LONG PRAIRIE TRAIL

Suggested Auto Routes

Chicago to Capron

Road	Direction	Miles
I-90 to US20	W	49.6
US20 to ST23	NW	10
ST23 to US14	N	10
US14 to ST173	N	2
ST173	W	7.7
Total: 79.3 miles; 1 hour, 20 minutes		

Springfield to Caledonia

Road	Direction	Miles
9th St. to Peoria	N	2
Peoria to I-55	NE	5.8
I-55 to US51	NE	58.7
US51 to I-39	N	36
I-39 to I-90	N	89.8
I-90 to US20	N	1.6
US20 to ST76	E	6
ST76	N	7.8
Total: 207.7 miles; 3 hours, 15 minutes		

Additional information sources:
John Kremer, Executive Director
Boone County Conservation District
7600 Appleton Road
Belvidere, IL 61008
(815) 547-7935

#6 MCHENRY COUNTY PRAIRIE TRAIL

Trail Uses:
North Segment - Bicycling, Horseback Riding, Hiking, Cross-country Skiing and Snowmobiling.
South Segment - Bicycling, Hiking, In-line Skating and Cross-country Skiing

Trail Heads:
North Segment:
North - Richmond
South - Ringwood

South Segment:
South - Algonquin
North - Crystal Lake

Length of Trail:
North - 7.5 miles
South - 7 miles

Surface:
North - Dirt & Ballast
South - Asphalt

Grade: Level

Date Established:
North - 1987
South - 1988

Trail Name Origin:
Trail was named for its location in McHenry County and the rich prairie landscape surrounding the trail.

Trail Highlights:
- Former Chicago & Northwestern Railroad.
- North segment crosses streams over original railroad bridges and offers easy access to Glacial Park home to Northern Illinois' most scenic wetlands.
- South segment is surrounded by formerly mined gravel pits and crosses the Fox River in Algonquin.
- South segment links to Fox River Trail.

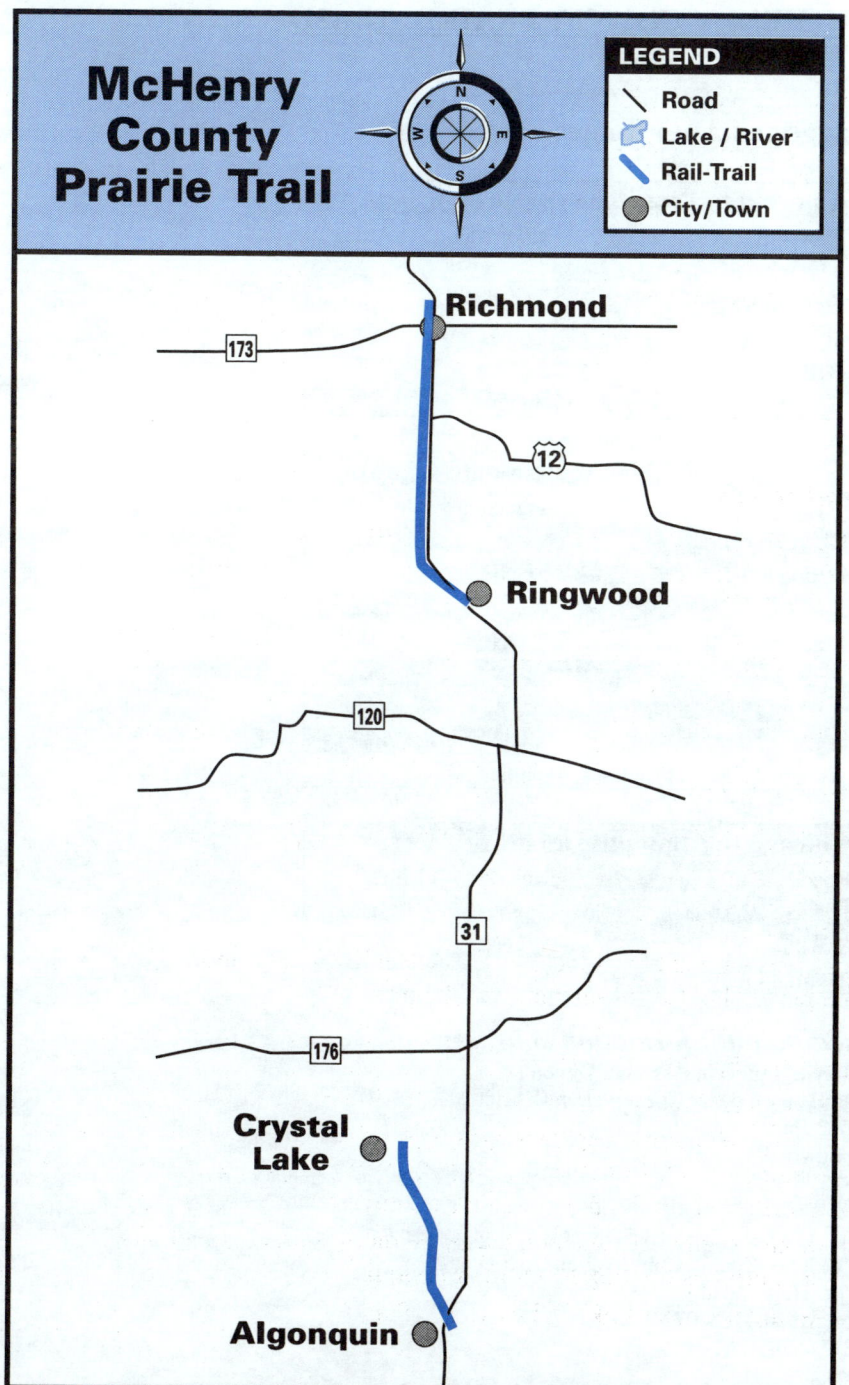

MC HENRY COUNTY PRAIRIE TRAIL

Suggested Auto Routes

Chicago to Ringwood (North Segment)

Roads	Direction	Miles
I-90 to ST53	NW	25
ST53 to US14	NE	3.1
US14 to ST31	NW	16.3
ST31	N	12
Total: 56.4 miles; 1 hours, 13 minutes		

Springfield to Algonquin (South Segment)

Road	Direction	Miles
9th St. to Peoria	N	2
Peoria to I-55	NE	5.8
I-55 to I-355	NE	160.6
I-355 to I-290	N	20.3
I-290 to I-90	N	6.6
I-90 to ST31	W	13.3
ST31	N	6.7
Total: 215.3 miles; 3 hours, 46 minutes		

Chicago to Algonquin (South Segment)

Roads	Direction	Miles
I-90 to ST31	NW	38.3
ST31	N	6.7
Total: 45 miles;		

Additional information sources:

Mary Eysenbach, Assistant Director
Mc Henry County Conservation District
6512 Harts Road
Ringwood, IL 60072
(815) 678-4431

Craig Hubert, Executive Director
Mc Henry County Conservation District
6512 Harts Road
Ringwood, IL 60072
(815) 678-4361

#7 VIRGIL L. GILMAN NATURE TRAIL

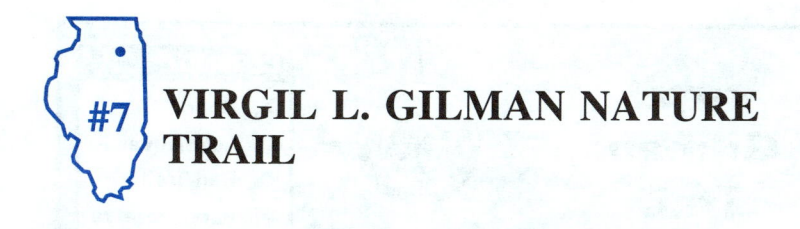

Trail Uses: Bicycling, Hiking, In-line Skating, Cross-country Skiing and Snowmobiling (in designated areas)

Trail Heads:
East - Montgomery
West - Sugar Grove

Length of Trail: 17.3 miles

Surface: Asphalt & Crushed Stone

Grade: Flat

Date Established: 1948

Trail Name:
Named after the first Park District Director.

Trail Highlights:
- Former Elgin, Joliet & Eastern Railroad and Chicago Milwaukee, St. Paul & Pacific Railroad.
- Trail presents a variety of countryside including Blisswood Forest Preserve, Blackberry historic farm village and trestle railroad bridge.
- Designated as a "National Heritage Trail"
- Links with the Fox River Trail.

Suggested Auto Routes

Chicago to Montgomery		
Road	Direction	Miles
I-290 to I-88	W	14.1
I-88 to ST31	W	20.2
ST31	S	5.4
Total: 39.7 miles; 44 minutes		

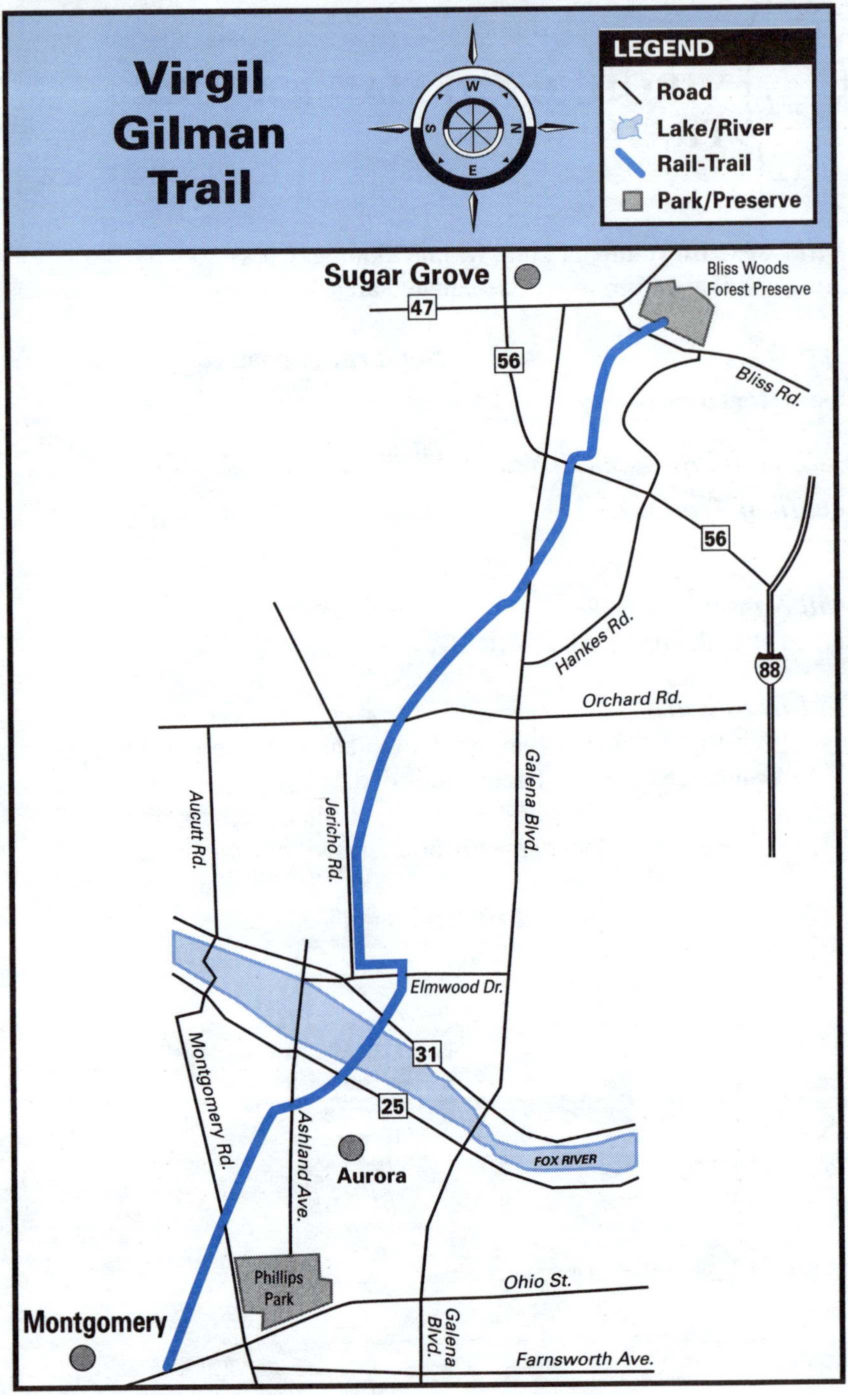
Virgil Gilman Trail
W
S
N
E
LEGEND
Road
Lake/River
Rail-Trail
Park/Preserve
Sugar Grove
47
56
Bliss Woods Forest Preserve
Bliss Rd.
56
Hankes Rd.
88
Orchard Rd.
Aucutt Rd.
Jericho Rd.
Galena Blvd.
Elmwood Dr.
31
25
Montgomery Rd.
Ashland Ave.
Aurora
FOX RIVER
Phillips Park
Ohio St.
Galena Blvd.
Montgomery
Farnsworth Ave.

VIRGIL L. GILMAN NATURE TRAIL

Auto Routes (cont.)

Springfield to Sugar Grove		
Road	Direction	Miles
9th St. to Peoria	N	2
Peoria to I-55	NE	5.8
I-55 to ST47	NE	113.6
ST47	N	47
Total: 168.4 miles; 2 hours, 45 minutes		

Additional information sources:
Bill Donnell, Landscape Architect
Fox Valley Park District
712 South River Street
Aurora, IL 60506
(630) 897-0516

Greater Aurora Chamber of Commerce
40 West Downer Place
Aurora, IL 60507
(630) 897-9214

Iowa

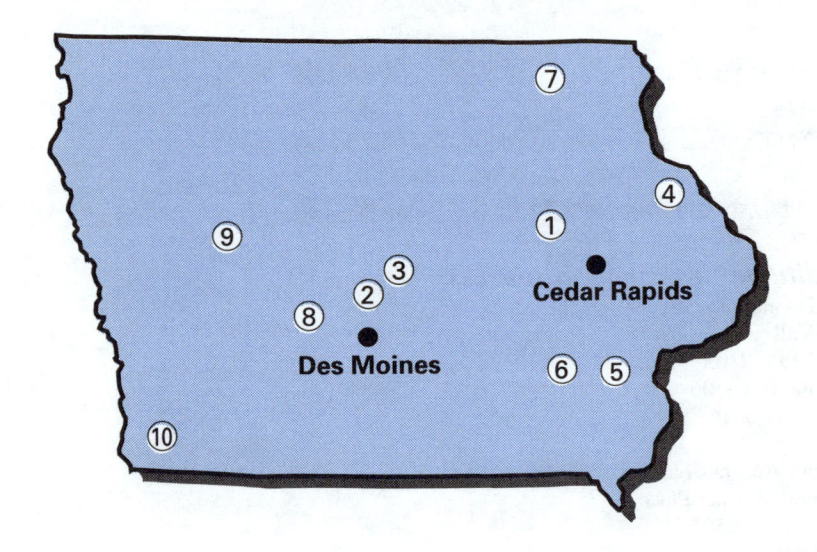

# 1	Cedar Valley	# 6	Kewash
# 2	Chichaqua Valley	# 7	Prairie Farmer
# 3	Heart of Iowa	# 8	Raccoon River Valley
# 4	Heritage	# 9	Sauk
# 5	Hoover	#10	Wabash Trace

FACTS ABOUT IOWA

Capital: Des Moines

Elevation:
Highest Point: Osceola Co. 1,670 ft.

Lowest Point: Mississippi River in Lee Co. 480 ft.

Largest City: Des Moines

Motto: Our liberties we prize and our rights we will maintain

Nickname: Hawkeye State

Population: 2,829,300

State Bird: Goldfinch

State Flower: Wild Rose

State Tree: Oak

Statehood: December 28, 1846 (29th state)

Time Zone: Central DST

Boasting Rights:
- More than 80 state park systems, providing more than 55,00 acres of scenic, historic, and recreation reserves, and lake reserves.
- 49 Rail trails, which comprise 484 miles developed trails.
- Future plans to develop 520 miles of rail-trails adding 520 trail miles.
- A leader in the conversion of railroads to recreational trail.

Geographic Center:
Story 5 miles northeast of Ames

PLACES OF INTEREST

Amana Colonies: Amana and six other villages in Iowa River valley; founded by German sect in 1855.
Backbone State Park: Near Strawberry Point; limestone bluffs; lake; scenic drives.
Burlington: Named Flint Hills by tribes who hunted for flint; temporary capital of state (1838); local Gothic architecture; Crapo Park.
Charles H. MacNider Museum: Near Mason City; collection of American art; puppet gallery; school of photography and painting.
Crystal Lake Cave: Near Dubuque; electrically lighted cave with stalactites and stalagmites; underground streams and lake.
Decorah: Limestone spires on Upper Iowa River; Twin Springs, Siewers Springs, Vesterheim, Norwegian-American Museum.
Effigy Mounds National Monument: Near Marquette; prehistoric Indian mounds in shapes of animals and birds.
Fishery Management Station: Near Guttenberg; hatchery and aquarium containing fish native to the Mississippi River.
Fort Atkinson Monument State Park: In Fort Atkinson; pioneer fort (1840); barracks; blockhouses.
Fort Dodge Historical Museum, Stockade and Fort: Near Fort Dodge; replica of fort built in 1850 houses museum exhibits of pioneer life and Indian artifacts.
Gardner Cabin Historic Site: Near Okoboji; restored log cabin built in 1856; relics of pioneer life.
Geode State Park: Near Burlington; unusual rocks formed by lime particles.
Grotto of the Redemption: In West Bend; built of stones, minerals, fossils, and shells collected from many states and countries.
Herbert Hoover National Historic Site: In West Branch; birthplace, restored boyhood home, burial place, and library museum of former president.
Iowa State Historical Museum and Archives: In Des Moines; exhibits of early farm life, mineral, and fossil collection.
Keokuk Dam: In Keokuk; dam and lock on Mississippi River for flood control and navigation.
Lacey-Keosauqua State Park: Near Keosauqua; Ely's Ford on Des Moines River; prehistoric Indian village; wildlife sanctuary.
LeClaire: Birthplace of Buffalo Bill (William Cody).
Ledges State Park: Near Boone; trails; sandstone walls and streams; wildlife research station.
Lewis and Clark State Park: Near Onawa; water and winter sports.

Little Brown Church in the Vale: Near Nashua; dedicated in 1864; known for popular hymn.
Living History Farm: Near Des Moines; working museum of farm history from 1700's to future; Farm of Today and Tomorrow; Walnut Hill Village.
Maquoketa Caves State Park: Near Maquoketa; limestone caves; site of prehistoric stone implements; natural bridge with 50-foot arch; balanced rock on cliff.
Mesquakie Indian Reservation: Near Tama; only reservation in Iowa.
Midwest Old Settlers and Threshers Heritage Museum: Near Mount Pleasant; antique farm equipment and home appliances; steam engine collection.
Pella: Historical Dutch farm village; annual Tulip Festival in May.
Pikes Peak State Park: Near McGregor; bluffs, sandstone, limestone, and fossilized walls; Bridal Veil Falls.
Pilot Knob State Park: Near Forest City; glacial formation; observation tower; Dead Man's Lake.
Pine Lake State Park: Near Eldora; Indian mounds.
Spillville: Antonin Dvorak Memorial in village where composer lived; Bily Clock Museum.
Springbrook State Park: Near Guthrie Center; various types of flora.
Stone State Park: In Sioux City; rolling wooded hills overlooking Missouri River valley; view of three states.
Wild Cat Den State Park: Near Muscatine; rock formations; picturesque mill and dam (1848)

Additional information sources:
Iowa Division of Tourism
200 East Grand Avenue
Des Moines, IA 50309
(800) 345-4692 (lower 48 states)
(515) 242-4705

Road Conditions Hotline
(515) 288-1047 (recording)

Iowa Dept. of Natural Resources
(515) 281-5145

Webpage:
http:/www.state.ia.us/

TRAIL COUNTIES

Cedar Valley: Benton, Blackhawk, Buchanan, & Linn

Chicaqua Valley: Jasper & Polk

Heart of Iowa: Marshall & Story

Heritage: Dubuque

Hoover: Cedar, Des Moines, & Johnson, Linn, Louisa, Muscatine

Kewash: Washington

Prairie Farmer: Winneshiek

Raccoon River Valley: Dallas & Guthrie

Sauk: Carroll & Sac

Wabash Trace: Fremont, Mills, Page & Pottawattamie

WEATHER CONDITIONS

	Temperature				Precipitation (inches)	
	Des Moines		Dubuque			
	High	Low	High	Low	DM*	Dub*
JAN	27	11	26	9	8S	8S
FEB	32	16	30	13	7S	7S
MAR	42	25	41	23	7S	10S
APR	60	39	58	37	3	4
MAY	71	51	68	47	4	5
JUNE	80	61	78	57	5	5
JULY	85	65	82	61	3	4
AUG	83	63	81	60	3	4
SEPT	75	54	72	51	3	5
OCT	65	44	62	41	2	3
NOV	46	29	44	27	1	3S
DEC	33	17	31	15	7S	11S

*DM – Des Moines; Dub – Dubuque; S – Snow

#1 CEDAR VALLEY NATURE TRAIL

Trail Uses: Bicycling, Hiking and Cross-country Skiing

Trail Heads:
South: Hiawatha
North: Evansdale

Surface: Chipped Limestone & Asphalt

Grade: Flat

Length of Trail: 52 miles

Date Established: 1984

Trail Name Origin:
Derived from the trail's location in the floodplain of the Cedar River.

Trail Highlights:
- Former Waterloo, Cedar Falls & Northern (WCF&N) electric Railroad line built in the early 1900's. Ownership changed several times. In February 1977 the Illinois Central Gulf Railroad was the authorized successor of the right-of-way.
- Trail follows the Cedar River, through woodlands, wetlands and rolling farmlands.
- Abundant in glacial deposits, fossils, limestone, wildlife and wildflowers.
- Historical landmarks, archaeological sites and two restored railroad depots.

Suggested Auto Routes

Dubuque to Hiawatha		
Road	Direction	Miles
US52 to US61	S	3.9
US61 to local road	S	.8
Local road to US151	SW	3.2
US151 to Collier Ave.	W	58.7
Collier Ave.	W	2.4
Total: 69 miles; 1 hours 15 minutes		

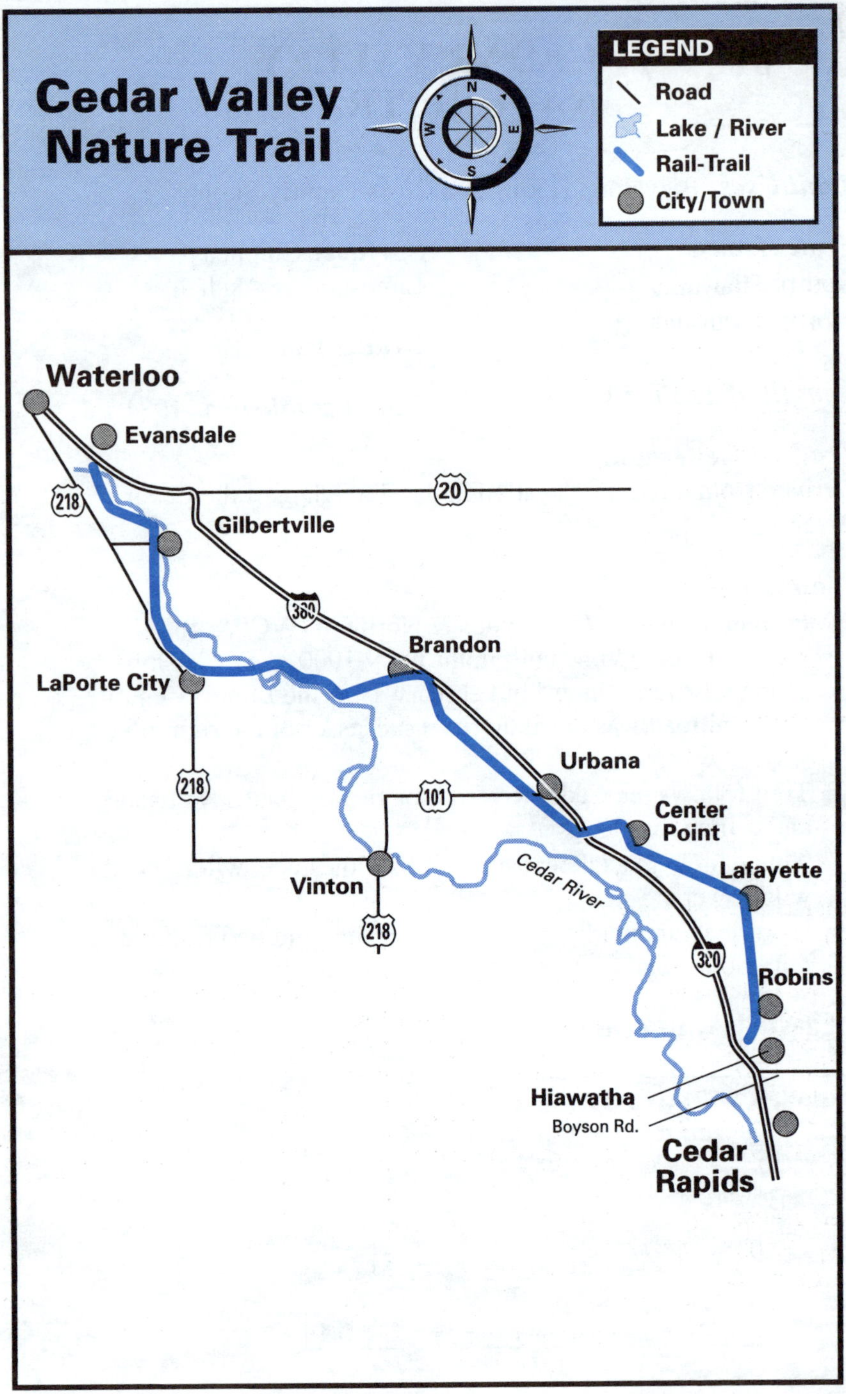
Cedar Valley
Nature Trail
N
E
S
W
LEGEND
Road
Lake / River
Rail-Trail
City/Town
Waterloo
Evansdale
218
20
Gilbertville
380
Brandon
LaPorte City
Urbana
218
101
Center
Point
Vinton
Cedar River
Lafayette
218
380
Robins
Hiawatha
Boyson Rd.
Cedar
Rapids

Cedar Valley Nature Trail

Auto Routes (cont.)

Des Moines to Evansdale		
Road	Direction	Miles
US 65 to US 69	N	2.3
US 69 I-80	N	1.6
I-80 to US 65	E	5.5
US 65 to ST 330	NE	13.2
ST 330 to ST 14	NE	26.1
ST 14 to E27	N	2
E27 to ST 229	E	12
ST 229 to US 63	E	6
US 63 to US 20	N	30.9
US 20 to I-380	E	4.9
I-380 to ST 297	E	4
ST 297 to Franklin	N	1
Franklin	W	2
Total: 111.5 miles; 2 hours 10 minutes		

Additional information sources:

Black Hawk & Buchanan County Section
Steve Finegan, Executive Director
Black Hawk County Conservation Board
2410 W. Lone Tree Road
Cedar Falls, IA 50613-1093
(319) 266-6813; (319) 277-1536

Waterloo Chamber of Commerce
215 East 4th Street
P.O. Box 1587
Waterloo, IA 50704
(319) 233-8431
(319) 233-4580 FAX

Linn & Benton County Sections
Dennis Goemaar, Deputy Director
Linn County Conservation Board
1890 County Home Road
Marion, IA 52302
(319) 398-3505

Cedar Rapids Area Chamber of Commerce
424 1st Avenue
Cedar Rapids, IA 52407
(319) 398-5317

Trail Fees:
Daily - $2.00
Annual - $5.00

CHICHAQUA VALLEY TRAIL

Trail Uses: Bicycling, Hiking and Cross-country Skiing

Trail Heads:
West: Bondurant
East: Baxter

Surface: Crushed Limestone & Blacktop

Grade: Flat

Length of Trail: 20 miles

Date Established: 1987

Trail Name Origin:
Derived from the trail location in the Chichaqua Valley, named by the Fox Indians.

Trail Highlights:
- Former Chicago and Northwestern Railroad line.
- Chichaqua crosses forested banks and timber bottomlands of the Skunk River.
- The effects of Iowa's ice ages and prairies provide scenic sites along the trail.

Suggested Auto Routes

Waterloo to Baxter		
Road	Direction	Miles
US 63 to St 229	S	37.7
ST 229 to E27	W	6
E27 to ST 14	W	12
ST 14	S	25.4
Total: 85.9 miles; 1 hour, 30 minutes		

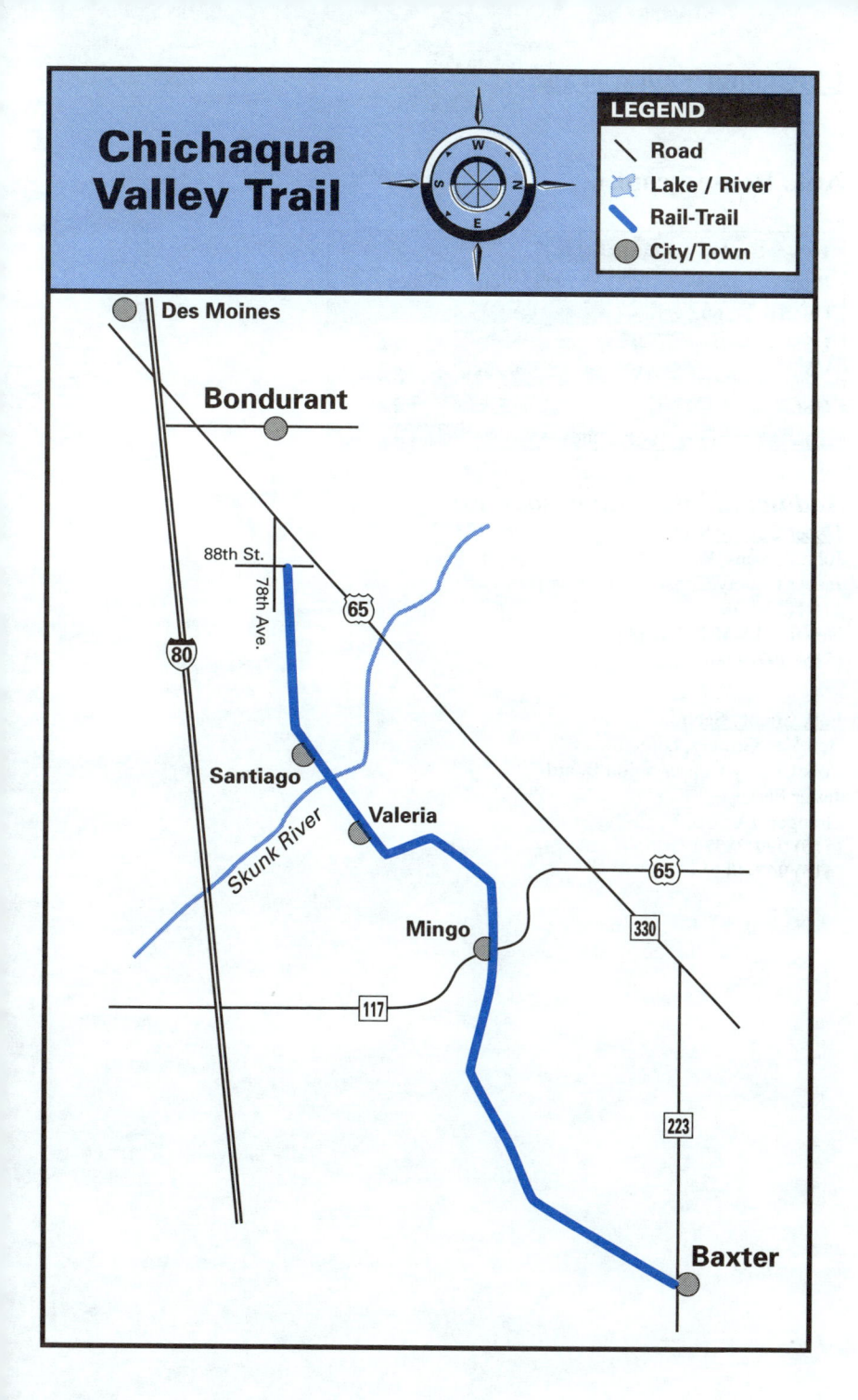

Chichaqua Valley Trail

Chichaqua Valley Trail

Auto Routes (cont.)

Des Moines to Bondurant		
Road	Direction	Miles
US65 to US69	N	2.3
US69 to I-80	N	1.6
I-80 to US65	E	5.5
US65	NE	2.4
Total: 11.8 miles; 14 minutes		

Additional information sources:
Jasper County Section
John Parsons, Parks Officer
Jasper County Conservation Board
115 N. 2nd Ave.
Newton, IA 50208
(515) 792-9780

Polk County Section
Ben Van Grundy, Director
Polk County Conservation Board
Jester Park
Granger, IA 50109
(515) 999-2557
(515) 967-4889

HEART OF IOWA NATURE TRAIL

#3

Trail Uses: Bicycling, Hiking, Horseback Riding, Cross-country Skiing and Snowmobiling

Trail Heads:
East - Rhodes
West - Slater

Surface: Crushed Limestone

Length of Trail: 32 miles portions undeveloped; Adjacent Equestrian trail

Grade: Flat

Date Established: 1989

Trail Name Origin:
Derived from trail location in central Iowa.

Trail Highlights:
- Former Milwaukee Railroad Line.
- Trail experience includes scenic prairie remnants, wetlands with native flora and fauna, an arboretum and a pioneer cemetery.
- Hoy Bridge 212 feet long, 60 feet high built in 1912 crosses Clear Creek
- Part of the "American Hiking Society's American Discover Trail." This trail system passes through several metropolitan areas and incorporates many trails as it passes from the East to the West Coast of the United States.

Future Plans:
- Connect the West portion to the existing Saylorville-Big Creek Trail in Des Moines.
- Connect the east portion to the Chichaqua Valley Trail.
- Future planned development will result in a 100-mile loop in central Iowa.

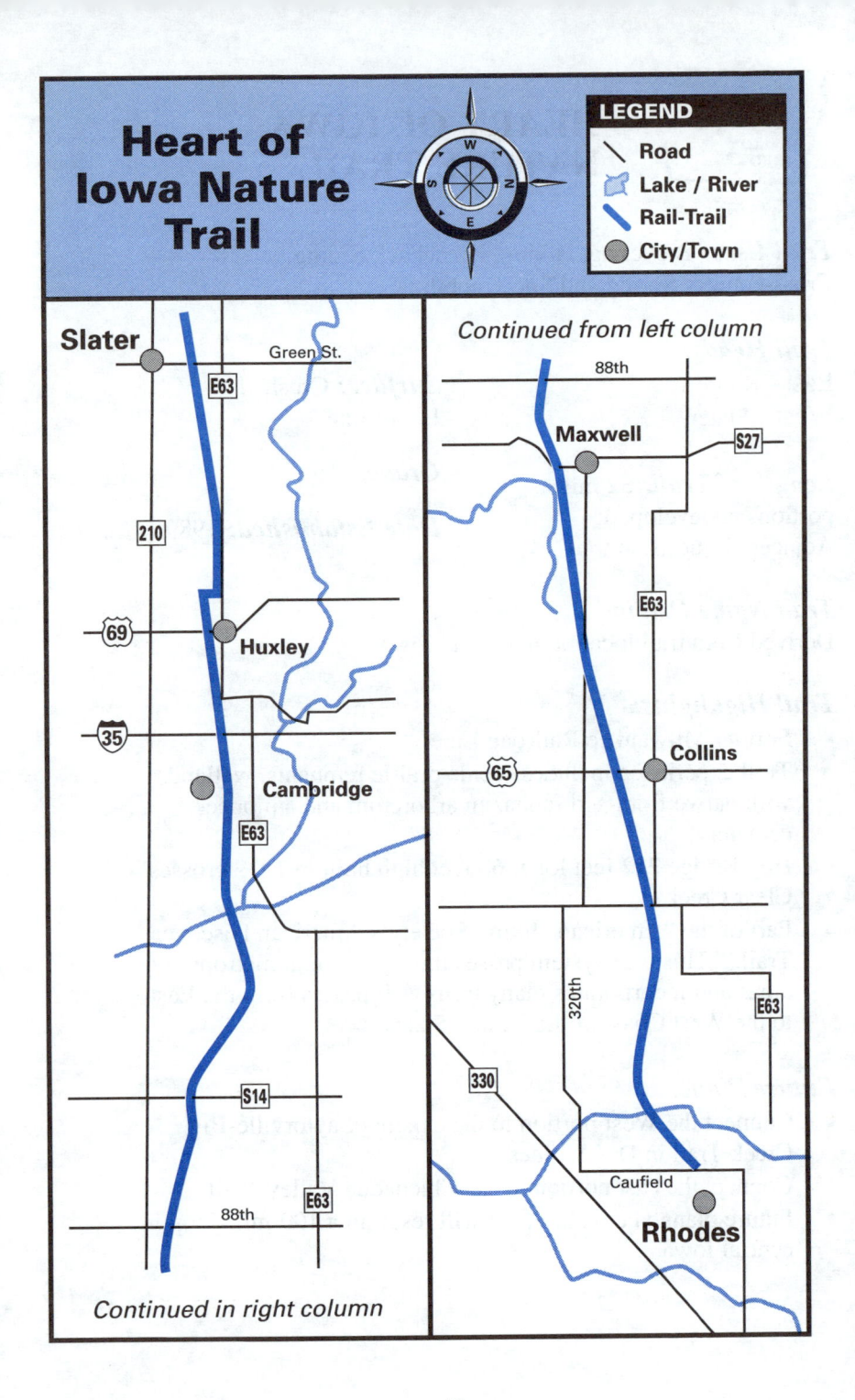

Heart of Iowa Nature Trail

Heart of Iowa Nature Trail

Suggested Auto Routes

Des Moines to Slater		
Road	Direction	Miles
US65 to US69	N	2.3
US69 to I-80	N	1.6
I-80 to I-35	E	1.5
I-35 to ST210	N	16
ST210	W	2
Total: 23.4 miles; 25 minutes		

Waterloo to Rhodes		
Road	Direction	Miles
US 63 to ST 229	S	37.7
ST 229 to E27	W	6
E27 to ST 14	W	12
ST 14 to ST 330	S	2
ST330	SW	15.6
Total: 75 miles; 1 hour, 30 minutes		

Additional information sources:
Steven Lekwa, Deputy Director
Story County Conservation Board
McFarland Park
R. R. 2, Box 272E
Ames, IA 50010-9651
(515) 232-2516

Gary Brandenburg
Marshall County Conservation Board
1302 East Olive St
Marshalltown, IA 50158
(515) 754-6303

Trail Fees:
Daily - $1.00
Annual - $5.00
Fees are not required within city limits or on Story County portion. Permits may be purchased at the Slater and Cambridge trailheads.

HERITAGE TRAIL #4

Trail Uses: Bicycling, Hiking, Cross-country Skiing and Snowmobiling

Trail Heads:
East - Dubuque
West - Dyersville

Surface: Limestone Screenings

Grade: 1 %

Length of Trail: 26 miles

Date Established: 1982

Trail Name Origin:
Derived from the legacy of Railroad history in northeast Iowa.

Trail Highlights:
- Former Chicago Northwestern Railroad Line.
- Heritage is a mountain trail in a prairie country; it boosts rugged woodlands, gently slopping grade, numerous river overlooks, limestone bluffs, railroad artifacts, fossils and old lead mines. Considered the Upper Midwest's most scenic all-season trail.
- Follows Little Maquoketa River

Suggested Auto Routes

Cedar Rapids to Dyersville		
Road	Direction	Miles
US151 to ST38	E	30.7
ST38 to X47	N	6
X47 to US20	N	10.7
US20 to ST136	E	5.1
ST136	N	2.3
Total: 54.8 miles; 1 hour, 19 minutes		

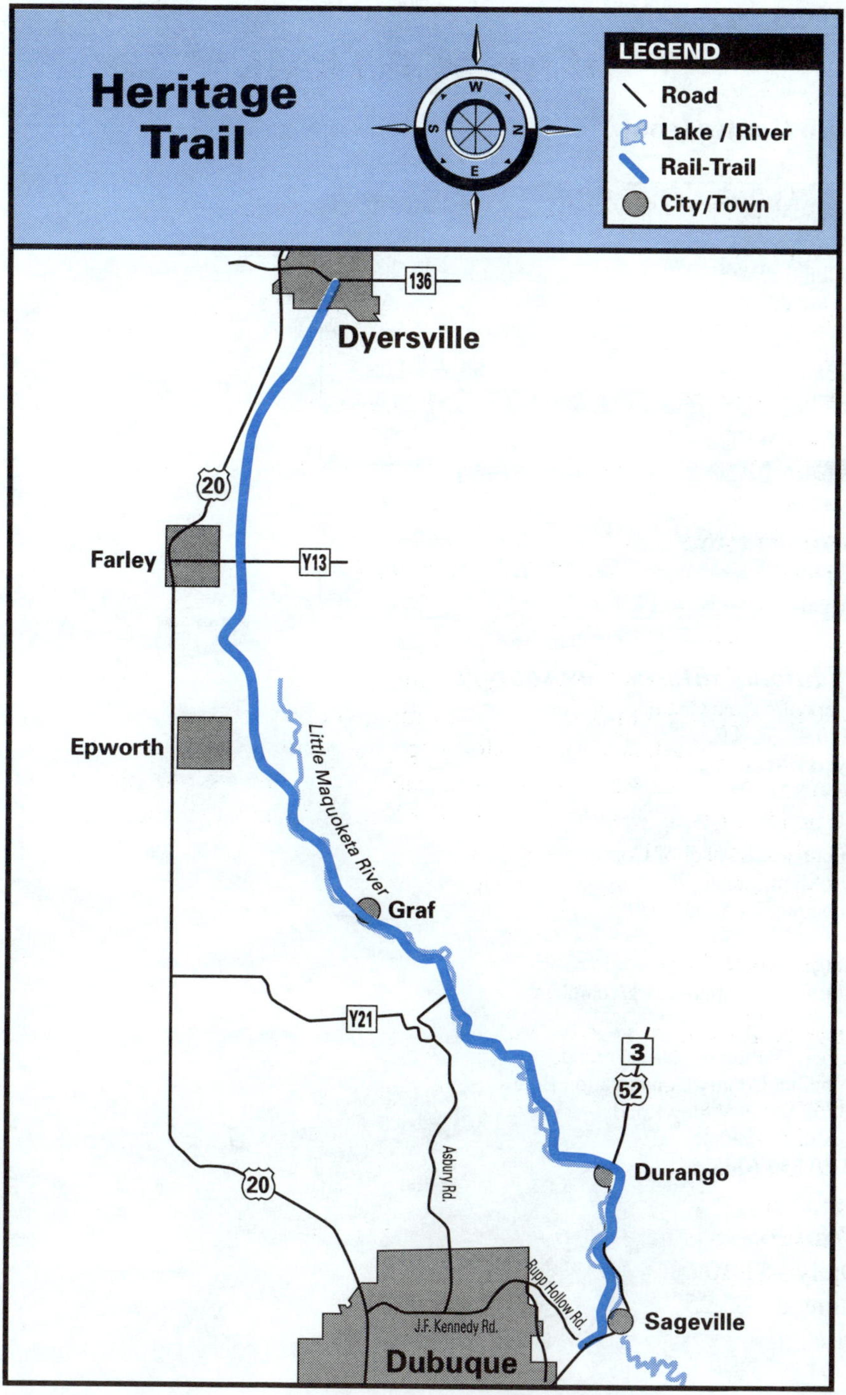
Heritage Trail
W
S
N
E
LEGEND
Road
Lake / River
Rail-Trail
City/Town
136
Dyersville
20
Farley
Y13
Epworth
Little Maquoketa River
Graf
Y21
3
52
Durango
Asbury Rd.
20
Rupp Hollow Rd.
Sageville
J.F. Kennedy Rd.
Dubuque

Heritage Trail

Auto Routes (cont.)

Des Moines to Dyersville		
Road	Direction	Miles
US65 to US69	N	2.3
US69 to I-80	N	1.6
I-80 to I-380	E	103
I-380 to 1st Ave.	N	17.8
1st Ave to US151	NE	4.3
US151 to ST38	E	30.7
ST38 to X47	N	6
X47 to US20	N	10.7
US20 to ST136	E	5.1
ST136	N	3.4
Total: 184.9 miles; 3 hours, 24 minutes		

Additional information sources:
Dyersville Area Chamber of Commerce
1410 9th St. S.E.
Dyersville, IA 52040
(319) 875-2311

Dubuque Chamber of Commerce
770 Main Street
Dubuque, IA 52004-0705
(319) 557-9200
(800) 798-8844
http://www.dubuque.org/chamber/

Robert Walton or Carol Freund
Dubuque County Conservation Board
13768 Swiss Valley Road
Peosta, IA 52068
(319) 556-6745

Trail Fees:
Daily - $1.10
Annual - $5.25

#5 HOOVER NATURE TRAIL

Trail Uses: Bicycling, Hiking, Horseback Riding, Cross-country Skiing and Snowmobiling (in designated areas)

Trail Heads:
North - Cedar Rapids
South - Burlington

Surface: Crushed Limestone & Original Ballast; Parallel dirt trail

Length of Trail: 115 miles (portions undeveloped)

Grade: Flat

Date Established: 1990

Trail Name Origin:
Trail runs through the hometown of Herbert Hoover.

Trail Highlights:
- Former Chicago, Rock Island and Pacific Railroad line.
- Designated as part of the "American Discovery Trail," a coast-to-coast national trails.
- Presidential Library in West Branch, the hometown of Herbert Hoover.

Future Plan:
- Establish a Railroad transportation museum/West Liberty history museum.
- Link with Cedar Valley Nature Trail.

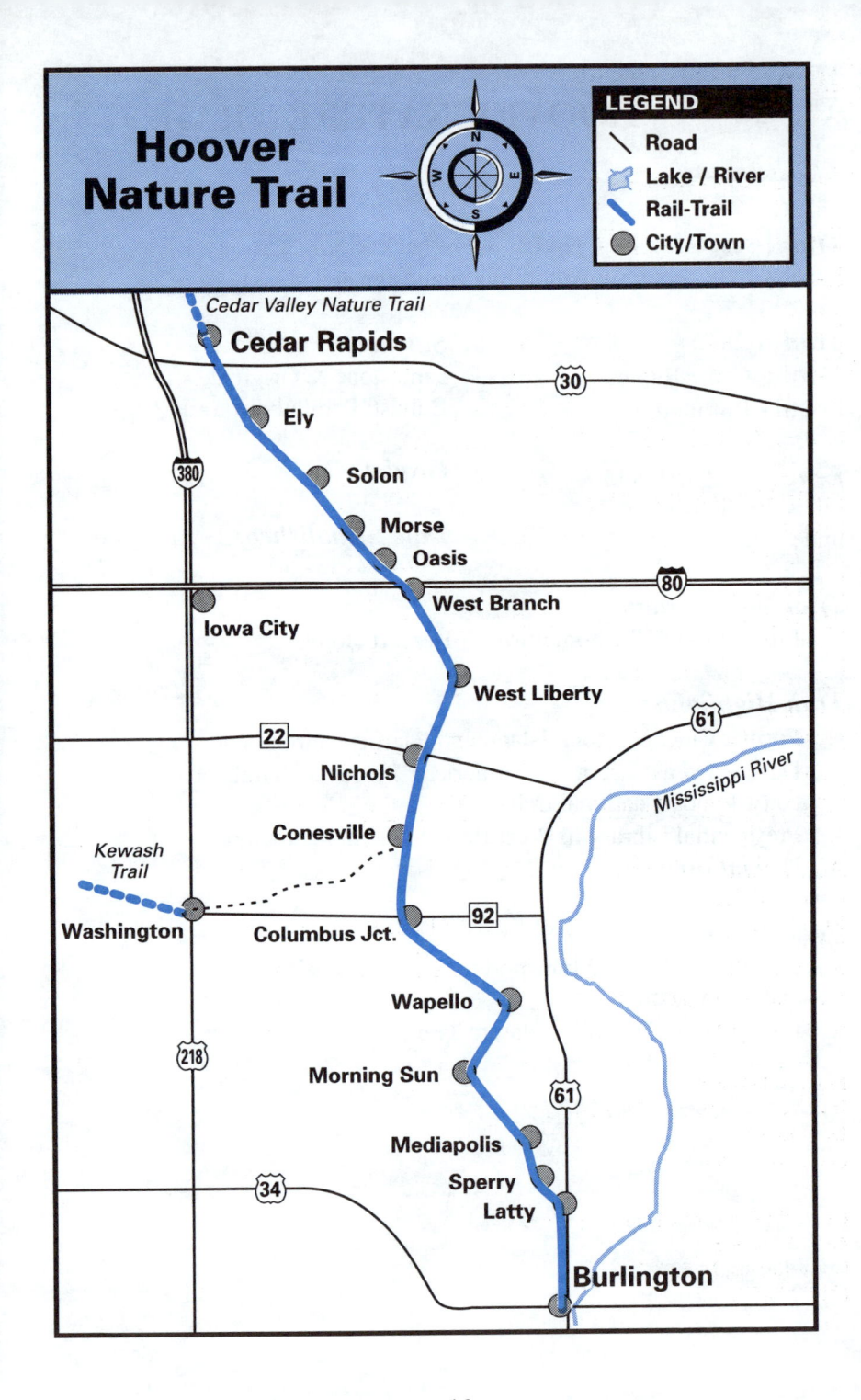

Hoover Nature Trail

LEGEND
- Road
- Lake / River
- Rail-Trail
- City/Town

Hoover Nature Trail

Suggested Auto Routes

Dubuque to Cedar Rapids

Road	Direction	Miles
US 52 to US 61	S	3.9
US 61 to local road	S	.8
Local road to US 151	SW	3.2
US 151	W	58.7
Total: 66.6 miles; 1 hour, 25 minutes		

Des Moines to Burlington

Road	Direction	Miles
I-235 to ST163	E	1.8
ST163 to ST92	SE	53.4
ST92 to ST21	E	11.3
ST21 to ST149	S	10
ST149 to ST78	E	6
ST78 to ST1	E	12
ST1 to US34	S	12
US34	E	50
Total: 156.5 miles; 3 hours		

Additional information sources:

Conrad Gregg,
Hoover Nature Trail, Inc.
%Liberty Realty
P. O Box 123
West Liberty, IA 52776-0123
(319) 627-2626.

Charlie Harper President
(319) 263-4043
(319) 263-9073 FAX

Mark Achelson
Iowa Natural Heritage Foundation
Des Moines, IA
(515) 288-1846

Cedar Rapids Area Chamber of Commerce
424 1st Avenue
Cedar Rapids, IA 52407
(319)398-5317

#6 KEWASH NATURE TRAIL

Trail Uses: Bicycling, Hiking and Cross-country Skiing

Trail Heads:
West: Keota
East: Washington

Surface: Crushed Limestone

Grade: Flat

Length of Trail: 13.8 miles

Date Established: 1991

Trail Name Origin:
Trail name was derived from the original railroad line.

Trail Highlights:
- Former Kewash Railroad line.
- Kewash is abundant with rare and unusual prairie plants, wildlife and wildflowers.

Suggested Auto Routes

Cedar Rapids to Washington		
Road	Direction	Miles
1st Ave. to I-380	SW	4.3
I-380 to US218	S	17.8
US218 to ST1	SE	6
ST1 to ST92	S	27.7
ST92	E	.6
Total: 56.4 miles; 1 hour, 5 minutes		

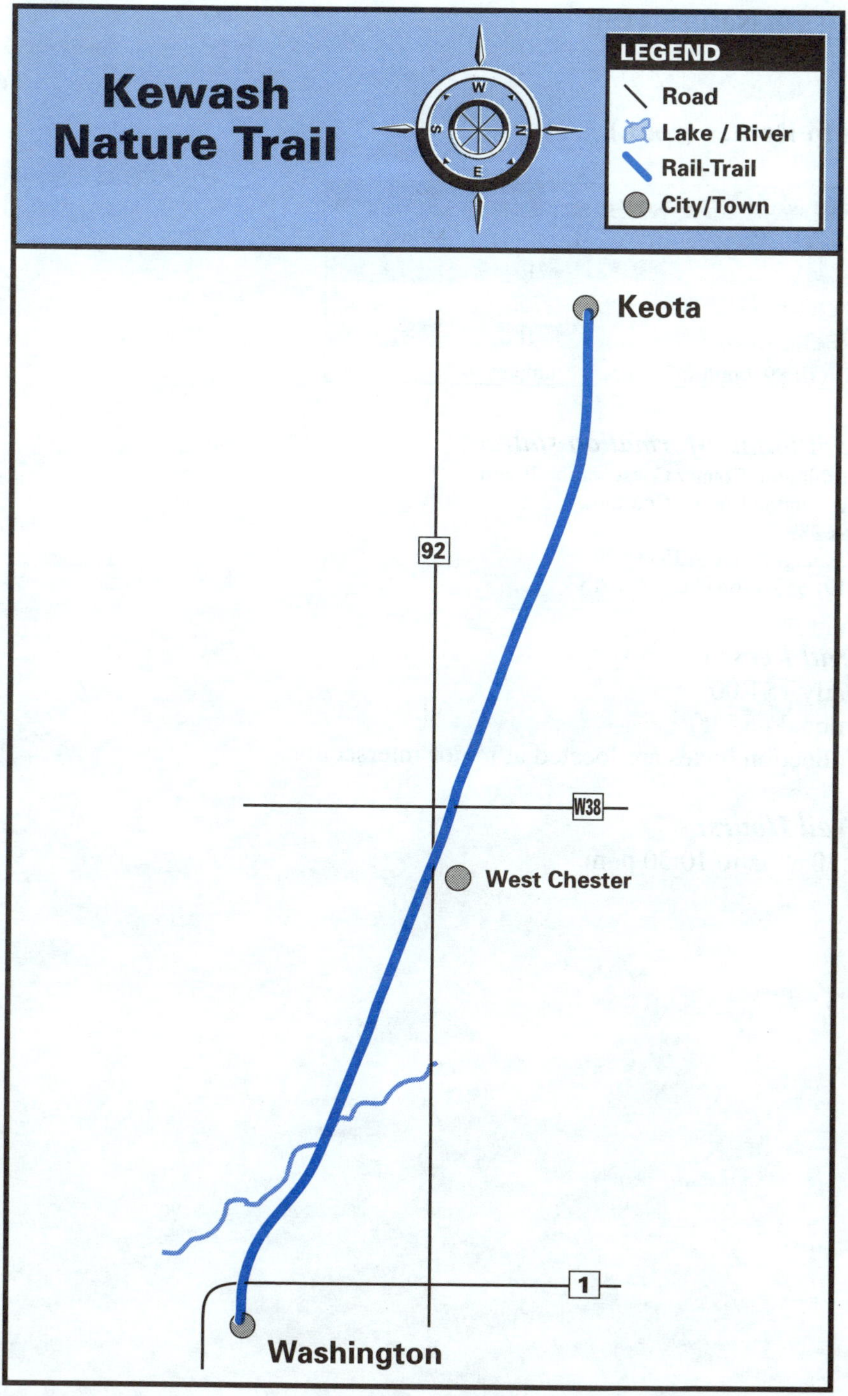
Kewash
Nature Trail
W
S
N
E
LEGEND
Road
Lake / River
Rail-Trail
City/Town
Keota
92
W38
West Chester
1
Washington

Kewash Nature Trail

Auto Routes (cont.)

Des Moines to Keota		
Road	Direction	Miles
I-235 to ST163	E	1.8
ST163 to ST92	SE	53.4
ST92	E	31.5
Total: 89.4 miles; 2 hours, 11 minutes		

Additional information sources:
Washington County Conservation Board
Washington County Courthouse
Box 889
Washington, IA 52353-0889
(319) 653-7765 phone & FAX

Trail Fees:
Daily - $1.00
Annual - $5.00
Collection boxes are located at major intersections.

Trail Hours:
4:30 a. m. to 10:30 p. m.

#7 PRAIRIE FARMER RECREATIONAL TRAIL

Trail Uses: Bicycling, Hiking, Cross-country Skiing and Snowmobiling (in designated areas)

Trail Heads:
South - Calmar
North - Cresco

Length of Trail: 18.2 miles

Surface: Compacted Limestone

Grade: Level

Date Established: 1989

Trail Name Origin:
Chosen by contest - Prairie Farmer was an old Chicago WLS radio show

Trail Highlights:
- Former Milwaukee Railroad Line.
- Prairie Farmer offers users picturesque farmland, prairie plants, wooded areas and abundant wildlife.

Suggested Auto Routes

Des Moines to Calmar		
Road	Direction	Miles
US65 to US69	N	2.3
US69 to I-80	N	1.6
I-80 to I-35	E	1.5
I-35 to ST3	N	84
ST3 to ST14	E	28.5
ST14 to US18	N	29
US18 to ST24	E	21.8
ST24	E	27.5
Total: 196.2 miles; 3 hours, 50 minutes		

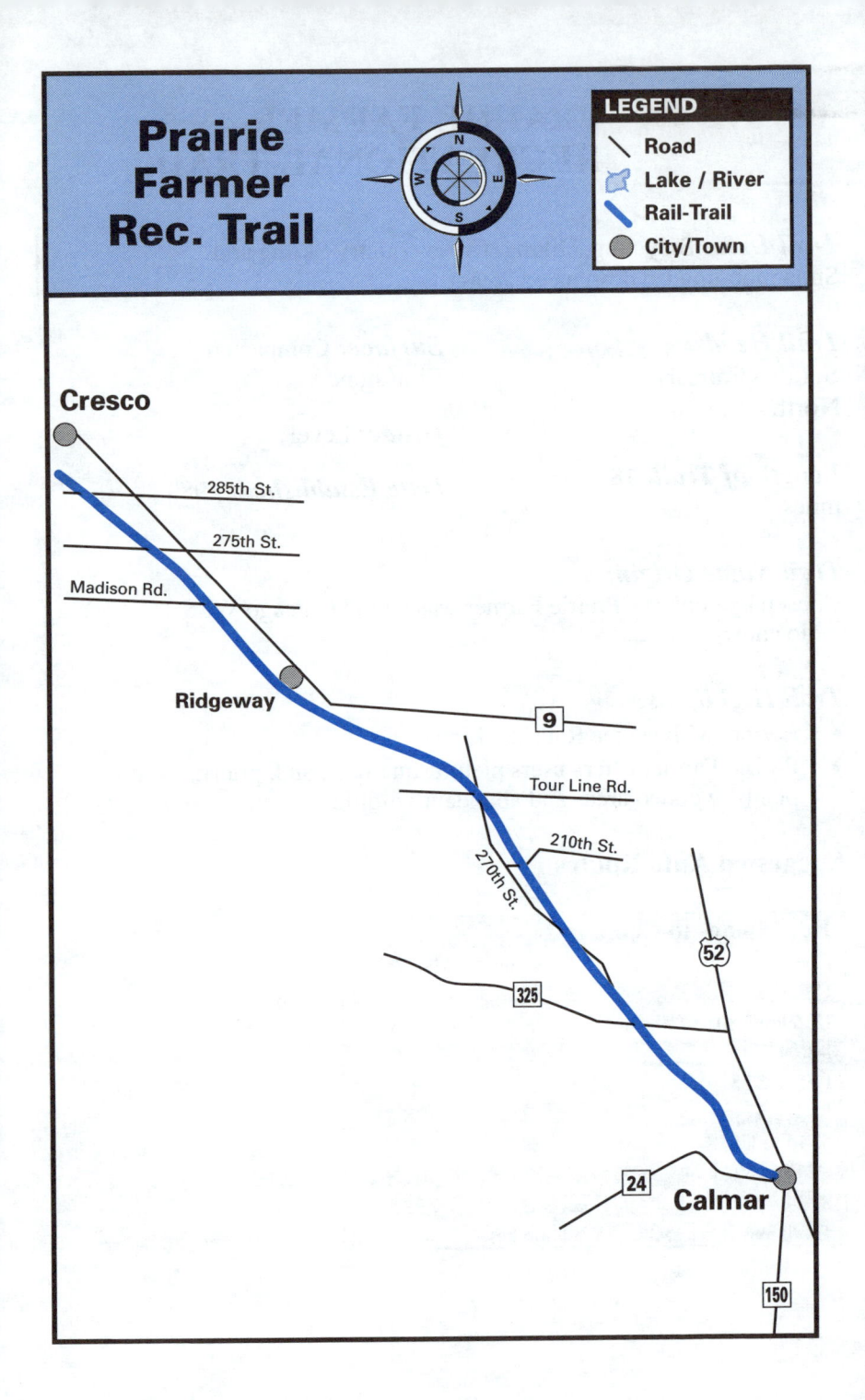

Prairie Farmer Rec. Trail

LEGEND
- Road
- Lake / River
- Rail-Trail
- City/Town

- Cresco
- 285th St.
- 275th St.
- Madison Rd.
- Ridgeway
- 9
- Tour Line Rd.
- 210th St.
- 270th St.
- 52
- 325
- 24
- Calmar
- 150

Prairie Farmer Recreational Trail

Auto Routes (cont.)

Cedar Rapids to Calmar		
Road	Direction	Miles
Collier Ave. to I-380	W	2.4
I-380 to ST150	NW	19.7
ST150	N	74
Total: 96.1 miles; 2 hours, 29 minutes		

Additional information sources:
David Oestmann, Director
Winneshiek County Conservation Board
2546 Lake Meyer Road
Ft. Atkinson, IA 52144
(319) 534-7145

Cresco Area Chamber of Commerce & Economic Development
101 2nd Avenue SW
P.O. Box 403
Cresco, IA 52136
(319) 547-3434 phone & FAX

RACCOON RIVER VALLEY TRAIL #8

Trail Uses: Bicycling, Hiking, In-line, and Cross-country Skiing

Trail Heads:
East - Waukee
West - Yale

Surface: Asphalt

Grade: 1-2 %

Length of Trail: 34 miles

Date Established: 1989

Trail Name Origin:
Derived from trail location, parallel to the Raccoon River.

Trail Highlights:
- Former Chicago Northwestern Railroad line.
- Trail winds through native prairie, scenic woodlands, Raccoon River, Lake Panorama, geological formations and six communities.
- Optional stops located on the trail: Brick and Tile Factory, French Castle Courthouse, Guthrie County Historical Village and Turn of the Century Museum.
- Three Bridges in Guthrie County crosses creeks along trail.

Suggested Auto Routes

Cedar Rapids Waukee		
Road	Direction	Miles
1st Ave. to I-380	SW	4.3
I-380 to I-80	S	17.8
I-80 to US6	W	115.6
US6	W	5.2
Total: 142.9 miles; 2 hours, 17 minutes		

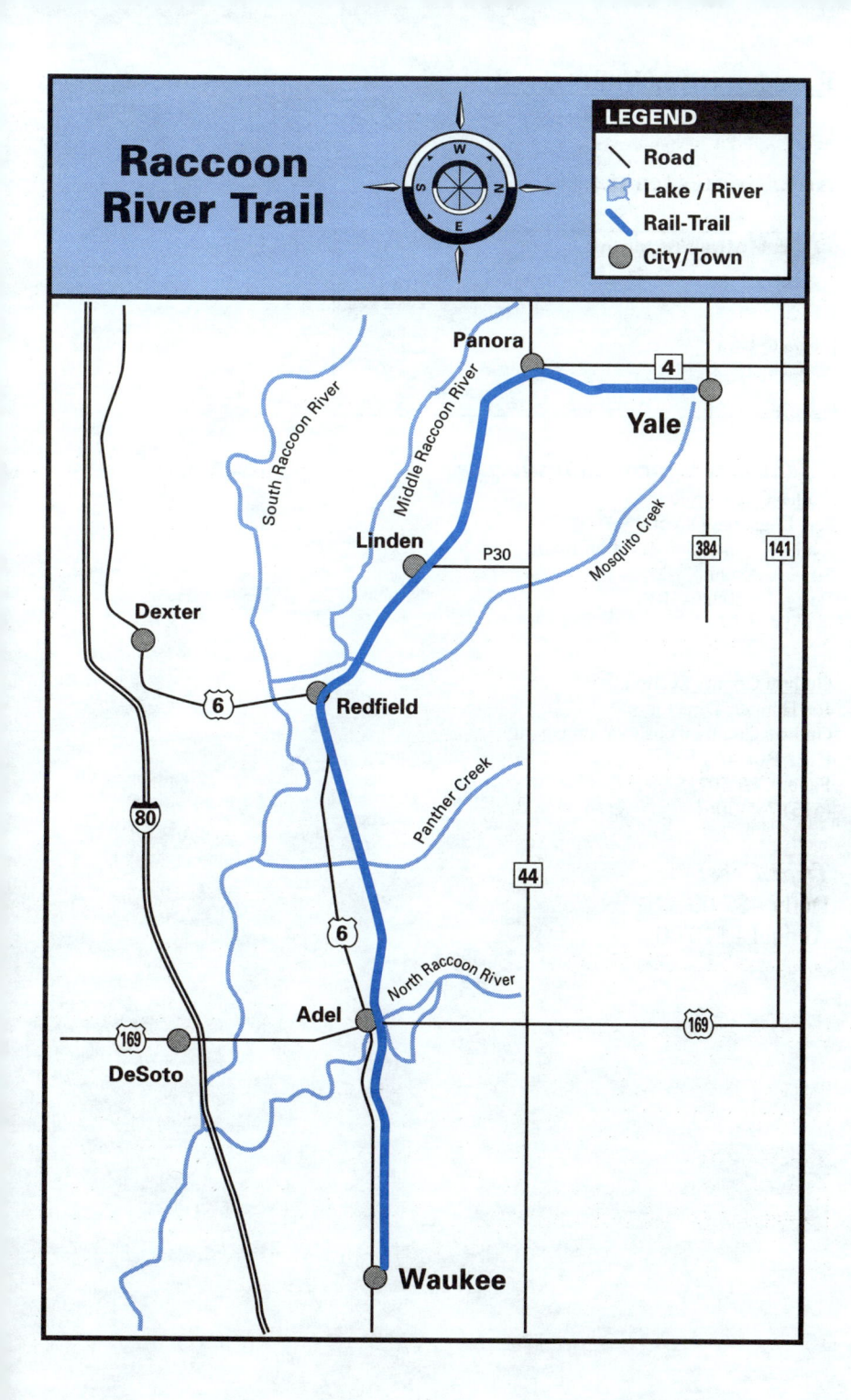

Raccoon River Trail

LEGEND
- Road
- Lake / River
- Rail-Trail
- City/Town

Raccoon River Valley Trail

Auto Routes (cont.)

Des Moines to Waukee		
Road	Direction	Miles
I-235 to I-80	W	9
I-80 to US6	N	1.7
US6	W	5.2
Total: 15.9 miles; 19 minutes		

Additional information sources:
Dallas County Section
Jeff Logsdon, Director
Dallas County Conservation Board
1477 K Avenue
Perry, IA 50220-8101
(515) 465-3577

Guthrie County Section
Joe Hanner, Director
Guthrie County Conservation Board
RR 2 Box 4A17
Panora, IA 50215-9802
(515) 755-3061

Trail Fees:
Daily - $2.00
Annual - $10.00

SAUK TRAIL

Trail Uses: Bicycling, Hiking, In-line Skating, Cross-country Skiing and Snowmobiling

Trail Heads:
South - Carroll
North - Lake View

Length of Trail: 33 miles

Surface: Asphalt & Crushed Limestone

Grade: Level

Date Established: 1989

Trail Name Origin:
Named after the Sauk Indians early settlers to this vicinity.

Trail Highlights:
- Former Chicago Central Pacific and Chicago Northwestern Railroad lines.
- Sauk traverses through farmlands, towns, four parks, Black Hawk marsh and Hazelbush Wildlife Area.
- Restored historic railroad depot in town of Breda.

Suggested Auto Routes

Des Moines to Carroll		
Road	Direction	Miles
US65 to US69	N	2.3
US69 to I-80	N	1.6
I-80 to ST141	W	9.7
ST141 to ST144	NW	25.2
ST144 to US30	NW	17
US30	W	34
Total: 89.8 miles; 1 hour, 46 minutes		

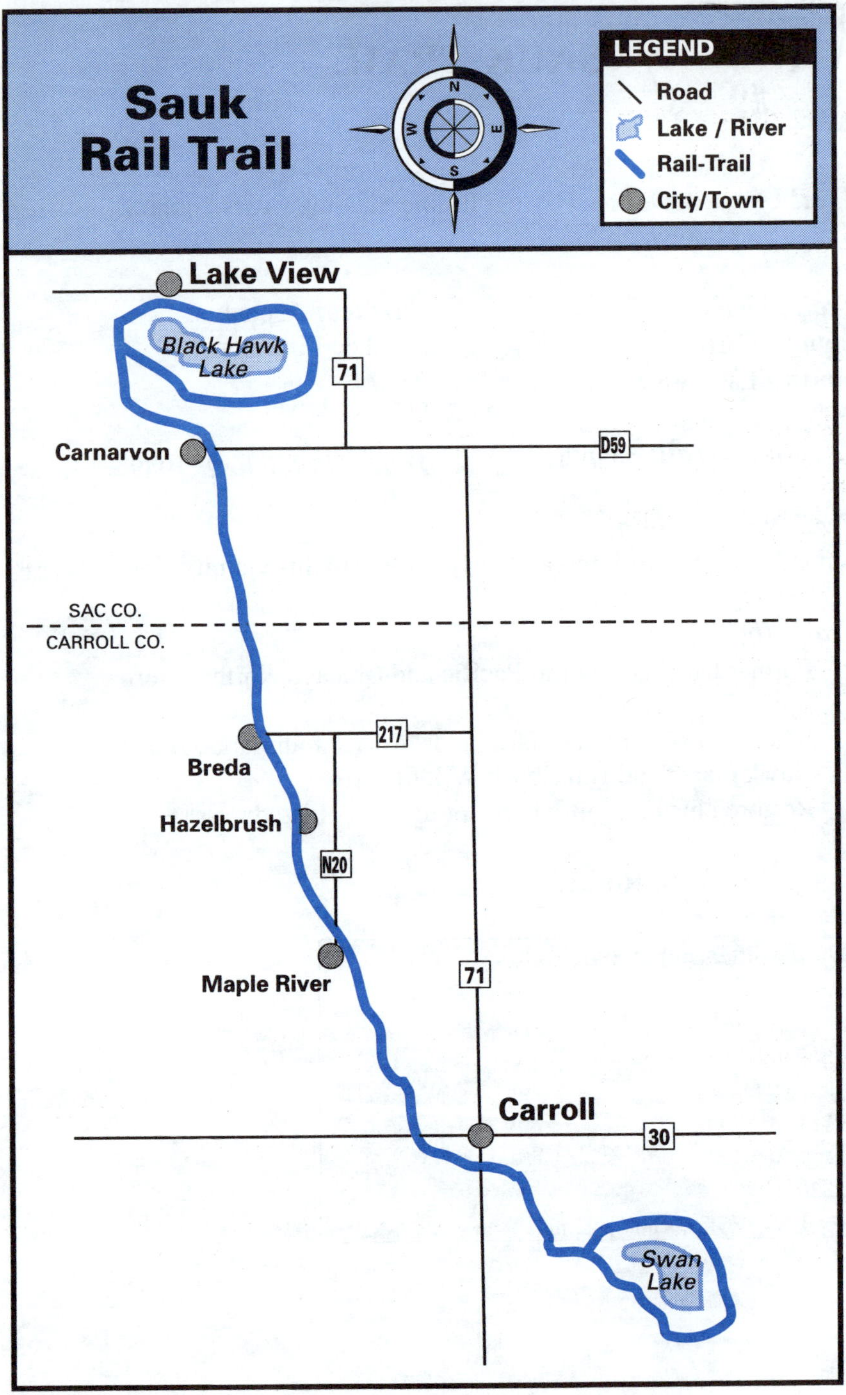
Sauk
Rail Trail
N
S
E
W
LEGEND
Road
Lake / River
Rail-Trail
City/Town
Lake View
Black Hawk
Lake
71
Carnarvon
D59
SAC CO.
CARROLL CO.
217
Breda
Hazelbrush
N20
Maple River
71
Carroll
30
Swan
Lake

Sauk Trail

Auto Routes (cont.)

Sioux City to Lake View		
Road	Direction	Miles
US 20 to US 59	E	46.8
US 59 to ST 175	S	11.6
ST 175	E	24.4
Total: 85.8 miles; 1 hours, 50 minutes		

Additional information sources:

Sac County Section
Chris Bass, Director
Sac County Conservation Board
2970 280th Street
Sac City IA 50583-7474
(712) 662-4530

Carroll County Section
David Olson, Director
Carroll County Conservation
Board RR 1, Box 240A
Carroll, IA 51401-9801
(712) 792-4614

Carroll Chamber of Commerce
223 West 5th Street
Carroll, IA 51401
(712) 792-4383

#10 WABASH TRACE NATURE TRAIL

Trail Uses: Bicycling, Hiking, Horseback Riding and Cross-country Skiing

Trail Heads:
North - Council Bluffs
South - Blanchard

Length of Trail: 63 miles
Parallel Equestrian trail

Surface: Crushed Limestone

Grade: Flat

Date Established: 1988

Trail Name Origin:
Derived from the Wabash Railroad line and the military trail called "Field Trace" located in the area.

Trail Highlights:
- Former Wabash Railroad line.
- Wabash winds through eight towns and crosses more than seventy bridges. Trail users will view picturesque loess hills unique to this area and Northern China.
- Restored Wabash Railroad Depot in Shenandoah is listed on the National Registry of Historic Places.

Suggested Auto Routes

Cedar Rapids to Council Bluffs		
Road	Direction	Miles
1st Ave. to I-380	SW	4.3
I-380 to I-80	S	17.8
I-80 to US6	W	236.2
US6	W	2.5
Total: 260.8 miles; 4 hours, 10 minutes		

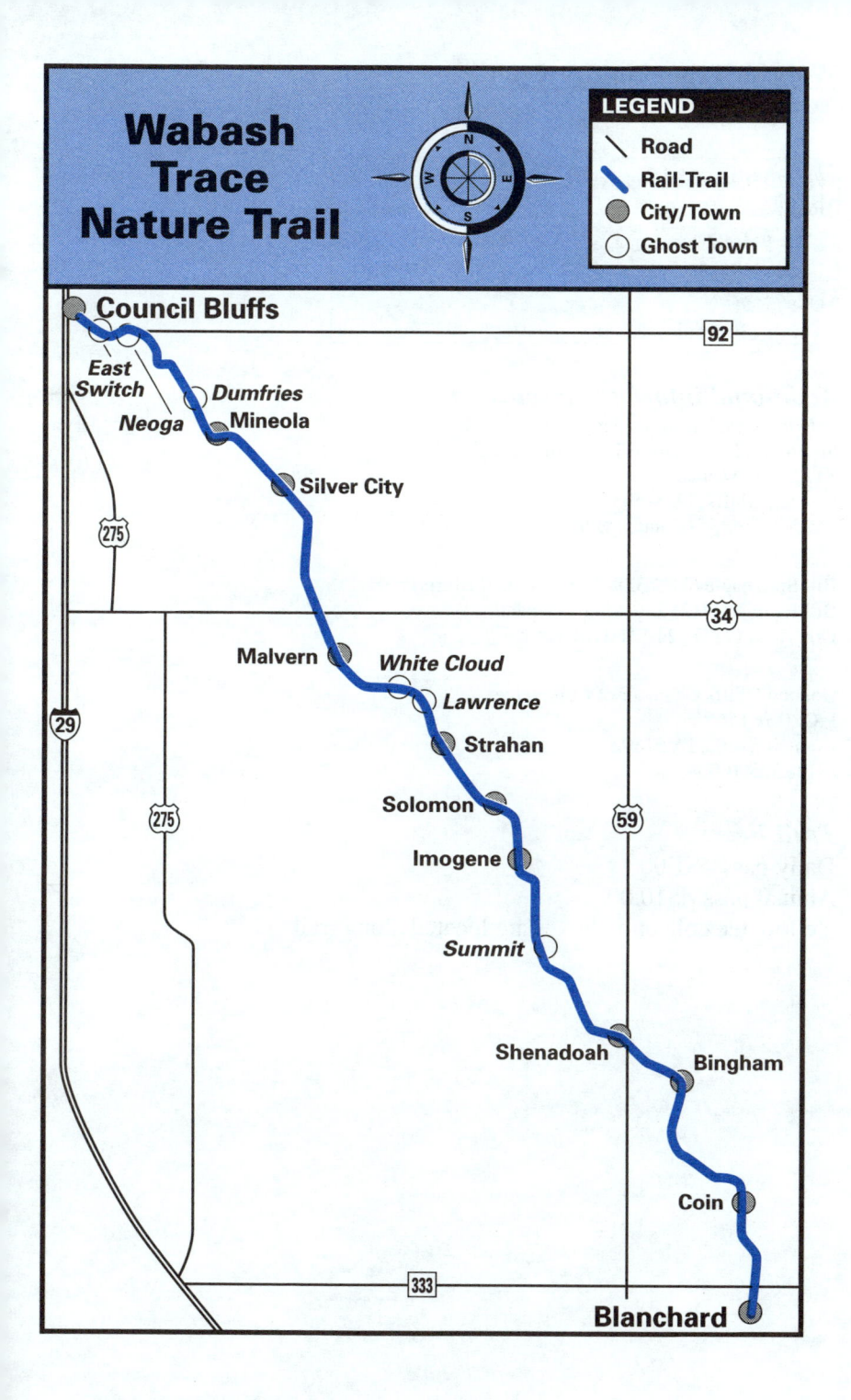

Wabash Trace Nature Trail

LEGEND
- Road
- Rail-Trail
- City/Town
- Ghost Town

- Council Bluffs
- East Switch
- Neoga
- Dumfries
- Mineola
- Silver City
- Malvern
- White Cloud
- Lawrence
- Strahan
- Solomon
- Imogene
- Summit
- Shenadoah
- Bingham
- Coin
- Blanchard

Wabash Trace Nature Trail

Des Moines to Council Bluffs		
Road	Direction	Miles
I-235 to I-80	W	9
I-80 to US6	W	118.9
US6	W	2.5
Total: 130.4 miles; 2 hour		

Additional information sources:
Pete Phillips, Vice President
Southwest Iowa Nature Trails, Inc.
347 Hyde Avenue
Council Bluffs, IA 51503
(712) 328-6836 (Council Bluffs)

Bill Spitznagle (712) 328-7460 (Council Bluffs)
Bill Hillman (712) 246-4444 (Shenandoah)
Don Reed (712) 624-8160 (Malvern)

Council Bluffs Chamber of Commerce
P.O. Box 1565
Council Bluffs, IA 51502
(712) 325-1000

Trail Fees:
Daily pass - $1.00
Annual pass - $10.00
Yellow fee collection boxes are located along trail.

Michigan

- #1 Bergland to Sidnaw
- #2 Bill Nicholls
- #3 Hancock/Calumet
- #4 Hart-Montague
- #5 Kal-Haven
- #6 Paint Creek
- #7 Peré Marquette Rail-Trail of Mid-Michigan
- #8 Stateline

FACTS ABOUT MICHIGAN

Capital: Lansing

Elevation:
Highest - Point: Mt. Arvon 1,979 ft.

Lowest Point - Lake Erie 572 ft.

Largest City: Detroit

Motto: Si quaeris peninsulam amoenam (If you seek a pleasant peninsula, look about you)

Nickname: Great Lake State; Wolverine State

Population: 9,496,100

State Bird: Robin

State Fish: Brook Trout

State Flower: Apple Blossom

State Tree: White Pine

Statehood: January 26, 1837 (26th state)

Time Zone:
Eastern/Central DST

Boasting Rights:
- 4 National Forests
- 6 major State Forests
- 89 State Parks
- Leads the nation as state with the most trails converted from abandoned rail corridors.
- 91 developed rail trails totaling 1,065 trail miles.
- Future plans to develop 38 rail trails totaling 514 miles.

Geographic Center:
Werford, 5 miles north-northwest of Cadillac

PLACES OF INTEREST

Battle Creek: Cereal factories; arboretum.
Bay City State Park: Near Bay City; beach on Saginaw Bay; nature museum; woods; fishing.
Benton Harbor: Mineral springs resort; House of David; open-air Municipal Fruit Market.
Cranbrook Institutions: In Bloomfield Hills; educational and cultural community.
D.H. Day State Park: Near Glen Arbor; beach; wooded campgrounds.
Dodge Brothers State Park No. 4: Near Pontiac; beach on Cass Lake; swimming, fishing, picnicking.
Tawas Point State Park: In East Tawas; beach on Tawas Bay; swimming, fishing, camping, hiking.
Fort Wilkins State Park: Near Copper Harbor; remains of old United State army outpost; shafts of an old copper mine nearby; camping.
Grand Haven State Park: Near Grand Haven; lake beach; swimming, fishing, camping.
Greenfield Village and Henry Ford Museum: In Dearborn; exhibits of Americana.
Harrisville State Park: On Lake Huron near Harrisville; scenic views; camping.
Holland: Tulip center of United States; Dutch historical exhibits in Netherlands Museum.
Holland State Park: Near Holland; Lake Michigan beach; sand dunes; camping.
Holly Recreation Area: Near Pontiac; winter sports.
Interlochen Center for the Arts: National music camp.
Interlochen State Park: Near Traverse City; beaches; virgin pine forest.
Iron Mountain: Winter sports; high ski slide.
Ironwood: Deep iron mines in Gogebic Range.
Island Lake Recreation Area: Near Brighton; Huron River winds through area; canoeing; beaches.
Isle Royale National Park: In northern Michigan; forested island, the largest in Lake Superior; ancient copper mines.
Ludington State Park: Near Ludington; Lake Michigan beach; trails; fishing, camping.
Mackinac Bridge: 5 miles long with approaches; connects Michigan's upper and lower peninsulas.
Mackinac Island: Resort; old fort (1780).
Muskegon State Park: Near North Muskegon; Lake Michigan beach; sand dunes; camping fishing.

Onaway State Park; Near Onaway: beach on Black Lake; densely wooded area; fishing, camping.
Ortonville Recreation Area: Near Ortonville; wooded hills; scenic views; lake fishing.
Palms Book State Park: Near Manistique; noted Kitch-iti-ki-pi spring; large, clear pool fed by underground spring.
Pictured Rocks National Lakeshore: On Lake Superior near Munising; colored rock formation.
Pickney Recreation Area: Near Gregory; camping, fishing.
Pontiac Lake Recreation Area: Near Pontiac; beaches.
Porcupine Mountains State Park: Near Ontonagon; winter sports, hiking, camping.
Sault Ste. Marie: "Soo" canal locks.
Sleeping Bear Dunes National Lakeshore: On Lake Michigan near Frankfort; sand dunes; forests.
Sterling State Park: Near Monroe; beach along Lake Erie.
Tahquamenon Falls State Park: Near Newberry; scenic views; Upper and Lower Falls; boat trips offer awesome view of Upper Falls.
Traverse City: Cherry center; Clinch Park Complex.
Walter J. Hayes State Park: Near Clinton in Irish Hills; camping, fishing, and picnicking.
Warren Dunes State Park: On Lake Michigan near St. Joseph; sand dunes; forest; swimming, camping.
Waterloo Recreation Area: Near Jackson; rolling hills; fishing, hiking, camping; nature center.
Yankee Springs Recreation Area: Near Hastings; rough wooded hills; camping, deer, and small-game hunting.

Additional information sources:
Michigan Travel Bureau
P. O. Box 30226
Lansing, MI 48909
(800) 543-2937

Michigan Dept. of Natural Resources
(517) 373-1230

Michigan Road Conditions
(800) 337-1334

Michigan Road Construction
(517) 373-2160

Webpage
http://www.state.mi.us/

TRAIL COUNTIES

Bergland to Sidnaw: Houghton & Ontonagon

•

Bill Nicholls: Houghton & Ontonagon

•

Hancock/Calumet: Houghton

•

Hart-Montague: Muskegon & Oceana

•

Kal-Haven: Kalamazoo & Van Buren

•

Paint Creek: Oakland

•

Pere-Marquette: Midland

•

Stateline: Gogebic & Iron

	WEATHER CONDITIONS					
	Temperature				**Precipitation**	
	Detroit		**Sault St. Marie**		(inches)	
	High	Low	High	Low	Detroit	SSM*
JAN	32	19	22	6	8S	27S
FEB	34	20	24	7	8S	19S
MAR	43	28	32	15	5S	15S
APR	58	39	47	29	3	5S
MAY	68	48	59	38	3	3
JUNE	79	59	70	47	3	3
JULY	83	63	75	52	3	3
AUG	82	62	73	53	3	3
SEPT	74	55	64	46	2	4
OCT	63	45	55	38	3	3
NOV	48	34	39	26	2	15S
DEC	35	24	27	13	7S	21S

*SSM – Sault St. Marie; S-Snow

BERGLAND to SIDNAW RAIL-TRAIL

Trail Uses: Hiking, Horseback Riding, Mountain Bicycling and Snowmobiling

Trail Heads:
East - Sidnaw
West - Bergland

Surface: Dirt, Gravel & Sand

Grade: Flat

Length of Trail:
45 miles

Date Established: 1991

Trail Name Origin:
Named for the towns at the east and west borders of the trail.

Trail Highlights:
- Former Soo Line Railroad.
- Bergland provides users with breathtaking views from five enormous bridges that overlook streams and the Ontonagon, Baltimore and Jumbo Rivers.
- Trail parallels Highway 28.

Suggested Auto Routes

Iron Mountain to Sidnaw		
Road	Direction	Miles
US2 to Wisconsin	N	4
US2 to Michigan	W	13.7
US2 to US141	NW	11
US141 to ST28	NW	36
ST28	W	12.4
Total: 77.1 miles; 1 hour, 45 minutes		

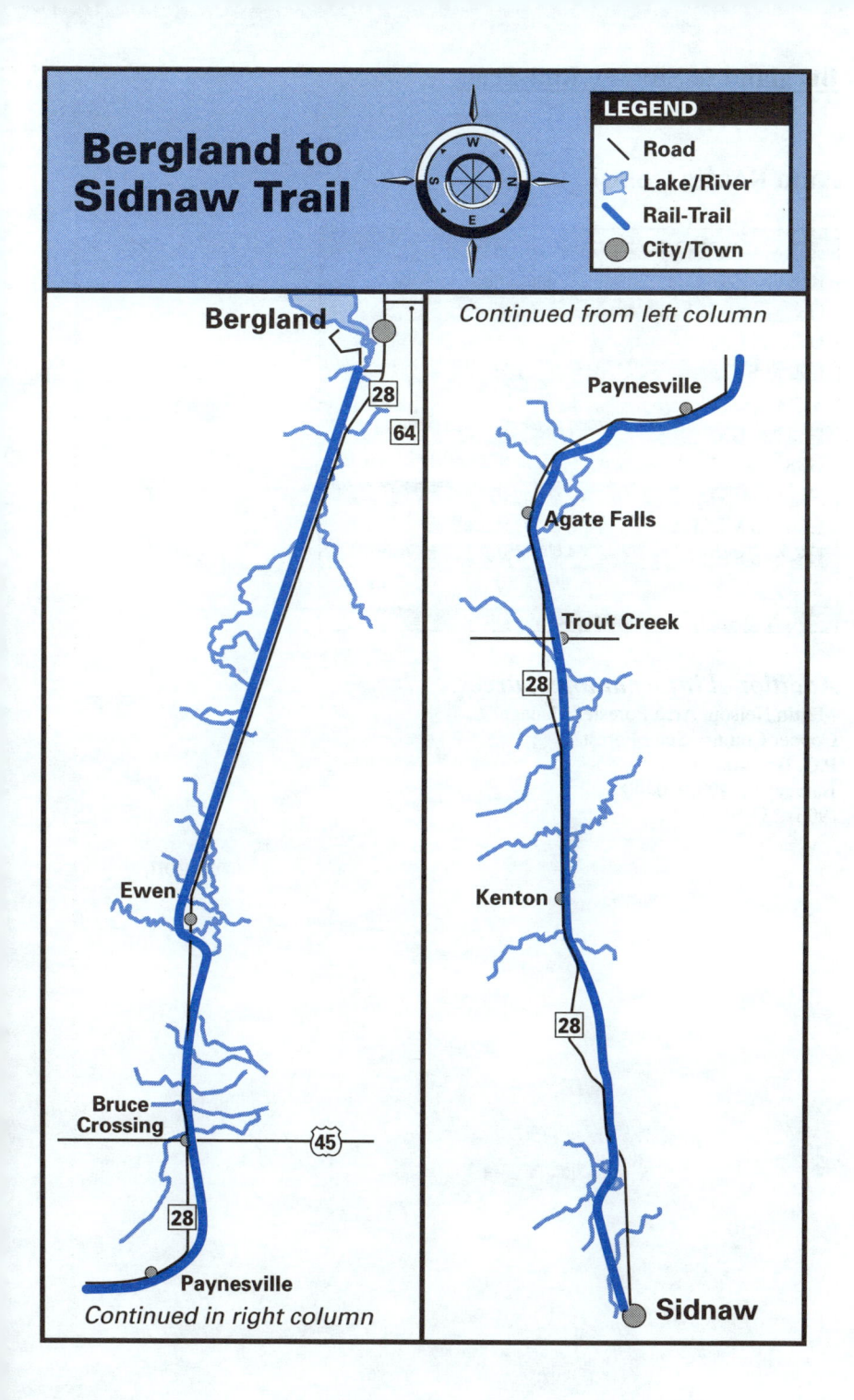

Bergland to Sidnaw Trail

LEGEND
- Road
- Lake/River
- Rail-Trail
- City/Town

Bergland
28
64
Ewen
Bruce Crossing
45
28
Paynesville
Continued in right column

Continued from left column
Paynesville
Agate Falls
Trout Creek
28
Kenton
28
Sidnaw

Bergland to Sidnaw Rail Trail

Auto Routes (cont.)

Madison, WI to Bergland, MI		
Road	Direction	Miles
US151 to US51	NE	3.8
US51 to I-90	N	3.4
I-90 to ST78	NW	24.3
ST78 to US51	N	7.9
US51 to US8	N	143.6
US8 to ST17	E	14.4
ST17 to US45	NE	25.6
US45 to Michigan	N	14.6
US45 to ST28	N	27
ST28	W	20
Total: 284.6 miles; 5 hours, 42 minutes		

Additional information sources:
Martin Nelson, Area Forester Manager
Copper Country State Forest
P.O. Box 400
Baraga, MI 49908-0400
(906) 353-6651

BILL NICHOLLS TRAIL

#2

Trail Uses: Hiking, Horseback Riding, Mountain Bicycling and Snowmobiling

Trail Heads:
North - Houghton
South - Mass City

Surface: Dirt, Gravel, Original Ballast & Sand

Grade: Flat

Length of Trail: 41 miles

Date Established: 1974

Trail Name Origin:
Named for the President of the Cooper Ridge Range Railroad, who was instrumental in the acquisition of the railroad corridor.

Trail Highlights:
- Former Cooper Range Railroad line.
- Bill Nichols is challenging but scenic as it winds through communities, old mining ruins, woodlands and crosses several small lakes. The trail crosses the Firesteel River via three bridges 65, 75 and 85 ft. high providing many scenic overlooks including the Portage Lake Ship Canal.
- Links to the Hancock/Calumet Rail-Trail and Keweenaw Rail-Trail.

Suggested Auto Routes

Iron Mountain to Mass City		
Road	Direction	Miles
US2 to Wisconsin	N	4
US2 to Michigan	W	13.7
US2 to U45	W	55
US45 to ST26	N	33
ST26	NE	5
Total: 110.7 miles; 2 hours, 25 minutes		

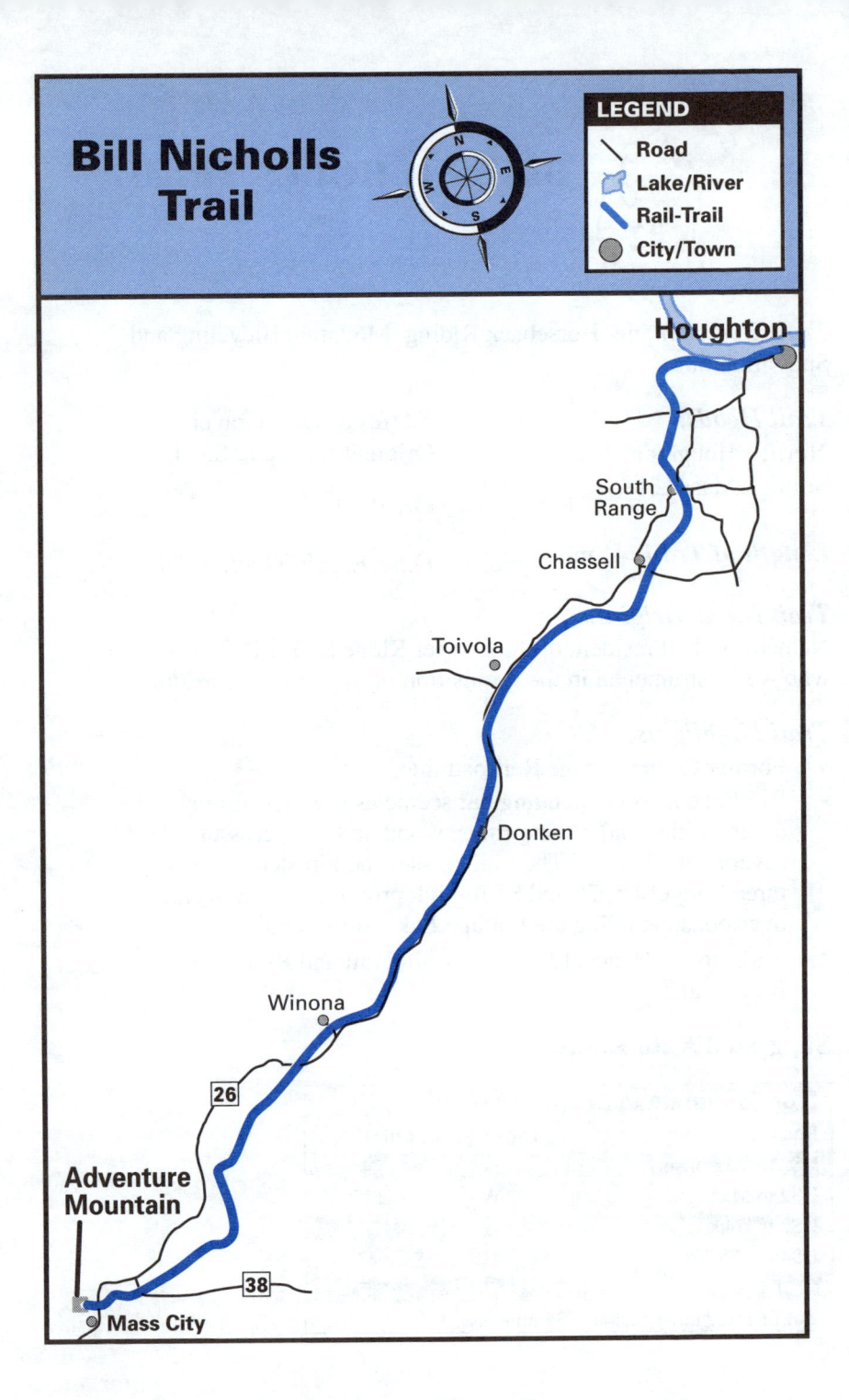

Bill Nicholls Trail

Bill Nicholls Rail-Trail

Auto Route (cont.)

Madison, WI to Mass City, MI

Road	Direction	Miles
US151 to US51	NE	3.8
US51 to I-90	N	3.4
I-90 to ST78	NW	24.3
ST78 to US51	N	7.9
US51 to US8	N	143.6
US8 to ST17	E	14.4
ST17 to US45	NE	25.6
US45 to Michigan	N	14.6
US45 ST26	N	41
ST26	N	5

Total: 283.6miles; 5 hours, 33 minutes

Additional information sources:
Martin Nelson, Forest Manager or Dave Tuovlia
Copper Country State Forest Area
Baraga Forest Area
P.O. Box 440
Baraga, MI 49908
(906) 353-6651

Houghton Lake Chamber of Commerce
1625 West Houghton Lake Drive
Houghton Lake, MI 48629
(517) 366-5644

HANCOCK/CALUMET TRAIL
#3

Trail Uses: Hiking, Horseback Riding, Mountain Biking and Snowmobiling

Trail Heads:
South - Hancock
North - Calumet

Surface: Sand & Gravel

Grade: 1-2 %

Length of Trail: 13.5 miles

Date Established: 1988

Trail Name Origin:
Name for the towns at the north and south borders of the trail.

Trail Highlights:
- Former Soo Line Railroad line.
- Hancock/Calumet begins at an abandoned depot, traverses through wetlands, Swedetown Pond and mining ruins. Trail ends at an observation deck overlooking a ship canal and Bill Nicholls Trail.
- Links with Bill Nicholls and Keweenaw Rail-Trails.

Suggested Auto Routes

Iron Mountain to Hancock		
Road	Direction	Miles
US2 to Wisconsin	N	4
US2 to Michigan	W	13.7
US2 to US141	N	11
US141 to US41	NW	40
US41	N	45.9
Total: 114.6 miles; 2 hours, 31 minutes		

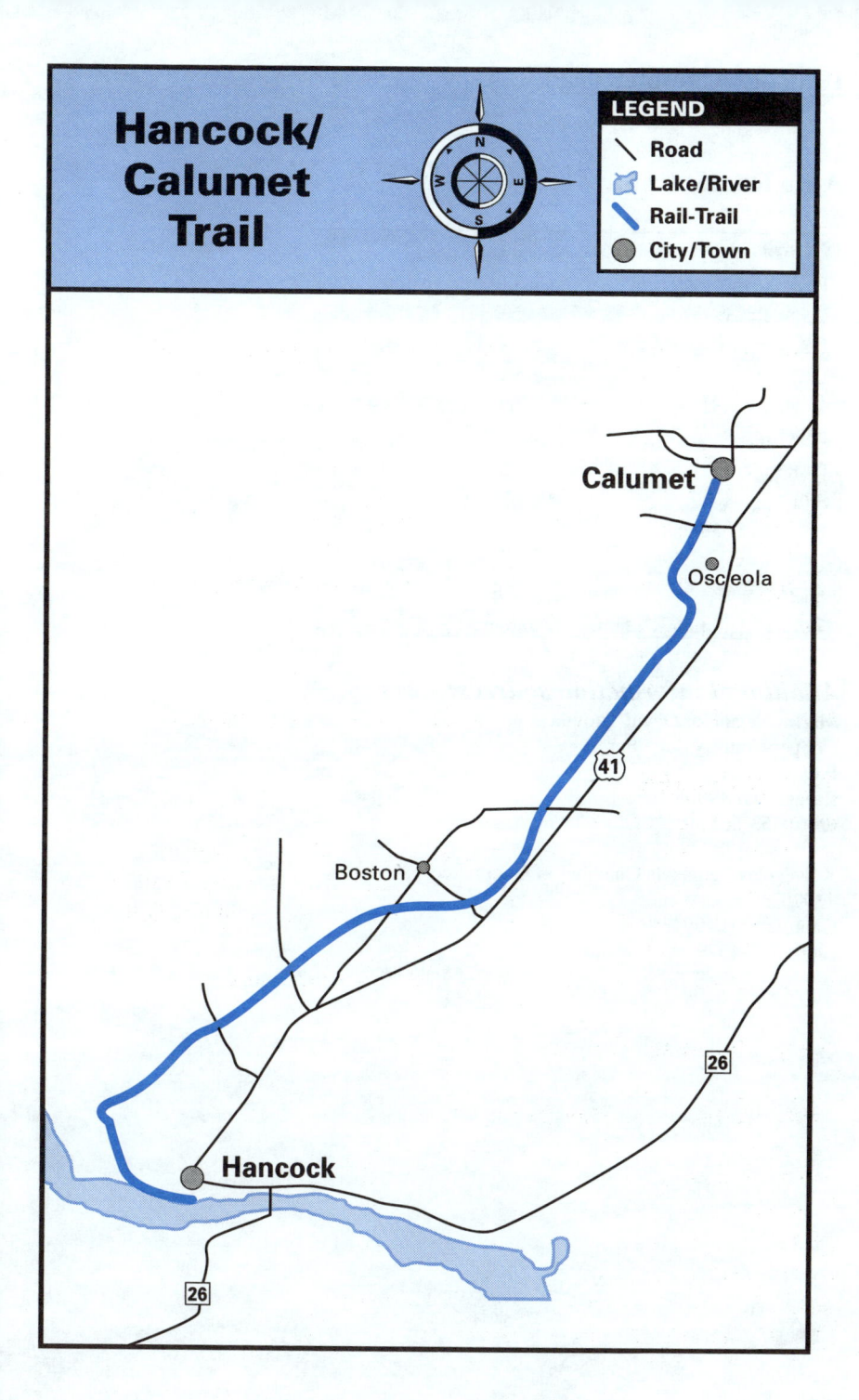

Hancock/Calumet Trail

Hancock/Calumet Trail

Auto Routes (cont.)

Madison, WI to Hancock, MI		
Road	Direction	Miles
US 151 to US51	NE	3.8
US51 to I-90	N	3.4
I-90 to ST78	NW	24.3
ST78 to US51	N	7.9
US51 to US8	N	143.6
US8 to ST17	E	14.4
ST17 to US45	NE	25.6
US45 to Michigan	N	14.6
US45 to ST26	N	41
ST26	NE	42.9
Total: 321.5 miles, 6 hour, 40 minutes		

Additional information sources:
Martin Nelson or David Tuovila
Copper Country State Forest
P.O. Box 400
Baraga, MI 49908
(906) 353-6651

Keweenaw Peninsula Chamber of Commerce
1197 Calumet Avenue
Calumet, MI 49913
(906) 337-4579

HART-MONTAGUE BICYCLE TRAIL STATE PARK

Trail Uses: Bicycling, Hiking, Horseback Riding (in designated areas), In-line Skating, Cross-country Skiing and Snowmobiling

Trail Heads:
North - Hart
South - Montague

Grade: Mostly Flat

Date Established: 1987

Length of Trail: 22.5 miles
Surface: Asphalt

Trail Name Origin:
Named for towns at the north and south borders of the trail.

Trail Highlights:
- Former C&O and Chicago & Western Michigan Railroad lines.
- Hart-Montague winds through a pleasant mix of orchards forests, farmland, parks and small communities.
- Scenic rest stop overlooks East Golden Pond.

Suggested Auto Routes

Detroit to Montague		
Road	Direction	Miles
I-75 to I-696	NW	7.3
I-696 to I-96	W	16.7
I-96 to US31	W	161.2
US31	NW	20
Total: 206.9 miles; 3 hours, 15 minutes		

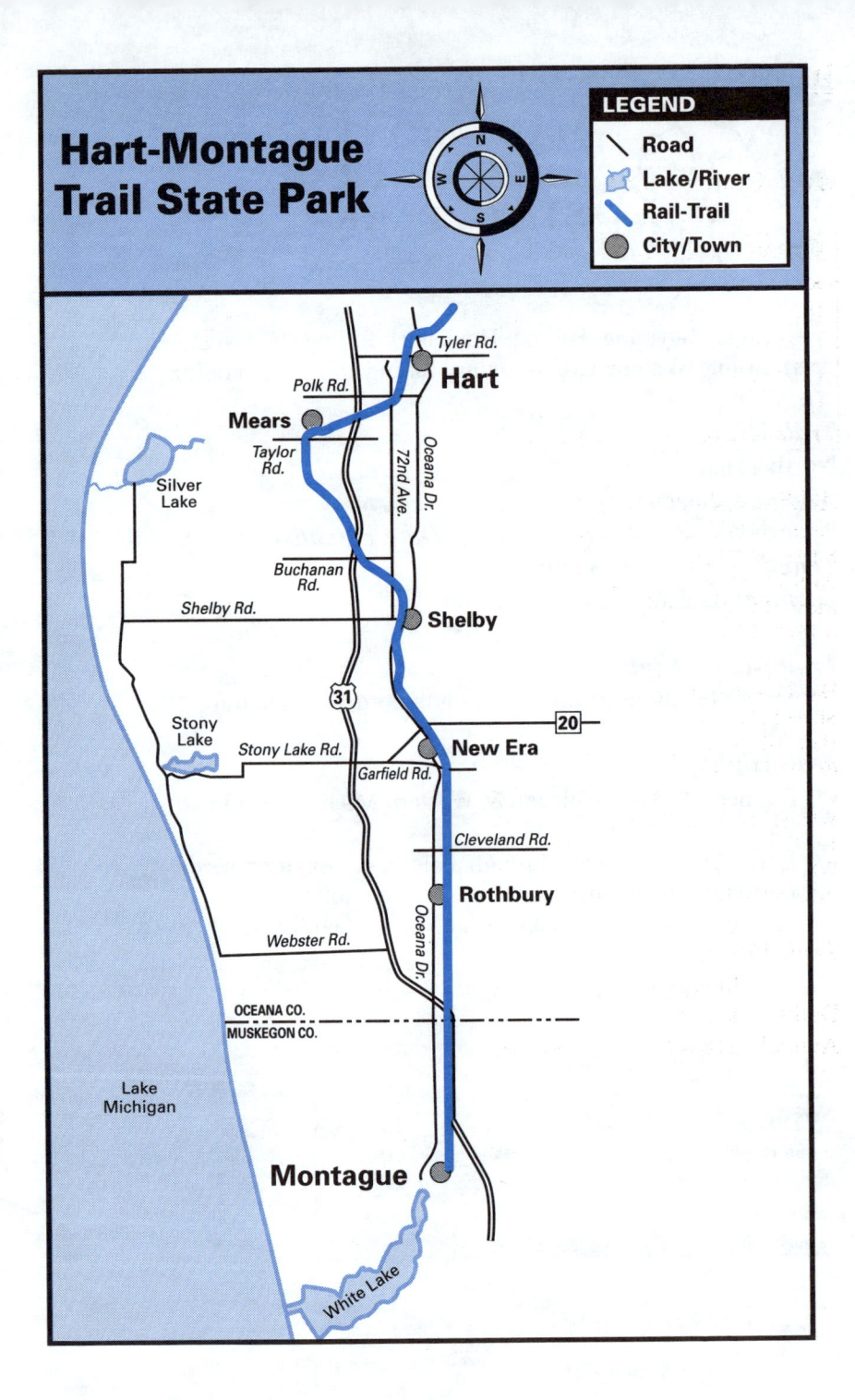

Hart-Montague Trail State Park

Hart-Montague Bicycle Trail State Park

Auto Routes (cont.)

Grand Rapids to Montague

Road	Direction	Miles
US131 to I-296	N	2.4
I-296 to I-96	NW	1.1
I-96 to US31	W	30.2
US31	NW	20
Total: 55.4 miles; 51 minutes		

Additional information sources:
Peter Lundberg, Park Manager
Silver Lake State Park
9679 West State Park Road
Mears, MI 49436 –9734
(616) 873-3083

Hart Chamber of Commerce
Silver Lake Road
Hart, MI 49420
(616) 873-2247

White Lake Area Chamber of Commerce
124 Hanson Street
Whitehall, MI 49461
(616) 893-4585

Trail Passes:

	Individual	Family
Daily	$ 2.00	$ 5.00
Annual	$10.00	$25.00

KAL-HAVEN TRAIL

Trail Uses: Bicycling, Hiking, Horseback Riding, Cross-country Skiing and Snowmobiling

Trail Heads:
East - Kalamazoo
West - South Haven

Length of Trail: 33.5 mile; 14 mile Equestrian trail

Surface: Crushed Limestone

Grade: Flat

Date Established: 1988

Trail Name Origin:
Named for the towns at the east and west borders of the trail.

Trail Highlights:
- Former South Haven to Kalamazoo and Penn Central Railroad lines.
- Kal-Haven traverses through apple orchards, blueberry fields, farmlands, glacial areas, wetlands and wooded areas. Trail crosses the Black River via a covered bridge and Baker Creek via Camel Back Bridge.
- The east trailhead in Kalamazoo is marked by a refurbished caboose, which serves as an office and information center. Midway through the trail in Bloomingdale is a restored depot, which serves as a museum and rest stop.

Suggested Auto Routes

Detroit to Kalamazoo		
Road	Direction	Miles
I-94	W	136.4
Total: 136.4 miles; 2 hours, 10 minutes		

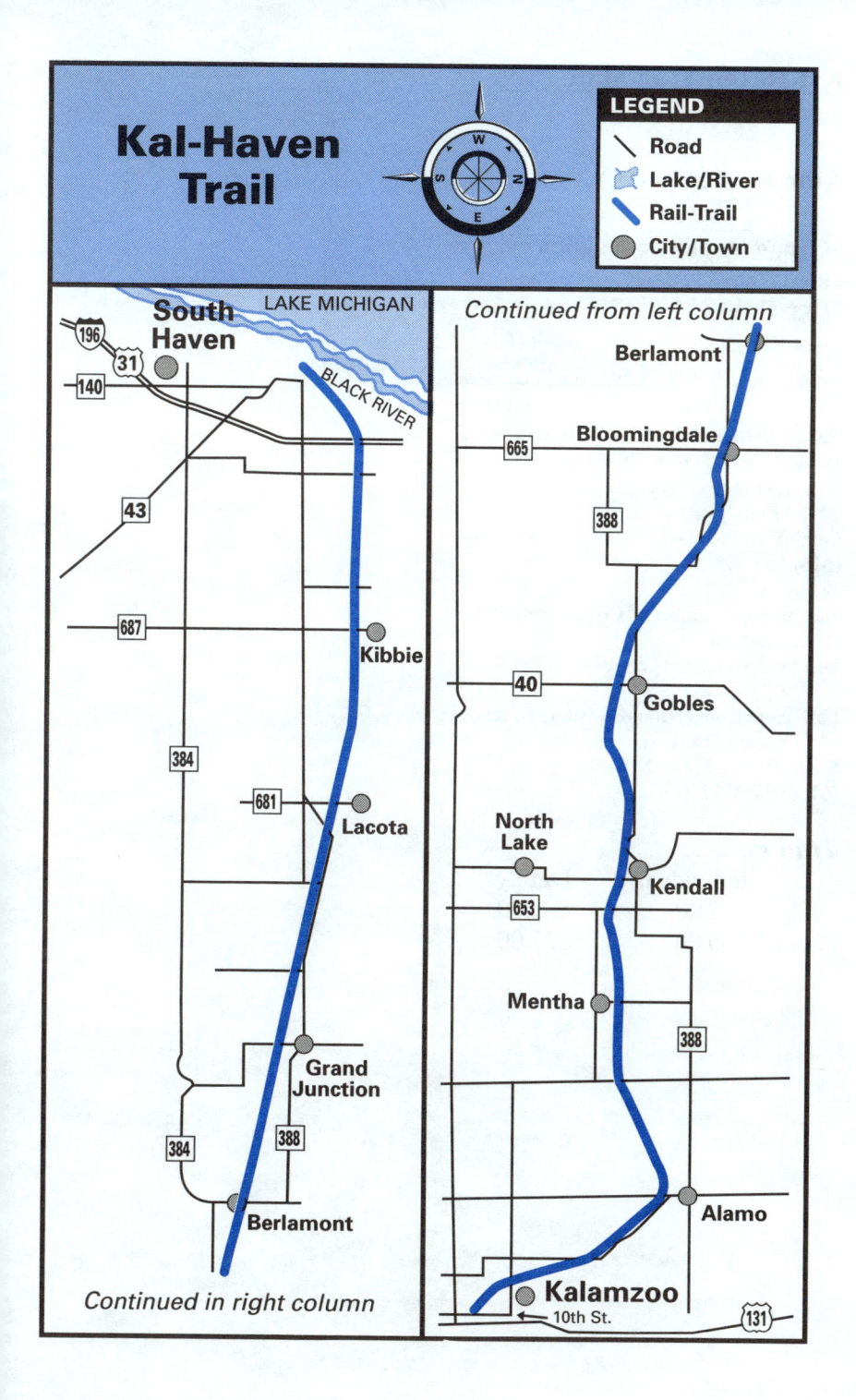

Kal-Haven Trail

LEGEND
- Road
- Lake/River
- Rail-Trail
- City/Town

LAKE MICHIGAN
South Haven
BLACK RIVER
Kibbie
Lacota
Grand Junction
Berlamont

Continued in right column

Continued from left column
Berlamont
Bloomingdale
Gobles
North Lake
Kendall
Mentha
Alamo
Kalamzoo
10th St.

Kal-Haven Trail State Park

Auto Routes (cont.)

Grand Rapids to Kalamazoo		
Road	Direction	Miles
US131 to I-94	S	51.7
I-94	E	1
Total: 52.7 miles; 52 minutes		

Additional information sources:
David Marsh, Trail Supervisor
Van Buren State Park
23960 Ruggles Road
South Haven, MI 49090
(616) 637-4984

Kalamazoo Chamber of Commerce
Kalamazoo, MI
http://www.kazoobiz.com/

Lakeshore Convention & Visitors Bureau
415 Phoenix Street
South Haven, MI 49090
(616) 637-5252

Trail Passes:

	Individual	Family
Daily	$ 2.00	$ 5.00
Annual	$10.00	$25.00

PAINT CREEK TRAILWAY

Trail Uses: Bicycling, Hiking, Horseback Riding (in designated areas) and Cross-country Skiing

Trail Heads:
North - Lake Orion
South - Rochester

Length of Trail: 10.5 miles

Surface: Crushed Stone, Original Ballast & Dirt

Grade: 1%

Date Established: 1990

Trail Name Origin:
Derived from trail location parallel to Paint Creek.

Trail Highlights:
- Former Detroit & Bay City and Penn Central Railroad lines.
- Paint Creek provides users with a tranquil environment of glacial rocks, cider mills and nearly a dozen bridges.
- Paint Creek Cider Mill is a popular rest stop for trail users seeking cider, donuts and other refreshments.

Suggested Auto Routes

Detroit to Rochester		
Road	Direction	Miles
I-75 to ST59	NW	24.2
ST59	E	4.5
Total: 31.8 miles; 32 minutes		

84

Paint Creek Trail

Auto Routes (cont.)

Grand Rapids to Rochester		
Road	Direction	Miles
I-196 to I-96	E	4
I-96 to I-69	E	52.7
I-69 to ST121	E	51.7
ST121 to I-75	E	.8
I-75 to ST59	SE	37.7
ST59	E	4.5
Total: 154.5 miles; 2 hours, 35 minutes		

Additional information sources:
Bill Stark, Trailways Coordinator
Paint Creek Trailways Commission
4393 Collins Road
Rochester, MI 48306-1619
(248) 651-9260

Orion Area Chamber of Commerce
c/o Pamela Little
P.O. Box 236
Lake Orion, MI 48361
(248) 693-6300

PERE MARQUETTE RAIL-TRAIL of MID-MICHIGAN

Trail Uses: Bicycling, Hiking and In-line Skating

Trail Heads:
East - Midland
West - Coleman

Surface: Asphalt

Grade: Flat

Length of Trail: 21 miles

Date Established: 1993

Trail Name Origin:
Named derived from the former railroad line.

Trail Highlights:
- Former Flint & Pere Marquette Railroad line.
- Pere Marquette offers users a charming look at railroad history, historical attractions and breathtaking views of the area. Trail crosses the Chippewa and Tittabawassee Rivers via the "Tridge' Bridge and three former railroad bridges.
- Optional historical stop: Centennial Museum (restored historic building with railroad artifacts), Herbert H. Dow Historical Museum and Bradley House.
- Links with White Pine Trail State Park.

Future Plan:
Extend trail through Clare, Farwell, Evart, Reed City, Baldwin and Ludington. This extension would include a link with Wisconsin via ferry service.
Link with Pine Haven Recreation Area.

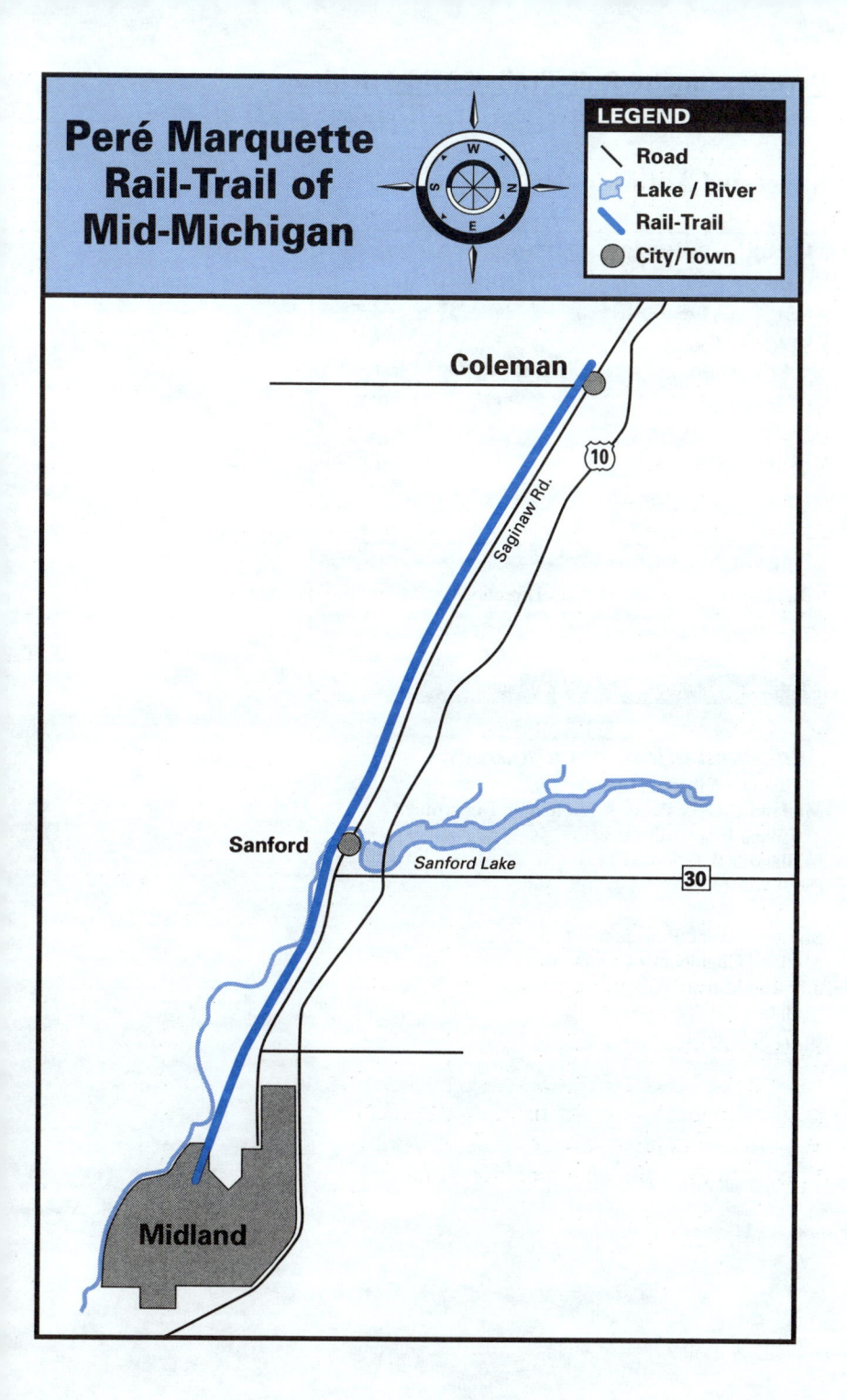

Peré Marquette Rail-Trail of Mid-Michigan

LEGEND
- Road
- Lake / River
- Rail-Trail
- City/Town

Coleman

Saginaw Rd.

10

Sanford

Sanford Lake

30

Midland

Pere Marquette Rail-Trail of Mid-Michigan

Suggested Auto Routes

Grand Rapids to Coleman

Road	Direction	Miles
US131 to ST46	NE	34.4
ST46 to ST66	E	18.7
ST66 to ST20	N	12
US20 to US27	E	19.9
US27 to US10	N	15.6
US10	E	9.1
Total: 109.7 miles; 2 hours, 9 minutes		

Detroit to Midland

Road	Direction	Miles
I-75 to US10	NW	109.6
US10	W	16.1
Total: 125.7 miles; 2 hours, 2 minutes		

Additional information sources:
William C. Gibson, Director
Midland County Parks & Recreation Department
220 West Ellsworth Street
Midland, MI 48640-5194
(517) 832-6870

Shirley Clwers, President
Midland Chamber of Commerce
300 Rodd Street
Midland, MI 48640-5126
(517) 839-9901

STATELINE TRAIL #8

Trail Uses: Hiking, Horseback Riding, Mountain Bicycling and Snowmobiling

Trail Heads:
West - Marenisco
East - Stager

Surface: Sand & Gravel

Grade: Flat

Length of Trail: 87 miles with detour

Date Established: 1984

Trail Name Origin:
Trail is named for its proximity to the Wisconsin border and Michigan.

Trail Highlights:
- Former Chicago & Northwestern Railroad line.
- Stateline provides users with magnificent scenery and rugged terrain. It traverses through iron red painted countryside passing lakes, farmland and old mines. More than fifty bridges provide incredible views of rivers and wildlife including a large population of Bald Eagles.
- Links with Stager Junction to Crystal Falls Trail.

Suggested Auto Routes

Iron Mountain to Stager		
Road	Direction	Miles
US2/US141	N	18
Iron Co 424 to Stager, MI	NW	2
Total: 20 miles; 28 minutes		

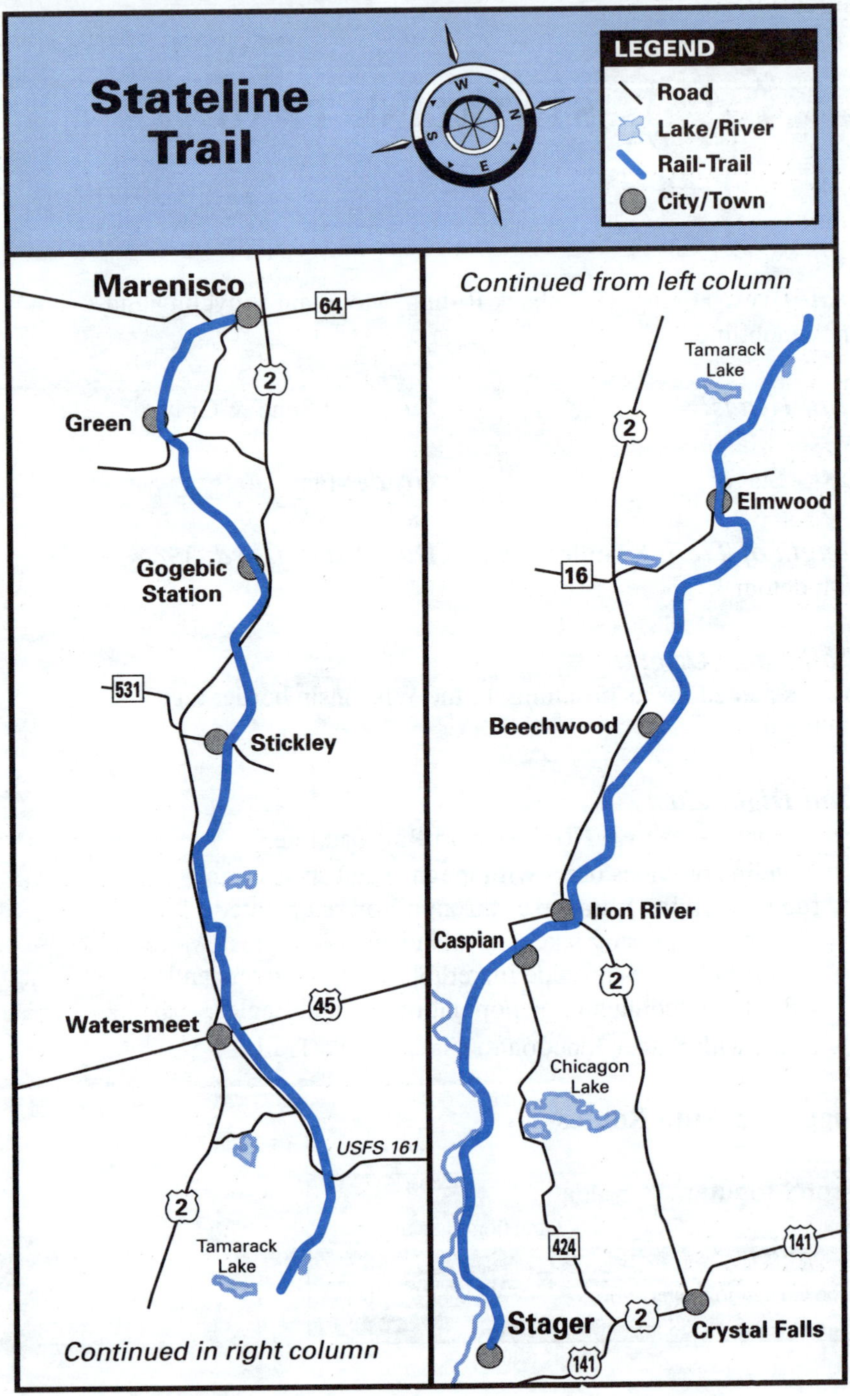
Stateline Trail
LEGEND
Road
Lake/River
Rail-Trail
City/Town
W
N
E
S
Marenisco
64
2
Green
Gogebic Station
531
Stickley
45
Watersmeet
USFS 161
2
Tamarack Lake
Continued in right column
Continued from left column
Tamarack Lake
2
Elmwood
16
Beechwood
Iron River
Caspian
2
Chicagon Lake
424
141
Stager
2
Crystal Falls
141

Stateline Rail-Trail

Auto Routes (cont.)

Madison, WI to Marenisco, MI		
Road	Direction	Miles
US151 to US51	NE	3.8
US51 to I-90	N	3.4
I-90 to ST78	NW	24.3
ST78 to US51	N	7.9
US51 to US8	N	143.6
US8 to Rte 17	E	14.4
Rte 17 to US45	NE	25.6
US45 to MI	N	14.6
US45 to US2	N	8
US 2	W	28
Total: 273.6 miles; 5 hours, 10 minutes		

Additional information sources:
Iron County Administrator
2 South 6th St.
Crystal Falls, MI 49920-1494

Martin Nelson
Copper Country State Forest
P.O. Box 400
Baraga, MI 49909
(906) 353-6651

Minnesota

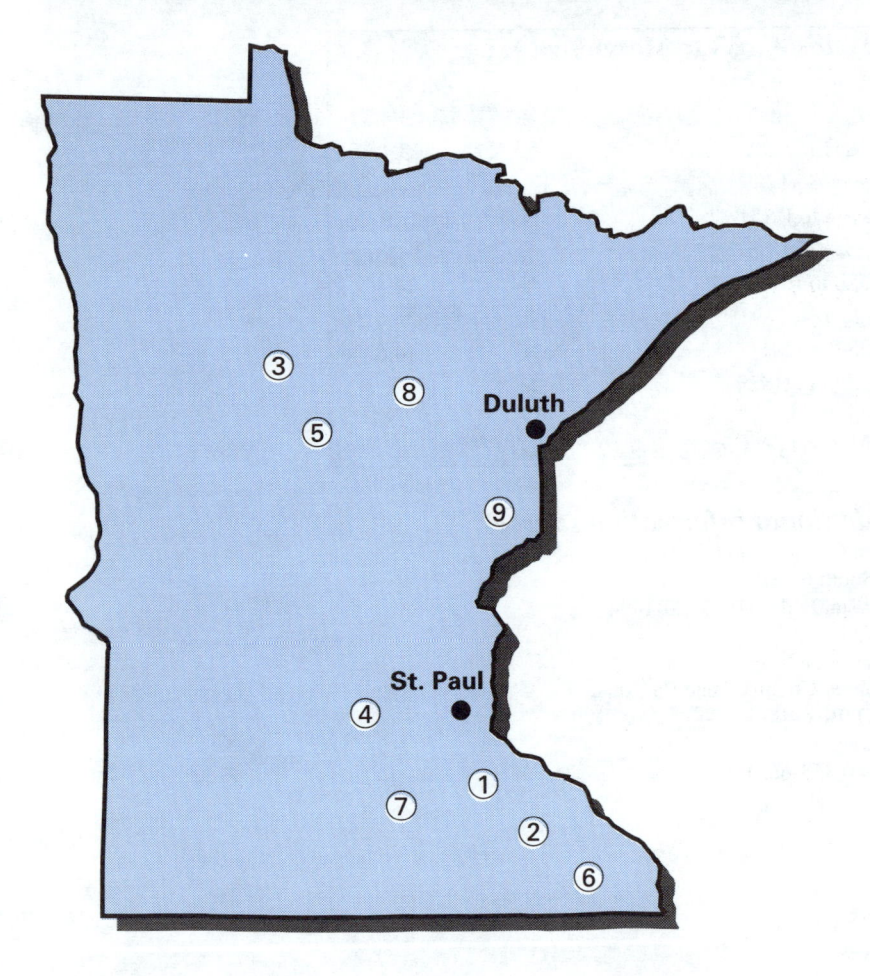

- #1 Cannon Valley
- #2 Douglas
- #3 Heartland
- #4 Luce Line
- #5 Paul Bunyan
- #6 Root River
- #7 Sakatah Singing Hills
- #8 Soo Line
- #9 Willard Munger

FACTS ABOUT MINNESOTA

Capital: St. Paul

Elevation:
Highest Point - Eagle Mountain 2,301 ft.

Lowest Point - Lake Superior 602 ft.

Largest City: Minneapolis

Motto: L'Etoile du Nord (The Star of the North)

Nickname: North Star State; Gopher State; Land of 10,000 lakes; Land of Sky Blue Waters

Population: 4,387,029

State Bird: Loon

State Fish: Walleye

State Flower: Pink and White Lady's Slipper (Norway Pine)

State Tree: Red Pine

Statehood: May 11, 1858 (32nd state)

Time Zone: Central DST

Boasting Rights:
- 890 miles of state owned trails one-third of which are built on old abandoned railroad grades.
- Over 10,000 lakes
- 50 developed rail trails totaling 964 miles.
- Future plans to develop 30 former railroads to rail trails, totaling 626 miles.

Geographic Center: Crow Wing, 10 miles southwest of Brainerd

PLACES OF INTEREST

Baptism River State Park: Near Two Harbors; scenic beauty, nature trails.
Bear Head Lake State Park: Near Ely; fishing, picnicking.
Beaver Creek Valley State Park: Near Caledonia; fishing, picnicking.
Birch Coulee State Memorial Park: Near Morton; site of Indian battle (1862).
Blue Mounds State Park: Near Luverne; unusual rock formations.
Bunyan House Information Center: In Bemidji; giant statues of legendary lumberjack and his blue ox.
Cascade River State Park: Near Grand Marais; series of rapids on Cascade River; fishing, picnicking.
Charles A. Lindbergh State Park: Near Little Falls; boyhood home of famous flier; dedicated as a memorial to his father.
Crow Wing State Park: Near Brainerd; pioneer town; scenic nature trails.
Ely: Iron mines; Echo Trail in Superior National Forest; starting point for wilderness canoe trips.
Father Hennepin State Memorial Park: Near Isle; scenic nature trails.
Fort Ridgely State Memorial Park: Near Fairfax; historic fort built in 1853.
Fort Snelling State Park: Near Minneapolis; historic fort built in 1820.
Gooseberry Falls State Park: Near Duluth; waterways; fishing, hiking, camping.
Grand Portage National Monument: In Grand Marais; old fur-trade trail and post.
Gunflint Trail: Begins near Grand Marais; in superior National Forest.
Hibbing: World's largest open-pit iron mine.
Kensington Runestone: In Alexandria; replica of stone once believed to have been left by Noresemen.
Kilen Woods State Park: Near Jackson; scenic hills; virgin timber.
Lake Vermillion: In northeastern Minnesota; largest lake in Arrowhead country.
McCarthy Beach State Memorial Park: Near Hibbing; lake beaches; virgin pine.
Mendota: Henry H. Sibley House (1835), oldest house in the state.
Mille Lacs Lake: In central Minnesota; scenic lake; Indian mounds.
Minnesota Museum of Mining: Near Chisholm.
Monson Lake State Memorial Park: Near Sunburg; Sioux massacre site (1862).

Niagara Cave: In Harmony; underground falls.
Northfield: Carleton and St. Olaf colleges.
North Shore Drive: Along Lake Superior.
Northwest Angle: Northernmost point in contiguous United States.
Old Mill State Park: Near Warren; old flour mill (1888).
Pipestone National Monument: Near Pipestone; Indian quarry for peace pipes.
Red Lake: In northwestern Minnesota; largest lake in the state.
Soudan Underground Mine State Park: Near tower; only underground state park in the United States; mining operations.
Split Rock Lighthouse: On Lake Superior near Duluth.
Temperance River State Park: Near Schroeder; fishing.
Traverse des Sioux: Ford near St. Peter.
Two Harbors: Iron-ore docks on Lake Superior.
Voyageurs National Park: In International Falls; old route of French-Canadian explores in beautiful northern lakes areas.
Whitewater State Park: Near Winona; River in wide, deep ravine.

Additional information sources:
Minnesota Office of Tourism
100 Metro Square
121 7th Place East
St. Paul, MN 55101-2112
(800) 657-3700
(612) 296-5029

Road Condition Hotlines
(800) 542-0220 (recording)
(612) 296-3076 (recording)

Dept. of Natural Resources
DNR Information Center
500 Lafayette Road
Saint Paul, MN 55155-4040
(612) 296-6157 (metro area)
(888) 646-6367 (MN toll free)
(612) 296-5484 (TDD metro area)
(800) 657-3929 (TDD)

Web Pages
http://www.state.mn.us/
http://www.dnr..state.mn.us/
http://www.state.mn.us/explore/index.html

TRAIL COUNTIES

Cannon Valley: Goodhue
•
Douglas: Goodhue & Olmsted
•
Heartland: Beltrami, Cass, Hubbard & Crow Wing
•
Luce Line: Carver, Hennepin & McLeod
•
Paul Bunyan: Beltrami, Cass, Hubbard & Crow Wing
•
Root River: Fillmore & Houston
•
Sakatah Singing Hills: Blue Earth, LeSueur & Rice
•
Soo Line: Cass, Aitkin, & Carlton
•
Willard Munger: Carlton, Pine & St. Louis

WEATHER CONDITIONS

	\multicolumn{4}{c	}{Temperature}	\multicolumn{2}{c	}{Precipitation (inches)}
	Duluth		St Paul			
	High	Low	High	Low	Dul.*	St P*
JAN	18	-1	21	3	17S	9S
FEB	22	2	26	7	12S	8S
MAR	33	14	37	20	14S	11S
APR	48	29	55	35	7S	2
MAY	60	39	68	46	3	3
JUNE	70	48	77	57	4	4
JULY	76	55	82	61	3	4
AUG	74	54	81	60	4	3
SEPT	64	45	71	49	3	3
OCT	54	36	61	39	2	2
NOV	35	21	41	24	10S	6S
DEC	22	6	27	11	16S	9S

*Dul – Duluth; St P- ST Paul; S - Snow

#1 CANNON VALLEY TRAIL

Trail Uses: Bicycling, Hiking, In-line Skating and Cross-country Skiing

Trail Heads:
West - Cannon Falls
East - Red Wing

Surface: Asphalt

Grade: Level

Length of Trail: 20 miles

Date Established: 1986

Trail Name Origin:
Derived from the trail location in the Cannon Valley.

Trail Highlights:
- Former Chicago Great Western Railroad Line.
- Cannon Valley winds along the Cannon River past woodlands, farms, hardwood forests, pastures and swamps.

Suggested Auto Routes

Duluth to Cannon Falls		
Road	Direction	Miles
I-35 to I-35E	S	133.4
I-35E to I-694	S	12.3
I-694 to I-494	S	10.7
I-494 to US52	SW	8.8
US52 to ST19	S	27.9
ST19	E	0.4
Total: 193.5 miles; 3 hours, 7 minutes		

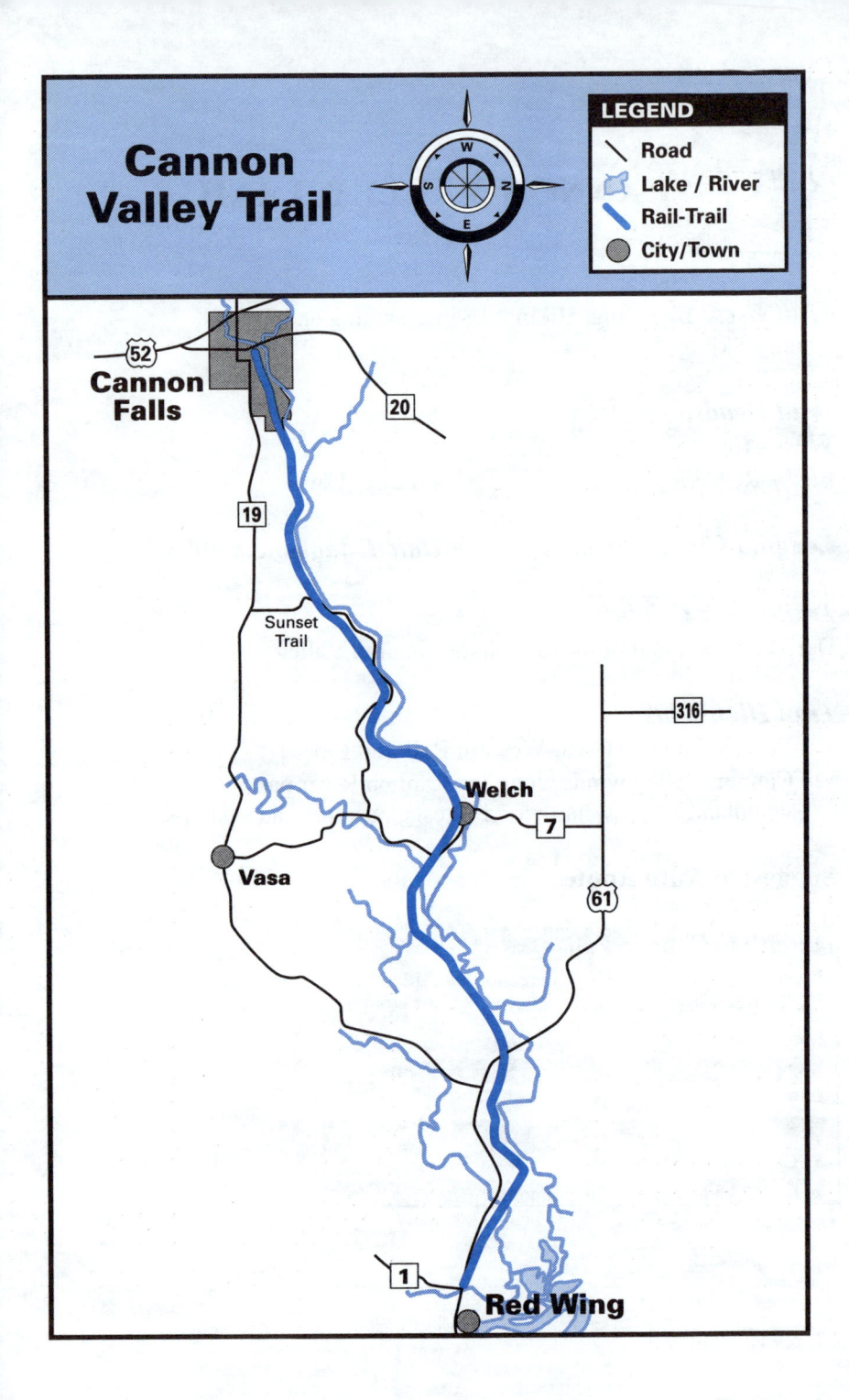

Cannon Valley Trail

LEGEND
- Road
- Lake / River
- Rail-Trail
- City/Town

Cannon Falls

Sunset Trail

Welch

Vasa

Red Wing

98

Cannon Valley Trail

Auto Routes (cont.)

St Paul to Cannon Falls		
Road	Direction	Miles
Lafayette Ave. to I-494	S	5.5
I-494 to US52	W	.7
US52 to ST19	S	27.9
ST19	E	.4
Total: 34.5 miles; 40 minutes		

Additional information sources:
Bruce Blair, Superintendent
Cannon Valley Trail
City Hall
306 West Mill Street
Cannon Falls, MN 55009
(507) 263-3954
(507) 263-5843 FAX

Pat Anderson
Cannon Falls Chamber of Commerce
P.O. Box 2
Cannon Falls, MN 55009
(507) 263-2289

Red Wings Area Chamber of Commerce
420 Levee Street
Red Wing, MN 55066
(612) 388-4719

#2 DOUGLAS STATE TRAIL

Trail Uses: Bicycling, Hiking, Horseback Riding, In-line Skating, Cross-country Skiing and Snowmobiling

Trail Heads:
South - Rochester
North - Pine Island

Surface: Asphalt

Grade: Flat

Length of Trail: 12.5 miles; Parallel Equestrian trail

Date Established: 1973

Trail Name Origin:
Derived from the town of Douglas, the midpoint town of the trail.

Trail Highlights:
- Former Chicago & Great Western Railroad line
- Douglas winds through beautiful rural scenery crossing some of the richest agricultural land in Minnesota.
- Three trestles cross the Zumbro River.

Suggested Auto Routes

Duluth to Pine Island		
Road	Direction	Miles
I-35 to I-35E	S	133.4
35E to I-694	S	12.3
I-694 to I-494	S	10.7
I-494 to US52	SW	8.8
US52	SE	54.6
Total: 219.8 miles; 3 hours, 50 minutes		

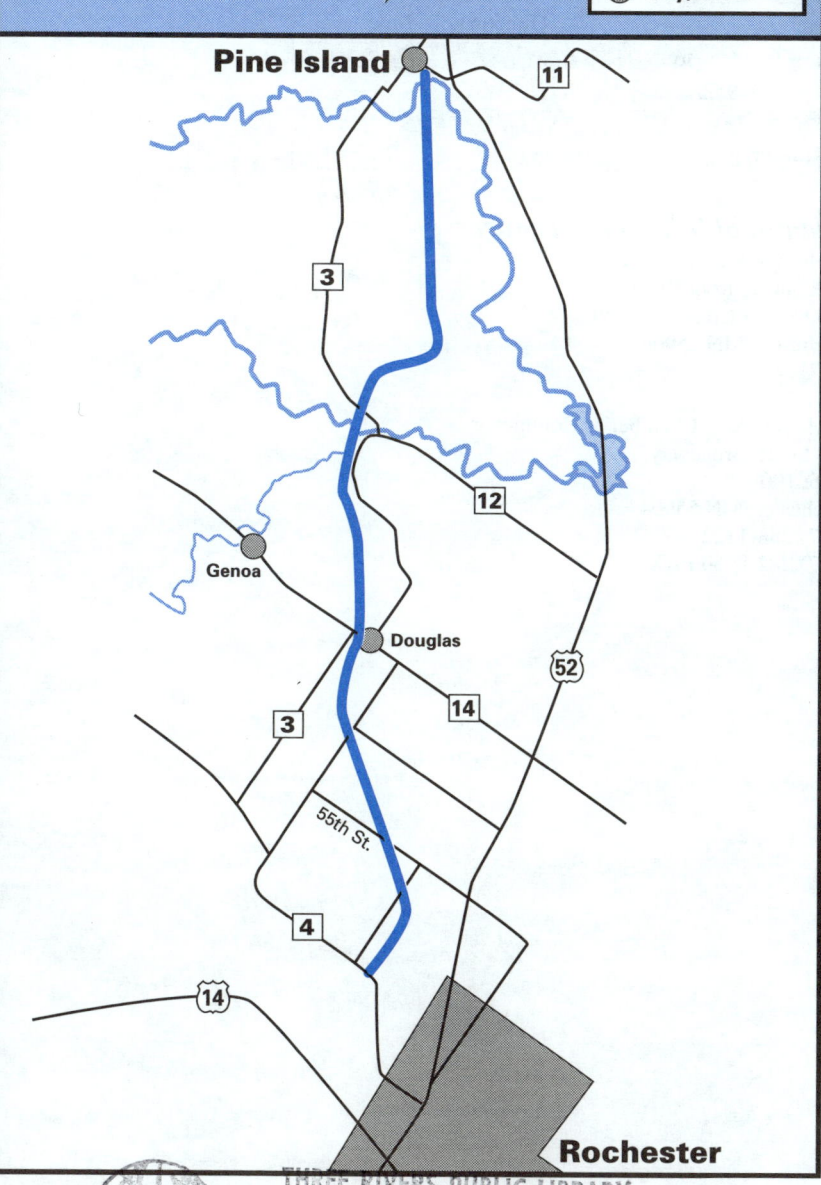

Douglas State Trail

Douglas State Trail

Auto Routes (cont.)

St Paul to Pine Island		
Road	Direction	Miles
Lafayette Ave. to I-494	S	5.5
I-494 to US52	W	.7
US52	SE	54.6
Total: 60.8 miles; 1 hour, 18 minutes		

Additional information sources:

Rochester Area Trails & Waterways
(Douglas & Root River Trails)
2300 Silver Creek Road NE
Rochester, MN 55906
(507) 285-7176

Rochester Area Chamber of Commerce
220 South Broadway
Suite 100
Rochester, MN 55904
(507) 288-1122
(507) 282-8960 FAX

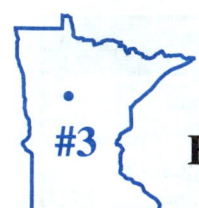

#3 HEARTLAND STATE TRAIL

Trail Uses: Bicycling, Hiking, Horseback Riding, In-line Skating, Cross-country Skiing and Snowmobiling

Trail Heads:
North - Cass Lake
South - Park Rapids

Surface: Asphalt, Compacted Gravel, Railroad Ballast & Sand

Length of Trail: 49 miles; Adjacent Equestrian trail

Date Established: 1974

Grade: Level & Sharply Rolling Terrain

Trail Name Origin:
Derived from the trail location in the North Central part of the state, which is also known as the "Heartland Region of Minnesota."

Trail Highlights:
- Former Burlington Northern Railroad line.
- Trail users will experience spectacular views of forests, lakes, rivers, streams, farms and rolling hills of the Chippewa National Forest Wildlife.
- Many varieties of wildlife are visible from Heartland trail including coyotes, mink, bobcat, black bear and bald eagle.
- One of the first rail-to-trail projects in the country.
- Links with Paul Bunyan Trail.

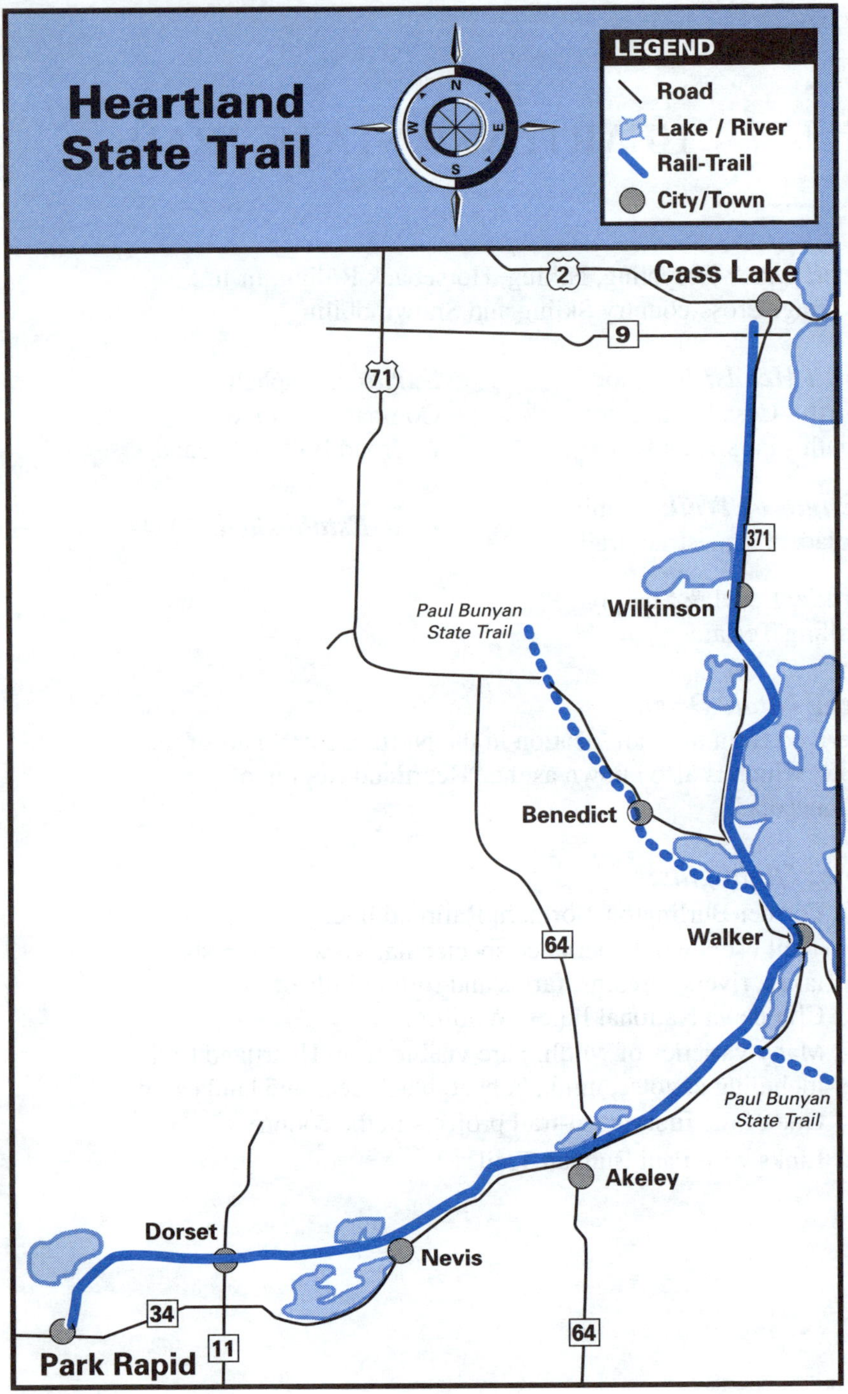
Heartland
State Trail
N
S
E
W
LEGEND
Road
Lake / River
Rail-Trail
City/Town
2
Cass Lake
9
71
371
Wilkinson
Paul Bunyan
State Trail
Benedict
64
Walker
Paul Bunyan
State Trail
Akeley
Dorset
Nevis
34
11
64
Park Rapid

Heartland State Trail

Suggested Auto Routes

Duluth to Cass Lake

Road	Direction	Miles
I-35 to US2	SW	10.4
US2	W	125.9

Total: 136.3 miles; 2 hours, 58 minutes

St Paul to Park Rapids

Road	Direction	Miles
I-94 to 35E	W	.7
35E to I-694	N	5.7
I-694 to I-94	W	10.1
I-94 to US71	W	96.8
US71	N	90.9

Total: 204.2 miles; 3 hours, 48 minutes*

Additional information sources:
Pat Tangeman, Trails & Waterways Technician
Heartland State Trail
P. O. Box 112
Nevis, MN 56467-0112
(218) 652-4054

Bemidji Area Trails & Waterways
(Heartland Trail)
2115 Birchmont Beach Road NE
Bemidji, MN 56601
(218) 755-2265

Park Rapids Area Chamber of Commerce
Highway 71 South
Park Rapids, MN 56470
(218) 732-4111

LUCE LINE TRAIL

Trail Uses: Bicycling (30 miles from Plymouth to Winsted), Hiking, Horseback Riding, Mountain Bicycling, Cross-country Skiing and Snowmobiling

Trail Heads:
East - Plymouth
West - Cosmos

Surface: Crushed Limestone (Winsted to Plymouth)

Length of Trail: 63 miles; 34-mile Parallel Equestrian trail (Eastern segment)

Grade: Flat

Date Established: 1973

Trail Name Origin:
Named after Mr. W.L. Luce, who founded the original electric railroad line that ran along this corridor.

Trail Highlights:
- Former Luce Line electric Railroad and Chicago Northwestern Railroad lines.
- Luce Line traverses through scenic rural and metropolitan countryside, which includes many varieties of prairie plants, wildlife, lakes and forests. Trail crosses the Crow River from Plymouth to Winstead.
- Remnants of railroading present on the trail allow users to experience the nostalgia of the railroading era.

Luce Line State Trail

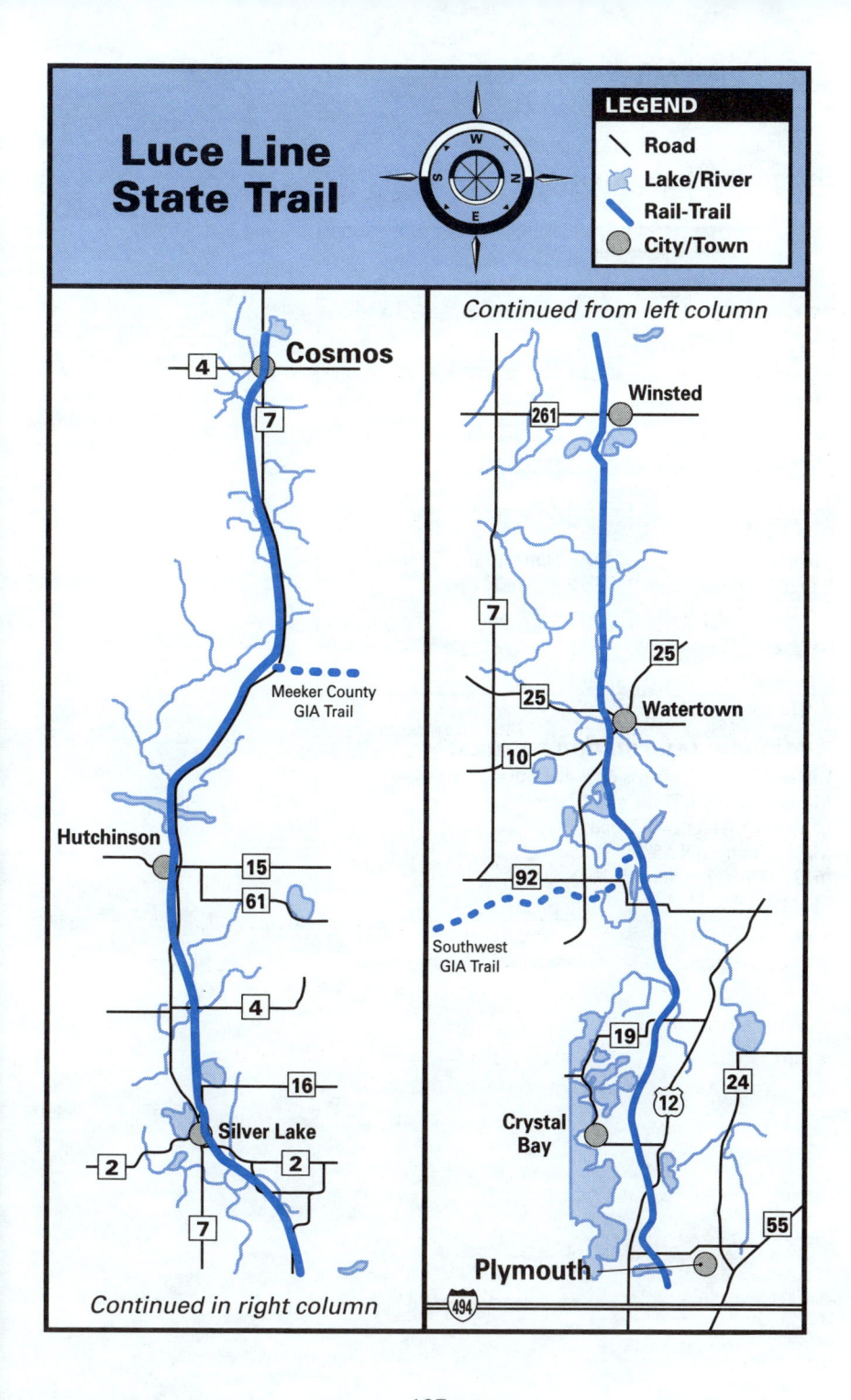

LEGEND
- Road
- Lake/River
- Rail-Trail
- City/Town

Cosmos
4
7
Meeker County GIA Trail
Hutchinson
15
61
4
16
Silver Lake
2
2
7

Continued in right column

Continued from left column

Winsted
261
7
25
25
Watertown
10
92
Southwest GIA Trail
19
24
12
Crystal Bay
55
Plymouth
494

Luce Line Trail

Suggested Auto Routes

Duluth to Plymouth

Road	Direction	Miles
I-35 to I-35W	S	133.4
I-35W to I-694	SW	13.8
I-694 to I-94	W	4.8
I-94 to I-494	W	7.8
I-494	SW	5.4

Total: 165.2 mile; 2 hours, 39 minutes

St Paul to Plymouth

Road	Direction	Miles
I-94 to I-394	W	11.4
I-394 to I-494	W	7.6
I-494	N	2.6

Total: 21.6 miles; 21 minutes

Additional information sources:
Richard Schmidt, Trails & Waterways Technician
Minnesota DNR Trails and Waterways
Unit 3980 Watertown Road
Maple Plain, MN 55359-9615
(612) 475-0371 phone & FAX

#5 PAUL BUNYAN TRAIL

Trail Uses: Bicycling, Hiking, In-line Skating and Snowmobiling

Trail Heads:
North - Bemidji
South - Brainerd

Length of Trail: 100 miles

Surface: Blacktop (48 miles); Railroad ballast, Stone, and Sand (52 miles)

Grade: Level

Date Established: 1988

Trail Name Origin:
Derived from the legendary logger Paul Bunyan believed to have traveled through the area.

Trail Highlights:
- Former Burlington Northern Railroad Line.
- Paul Bunyan offers users beautiful views of 21 lakes, wildflowers, wildlife, woodlands and streams in the Chippewa National Forest. Trail region is rich in history with thirteen recorded prehistoric sites near the trail.
- Trail Links with the Heartland Trail.

Future Plan:
Link with the Blue Ox Trail forming a 210-mile trail to the Canadian border. The completion of this extension will create a trail system of the longest rail to trail conversion in North America.

Suggested Auto Routes

Duluth to Brainerd		
Road	Direction	Miles
I-35 to ST210	W	24.7
ST210	W	90.9
Total: 115.6 miles; 2 hours, 57 minutes		

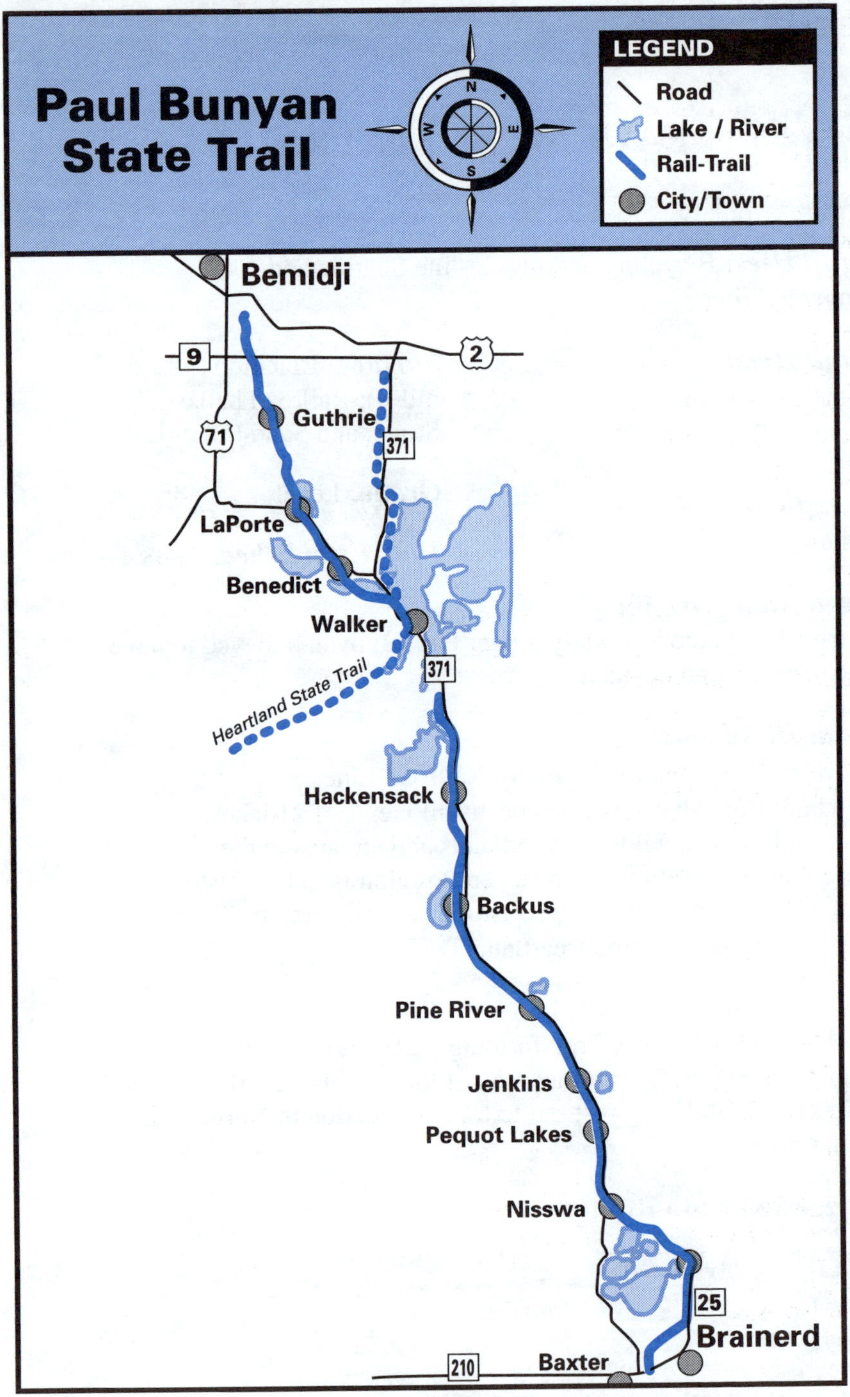
Paul Bunyan State Trail
N
E
S
W
LEGEND
Road
Lake / River
Rail-Trail
City/Town
Bemidji
9
2
Guthrie
71
371
LaPorte
Benedict
Walker
371
Heartland State Trail
Hackensack
Backus
Pine River
Jenkins
Pequot Lakes
Nisswa
25
Brainerd
210
Baxter

Paul Bunyan Trail

Auto Routes (cont.)

St Paul to Brainerd		
Road	Direction	Miles
I-94 to I-35E	W	.7
I-35E to I-694	N	5.7
I694 to I-94	W	10.1
I-94 to ST15	NW	57.4
ST15 to ST23	NE	1.9
ST23 to County Rd 1	E	4.1
County Rd 1 to ST25	N	13
ST25 to ST18	N	42.9
ST18 to ST371	W	1.1
ST371	N	.5
Total: 137.4 miles; 2 hours, 59 minutes		

Additional information sources:
Minnesota Bikeways Maps
Minnesota Department of Transportation
Boulevard Room B-2
Saint Paul, MN 55155
(612) 296-2216

Brainerd Area Trails & Waterways
(Paul Bunyan Trail)
1601 Minnesota
Brainerd, MN 56401
(218) 828-2557

Bemidji Area Chamber of Commerce
300 Bemidji Avenue
Bemidji, MN 56601
(218) 751-3540
(218) 759-0810

Terry McGaughey, Volunteer Coordinator
Brainerd Area Chamber of Commerce
124 North 6th Street
Brainerd, MN 56401
(800) 450-2838

ROOT RIVER STATE TRAIL

#6

Trail Uses: Bicycling, Hiking, In-line Skating, Cross-country Skiing and Snowmobiling

Trail Heads:
East - Rushford
West - Fountain

Surface: Asphalt

Grade: Flat

Length of Trail: 36 miles

Date Established: 1981

Trail Name Origin:
Derived from the Root River, which parallels the trail.

Trail Highlights:
- Former Chicago Milwaukee & St. Paul & Pacific Railroad lines.
- One of the states most scenic bicycle routes.
- Root River runs through the Root River Valley providing outstanding views of wooded hillsides and high limestone bluffs, abundant wildlife, historical buildings and rural communities. Trail users will cross 46 major and miner bridges, one approximately 500-ft long.
- Links with Harmony-Preston Valley State Trail.

Future Plan:
Network of trails called Blufflands trail system in Fillmore and Houston Counties.

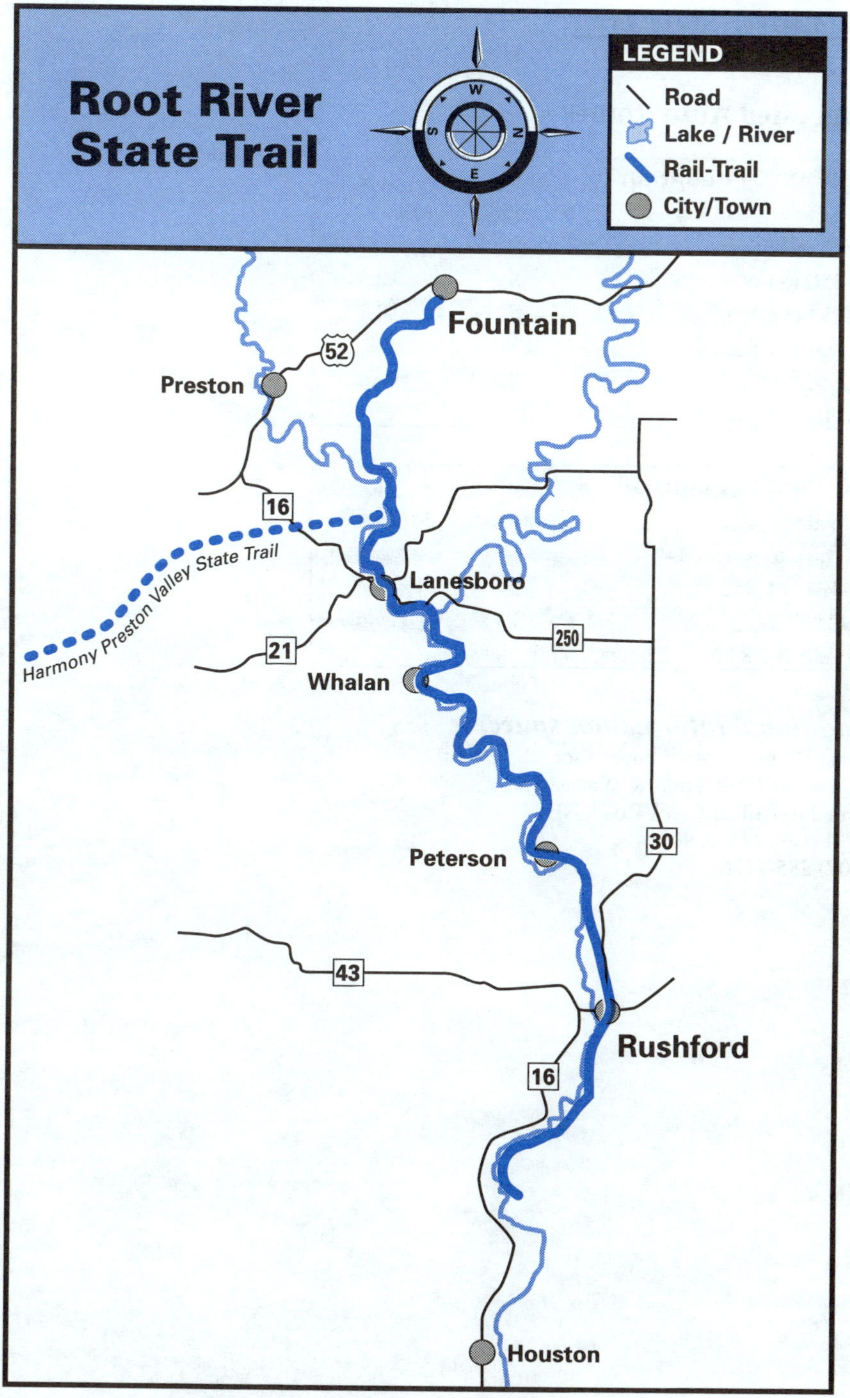
Root River State Trail
W
S
N
E
LEGEND
Road
Lake / River
Rail-Trail
City/Town
Fountain
52
Preston
16
Harmony Preston Valley State Trail
Lanesboro
21
250
Whalan
Peterson
30
43
Rushford
16
Houston

Root River State Trail

Suggested Auto Routes

Duluth to Fountain

Road	Direction	Miles
I-35 to I-35E	S	133.4
I-35E to I-694	S	12.3
I-694 to I-494	S	10.7
I-494 to US52	SW	8.8
US52	SE	99.6

Total: 264.8 miles; 4 hours, 45 minutes

St Paul to Fountain

Road	Direction	Miles
Lafayette Ave. to I-494	S	5.5
I-494 to US52	W	.7
US52	SE	99.6

Total: 105.8 miles; 2 hours, 15 minutes

Additional information sources:
Craig Blummer, Area Supervisor
Minnesota DNR Trails & Waterways
Unit 2300 Silver Creek Road, NE
Rochester, MN 55906
(507) 285-7176

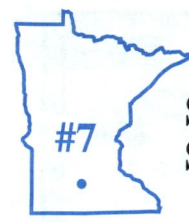

SAKATAH SINGING HILLS STATE TRAIL

#7

Trail Uses: Bicycling, Hiking, Horseback Riding, In-line Skating, Cross-country Skiing and Snowmobiling

Trail Heads:
East - Faribault
West - Mankato

Length of Trail: 39 miles; Parallel Equestrian trail

Surface: Asphalt

Grade: 2%

Date Established: 1980

Trail Name Origin:
Trail runs through the Sakatah State Park, which was inhabited by Dakota Nation and Wahpekita tribes. They named the area Sakatah, which translates to "Singing Hills."

Trail Highlights:
- Former Chicago and Northwestern Railroad line.
- Landscape surrounding Sakatah is a transition zone between the once "Big Woods" and the vast prairies. Trail users will experience tranquil views of wetlands, fields, forests and lakes that provide the perfect habitat for the abundant wildlife population.
- Glacial activity 14,000 years ago shaped the trail landscape. Sakatah rests on glacial remnants – moraine, rock and mineral debris deposits.

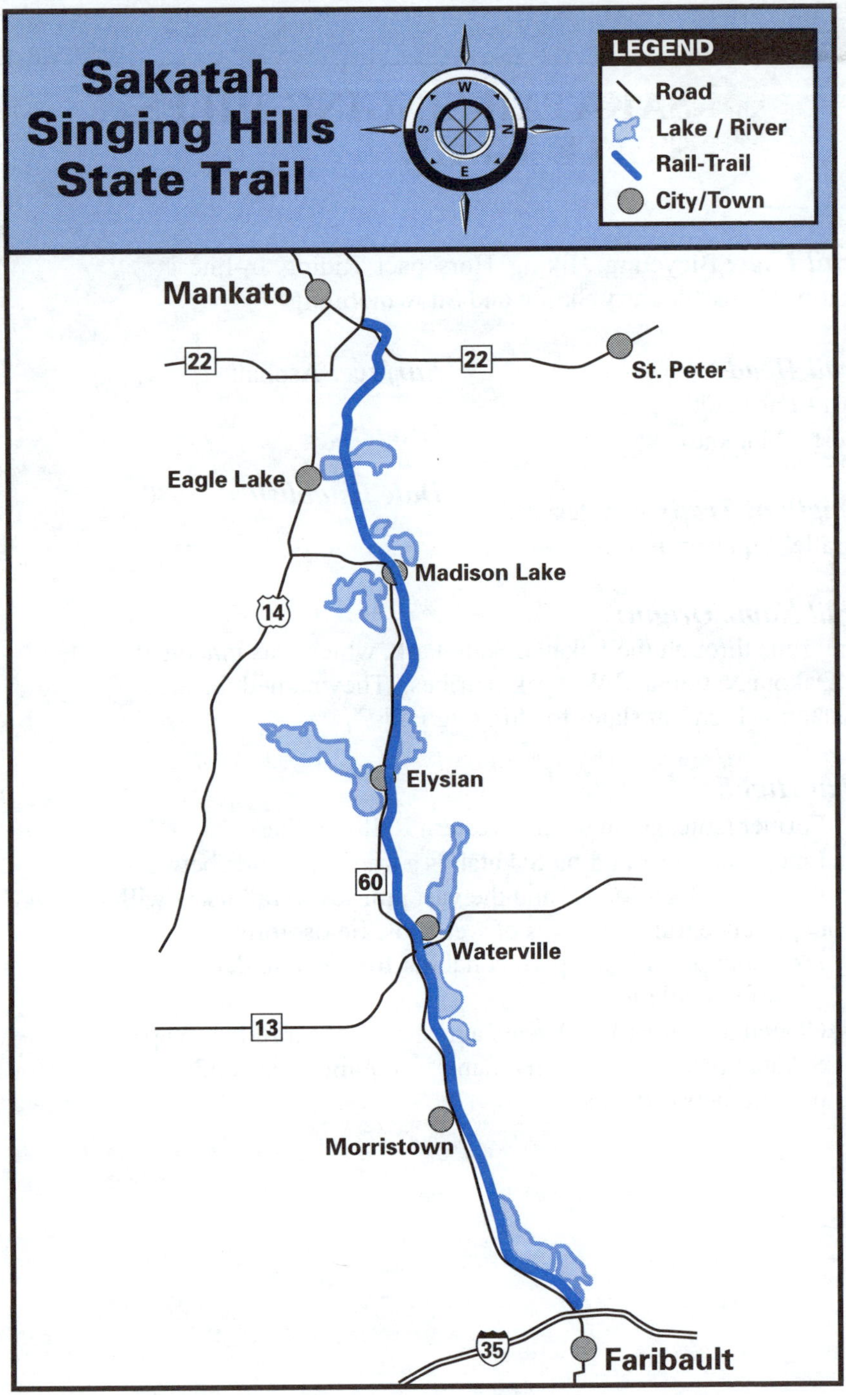

Sakatah Singing Hills State Trail
W
S
N
E
LEGEND
Road
Lake / River
Rail-Trail
City/Town
Mankato
22
22
St. Peter
Eagle Lake
Madison Lake
14
Elysian
60
Waterville
13
Morristown
35
Faribault

Sakatah Singing Hills State Trail

Suggested Auto Routes

Duluth to Faribault		
Road	Direction	Miles
I-35 to I-35E	S	133.4
I-35E to I-35	S	38.1
I-35 to ST99	S	29.7
ST99 to ST3	SE	1
ST3	SE	1.5
Total: 203.7 miles; 3 hours, 6 minutes		

St Paul to Faribault		
Road	Direction	Miles
I-94 to I-35E	W	1.3
I-35E to I-35	SW	18.1
I-35 to ST99	S	29.7
ST99 to ST3	SE	1
ST3	SE	1.5
Total: 51.6 miles; 50 minutes		

Additional information sources:

Sakatah Trail Improvement Association
(800) 507-7787 (trail information)

Randy Schorneck, Trail Technician
Sakatah State Park
P.O. Box 11
Elysian, MN 56028-0011
(507) 267-4772

#8 SOO LINE TRAIL

Trail Uses: Hiking. Horseback Riding, Mountain Bicycling and Snowmobiling

Trail Heads:
North - Cass Lake
South - Moose Lake

Length of Trail: 114 miles

Surface: Gravel & Original Ballast

Grade: Flat

Date Established: 1988

Trail Name Origin:
Named after the former Soo Railroad Line.

Trail Highlights:
- Former Soo Line Railroad.
- Soo line passes over many waterways including the Leech, Bog and Willow Rivers.
- Willard Mungar State Trail crosses Soo Line.

Suggested Auto Routes

Duluth to Moose Lake

Road	Direction	Miles
I-35	SW	44.3

Total: 44.3 miles; 44 minutes

St Paul to Moose Lake

Road	Direction	Miles
I-94 to I-35 E	W	.7
I-35E to I-35	N	19.4
I-35	N	89.1

Total: 109.2 miles; 1 hours, 47 minutes

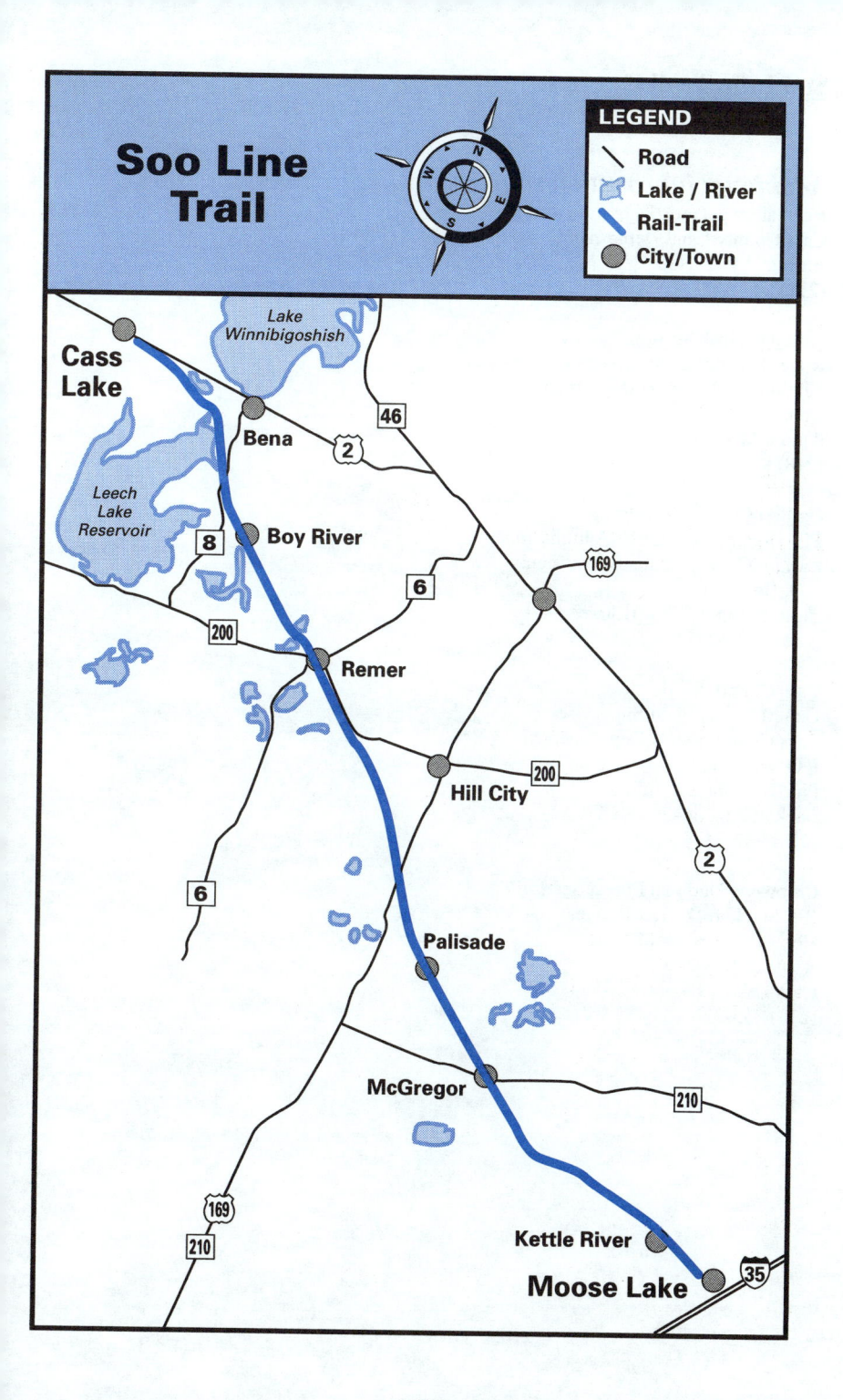

Soo Line Trail

LEGEND
- Road
- Lake / River
- Rail-Trail
- City/Town

- Cass Lake
- Lake Winnibigoshish
- Bena
- Leech Lake Reservoir
- Boy River
- Remer
- Hill City
- Palisade
- McGregor
- Kettle River
- Moose Lake

119

Soo Line Trail

Additional information sources:
Recreational Trails Department
Cass County Land Department
Backus, MN 56435
(218) 947-3338

Aitkin County Section
Roger Howard Commissioner
Aitkin County Lands Department
Courthouse
Aitkin, MN 56431
(218) 927-2102

Carlton County Section
Milo Rasmussen, Land Commissioner
Carlton County Lands Department
P.O. Box 130
Carlton, MN 55718-0130
(218) 384-4281

Cass County Section
Dan Marcum, Field Supervisor
Cass County Lands Department
P.O. Box 25
Pine Mountain Building
Backus, MN 56435-0025
(218) 947-3338

Chippewa National Forest Section
Bill Stocker, District Ranger
Chippewa National Forest
Route 3, Box 219
Cass Lake, MN 56633-8924
(218) 335-2283

WILLARD MUNGAR STATE TRAIL

#9

Trail Uses: Bicycling, Hiking, Horseback Riding, In-line Skating and Snowmobiling

Trail Heads:
North - Duluth
South - Hinckley

Surface: Asphalt & grass

Grade: Flat

Length of Trail: 75 miles; Parallel Equestrian trail

Date Established: 1973

Trail Name Origin:
Named for Willard Mungar, an Environmentalist and State Legislature who started the trail movement in Minnesota.

Trail Highlights:
- Former Lake Superior & Mississippi, St. Paul & Duluth, Northern Pacific and Burlington Northern Railroad lines.
- Willard Mungar is a scenic trail providing many opportunities to view wildlife, rivers, streams and lakes.
- Trail passes two fire museums, which provide a look at the greatest natural disasters in Minnesota's history, the Great Hinckley Fire of 1894 and the fire of 1918 in Moose Lake.
- "Recreational link to the many communities that it serves." Longest paved trail in the world.
- Willard Mungar crosses Soo Line trail.

Future Plan:
Organize a shuttle service to accommodate trail users.
Acquire and pave the three-mile section between Douglas Road to Carlton

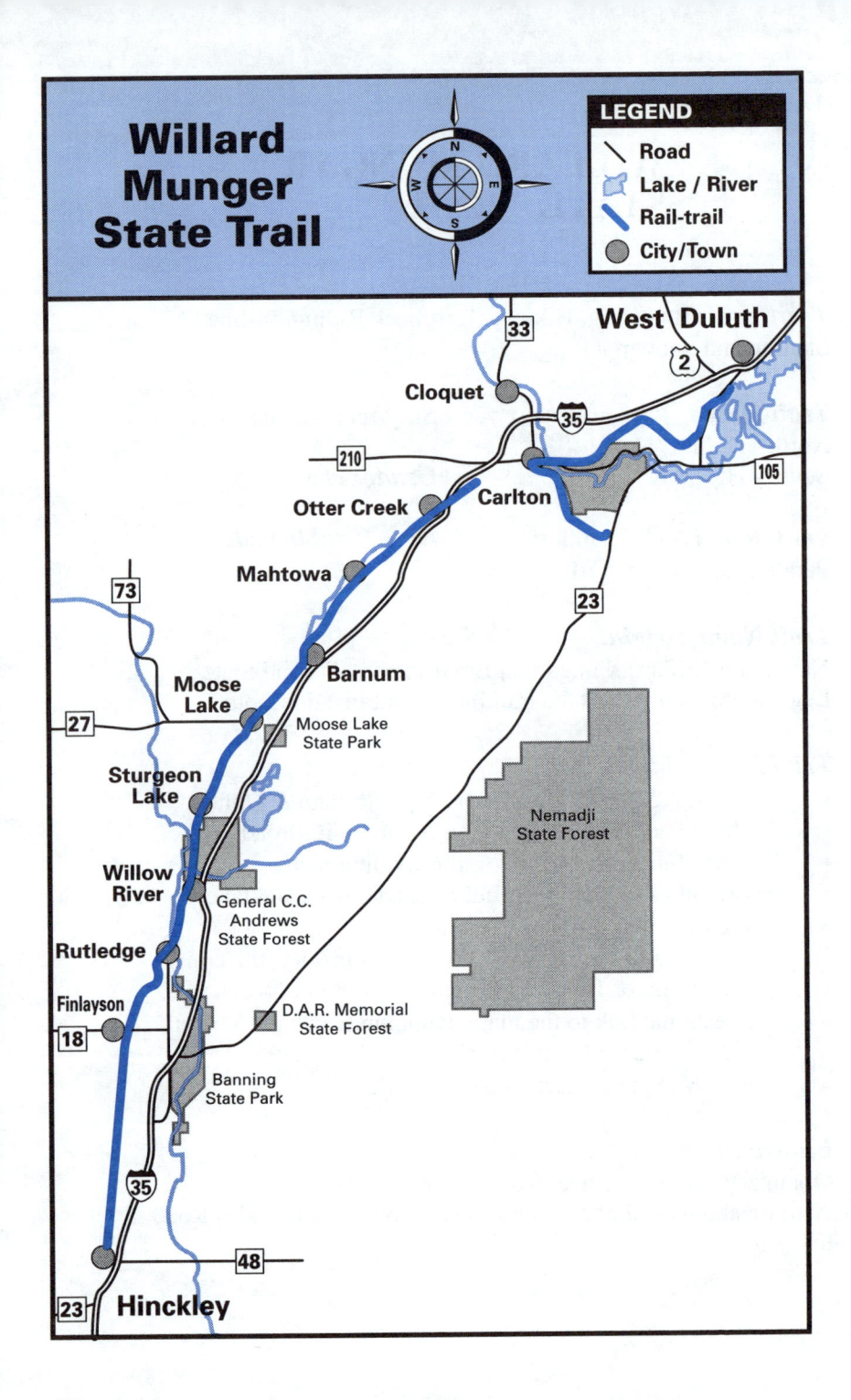

Willard Munger State Trail

Willard Mungar State Trail

Suggested Auto Routes

St Paul to Hinckley		
Road	Direction	Miles
I-94 to 35E	W	.7
I-35E to I-35	N	19.4
I-35 to ST48	N	56.1
ST48	NW	1.4
Total: 77.6 miles; 1 hour, 15 minutes		

Additional information sources:
Len Schmidt, President
Munger Trail Town Association
P.O. Box 176
Moose Lake, MN 55767
(888) 263-0586

Moose Lake Area Chamber of Commerce
P.O. Box 110
Moose Lake, MN 55767
(218) 485-4145

Hinckley Chamber of Commerce
Box 189
Hinckley, MN 55037
(612) 384-7837

Kevin Arends
Minnesota DNR Trails and Waterways Unit
Route 2, 701 S. Kenwood
Moose Lake, MN 55767
(218) 485-5410

Internet Website:
www.northwoods-exposure.com/munger-trail

Wisconsin

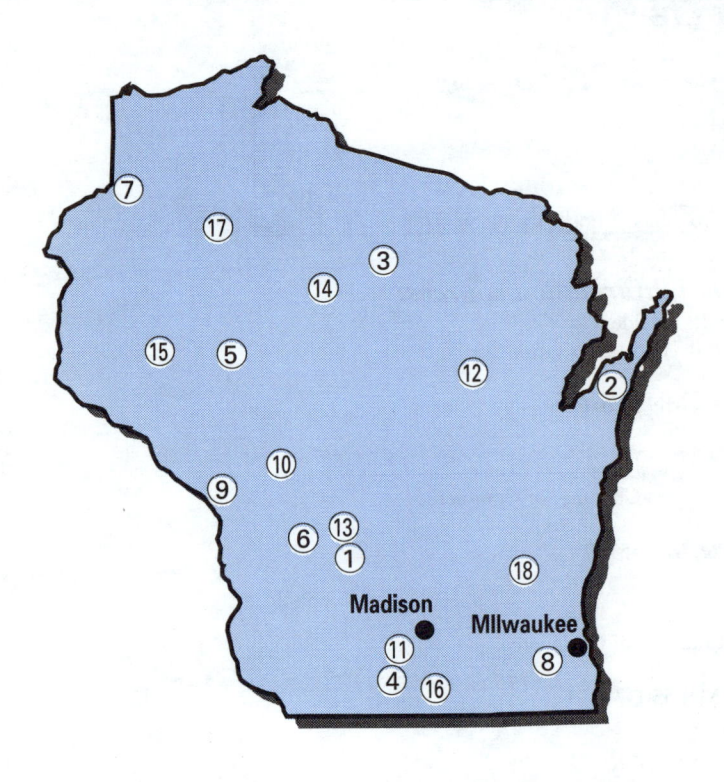

# 1	"400" State	#10	La Crosse River
# 2	Ahnapee	#11	Military Ridge
# 3	Bearskin	#12	Mountain-Bay
# 4	Cheese Country	#13	Omaha
# 5	Chippewa River	#14	Pine Line
# 6	Elroy-Sparta	#15	Red Cedar
# 7	Gandy Dancer	#16	Sugar River
# 8	Glacial Drumlin	#17	Tuscobia
# 9	Great River	#18	Wild Goose

FACTS ABOUT WISCONSIN

Capital: Madison

Elevation:
Highest Point - 1,953 ft.
Timms Hill

Lowest Point - 581 ft.
Lake Michigan

Largest City: Milwaukee

Motto: Forward

Nickname: Badger State

Population: 5,081,700

State Animal: Badger

State Bird: Robin

State Fish: Muskellunge (Muski)

State Flower: Wood Violet

State Tree: Maple

Statehood: May 29, 1848 (30th state)

Time Zone: Central DST

Boasting Rights:
- 65 State Parks.
- 4 Public Recreational Forests totaling 125,000 acres.
- National leader in bicycle trail development with over 10,000 miles on state, county and local roads.
- 3,597 miles of hiking trails.
- 1,601 miles of horse trails.
- 1,236 miles of ATV trails.
- 1,097 miles of developed rail-trails.
- Future plans to develop 522 miles of Rail-Trails.

Geographic State Center:
Wood County, 9 miles southeast of Marshfield

PLACES OF INTEREST

Amnicon Falls State Park: Near Superior; scenic waterfalls.
Apostle Islands: In Lake Superior near Bayfield; fishing; cliffs; Madeline Island Historical Museum.
Aztalan State Park: Near Lake Mills; site of ancient Indian village.
Big Foot Beach State Park: Near Lake Geneva
Blue Mound State Park: Near Blue Mounds; recreational area.
Brunet Island State Park: On Chippewa River near Cornell.
Cave of the Mounds: Near Blue Mounds; colorful formations.
Circus World Museum: In Baraboo; exhibits re-create the world of the American circus.
Copper Culture Mounds Historical-Memorial Park: Near Oconto; picnicking.
Copper Falls State Park: Near Mellen; river gorges; falls.
Cushing Memorial Park: In Waukesha; shaft honors Civil War heroes.
Dells of the Wisconsin: Near Wisconsin Dells; picturesque sandstone rocks; boat rides; footpaths; Indian dances.
Devil's Lake State Park: Near Baraboo; mountain lake; hills.
First Capitol State Park: Near Belmont; first territorial Capitol.
Governor Dodge State Park: Near Dodgeville; rocky promontories.
High Cliffs State Park: Near Menasha; Lake Winnebago.
Interstate State Park: Near St. Croix Falls; Dalles of St. Croix River.
Lake Geneva: Summer-winter resort.
Little Norway: Near Mount Horeb; pioneer village.
Lizard Mound Historical-Memorial Park: Near West Bend; ancient Indain mounds.
Neenah and Menasha: Cities on Lake Winnebago; paper mills; Grand Loggery, Governor Doty house.
Nelson Dewey Historical-Memorial Park: Near Cassville; home of first governor.
New Glarus: Swiss village; annual festival in September.
Newport State Park: Near Ellison Bay; sand dunes; wilderness camping.
Octagon House: In Watertown; museum of first kindergarten.
Old Wade House: Near Greenbush; early stagecoach inn.
Pattison State Park: Near Superior; state's highest waterfall.
Peninsula State Park: Near Ephraim; forested bluffs on Green Bay.
Perrot State Park: Near Trempealeau; Mississippi River bluffs.
Portage: Old Indian Agency House (1832); Surgeon's Quarters, Fort Winnebago (1828).

Potawatomi State Park: Near Sturgeon Bay; bluffs.
Prairie de Chien: Villa Louis, H. L. Dousman house (1870), Museum of Prairie du Chien.
Rhinelander: Lakes resort; Logging Museum.
Rib Mountain State Park: Near Wausau; scenic high point.
Roche a Cri State Park: Near Friendship; craggy rock.
Rock Island State Park: In Lake Michigan; wilderness camping; Great Hall; Potawatomi Lighthouse, first lighthouse (1837) on Lake Michigan.
Rocky Arbor State Park: Near Wisconsin Dells; rock formations; trails.
Superior: Iron-ore docks; grain elevators.
Terry Andrae-John M. Kohler State Park: Lake Michigan beach near Sheboygan; dunes.
Tower Hill Historical-Memorial Park: Near Spring Green; shot tower; Wisconsin River.
Wildcat Mountain State Park: Near Ontario; Kickapoo River bluffs.
Wyalusing State Park: Near Prairie du Chien.
Yerkes Observatory: At Williams Bay; world's largest refracting telescope

Additional information sources:

Wisconsin Department of Tourism
P.O. Box 7976
Madison, WI 53707
(800) 432-8747
(800) 372-2737
(608) 266-2161

Road Condition Hotline (winter)
(800) 762-3947 (WI)
(608) 246-7580 (Madison area)
(414) 785-7140 (Milwaukee area)

Road Construction Hotline (summer)
(800) 762-3947 (WI)
(608) 246-7580 (Madison area)
(414) 785-7140 (Milwaukee area)

Wisconsin Department of Natural Resources
Bureau of Parks & Recreation
Box 7921
Madison, WI 53707
(608) 266-2181 TDD (608) 267-2752
(608) 266-1877

Webpage:
http:/www.state.wi.us/

TRAIL COUNTIES

"400," The: Juneau & Sauk

Ahnapee: Door & Kewaunee
•
Bearskin: Oneida
•
Cheese County: Green, Iowa, & Lafayette
•
Chippewa: Dunn & Eau Claire
•
Elroy-Sparta: Juneau & Monroe
•
Gandy Dancer: Burnett, Douglas, Polk & Pine, MN
•
Glacial-Drumlin: Dane, Jefferson, & Waukesha
•
Great River: Buffalo, La Crosse, & Trempealeau
•
La Crosse River: La Crosse & Monroe
•
Military Ridge: Dane & Iowa
•
Mountain-Bay: Brown, Marathon & Shawano
•
Omaha: Juneau
•
Pine Line: Price & Taylor
•
Red Cedar: Dunn
•
Sugar River: Green
•
Tuscobia: Barron, Price, Sawyer & Washburn
•
Wild Goose: Dodge & Fond du Lac

HOURS

Trails are open daily
6:00 a.m. to 11:00 p.m.

Wisconsin State Trail Admission Fees:
(On certain Wisconsin State Trails Bicyclists, Equestrians and Skiers 17 and over must have a trail pass.)

Resident and Non-Resident Season Fee: $10.00
Resident and Non-Resident Daily Fee: $3.00
(trail fees may vary)

Trail admission cards may be purchased by mail or in person from the Department of Natural Resources, local businesses located near the trails, trail headquarters and local park rangers or contact:

>Bureau of Parks & Recreation
P. O. Box 1921
Madison, WI 53707
(608) 266-2181 (7:45 a.m. to 4:30 p.m. Mon. – Fri)

WEATHER CONDITIONS

	Temperature				Precipitation (inches)	
	Green Bay		Milwaukee			
	High	Low	High	Low	GB*	Mil*
JAN	24	7	27	11	10S	12S
FEB	27	9	30	15	8S	9S
MAR	37	20	39	23	9S	9S
APR	54	33	55	35	3	3
MAY	66	43	65	43	3	3
JUNE	76	53	75	54	3	4
JULY	81	58	80	59	3	3
AUG	79	56	80	59	3	3
SEPT	70	48	71	51	3	3
OCT	60	39	61	41	2	2
NOV	42	26	44	28	4S	3S
DEC	29	13	31	17	10S	11S

*GB - Green Bay; Mil - Milwaukee; S-Snow

#1 "400" State Trail

Trail Uses: Bicycling, Hiking, Horseback Riding and Snowmobiling

Trail Heads:
North - Elroy
South - Reedsburg

Length of Trail: 22 miles; Parallel 7-mile Equestrian trail

Surface: Packed Limestone Screenings

Grade: 2%

Date Established: 1993

Trail Name Origin:
Named for the Chicago Northwestern passenger train, which formerly ran on this grade. The train traveled 400 miles from Chicago to Minnesota/St. Paul in 400 minutes.

Trail Highlights:
- Former Chicago Northwestern Railroad line.
- "400" Trail winds through rolling farmlands, pastures, sandstone, bluffs and wetlands.
- Baraboo River parallels the entire trail length.
- Links with the Elroy-Sparta, Omaha, La Crosse and Great River Trails resulting in a one hundred twelve-mile recreational trail experience.

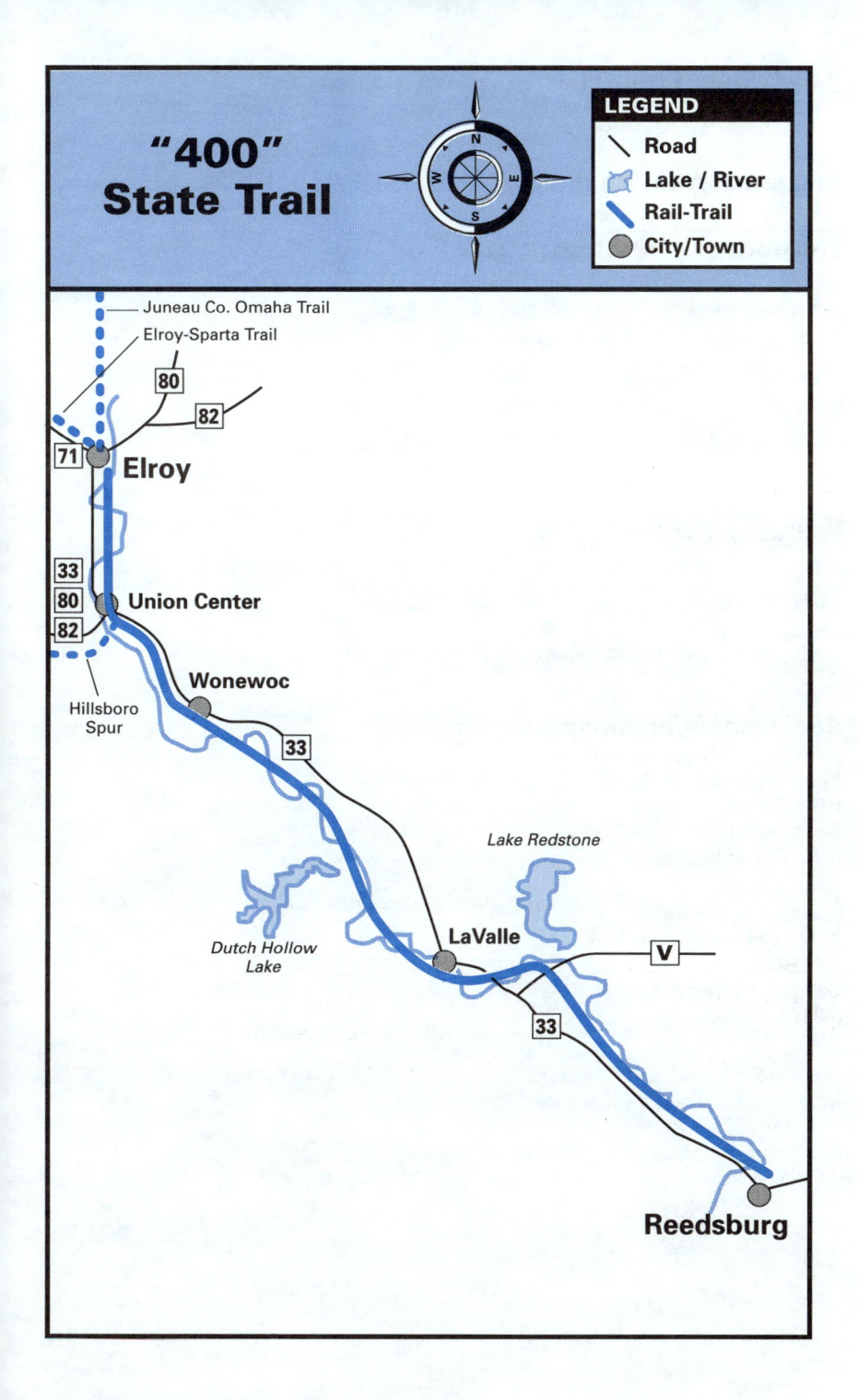

"400" State Trail

"400" State Trail, The

Suggested Auto Routes

Madison to Reedsburg

Road	Direction	Miles
US151 to US51	NE	3.8
US51 to I-90	N	3.4
I-90 to ST23	NW	42
ST23	W	13.9
Total: 63.1 miles; 1 hour, 15 minutes		

Milwaukee to Reedsburg

Road	Direction	Miles
I-94 to ST23	W	119.3
ST23	W	13.9
Total: 133.2 miles; 2 hours, 14 minutes		

Additional information sources:
Jerry Trumm, Superintendent
Mirror Lake State Park
E10320 Fern Dell Road
Baraboo, WI 53913-9341
(608) 254-2333

Ron Nelson, Superintendent
Wildcat Mountain State Park
P.O. Box 99
Ontario, WI 54651-0099
(608) 337-4775

The 400 State Trail
Reedsburg Chamber of Commerce
P.O. Box 142
Reedsburg, WI 53959
(608) 524-2850

#2 AHNAPEE STATE PARK TRAIL

Trail Uses: Bicycling, Hiking, Horseback Riding and Snowmobiling

Trail Heads:
North - Sturgeon Bay
South - Algoma

Length of Trail: 15.3 miles

Surface: Limestone Screenings

Grade: Mostly Level

Date Established: 1971

Trail Name Origin:
Derived from the Ahnapee River, which borders the trail for about five miles.

Trail Highlights:
- Former Ahnapee & Western Railroad.
- Ahnapee winds through a county park, farmlands, wetlands, wildlife area and the villages of Maplewood and Forestville.
- 8-ft. wide trail surface.
- No admission fee to use trail.
- Wisconsin's third recreational trail to be built on a former railroad route.
- Certified segment of the Ice Age National Scenic Trail.

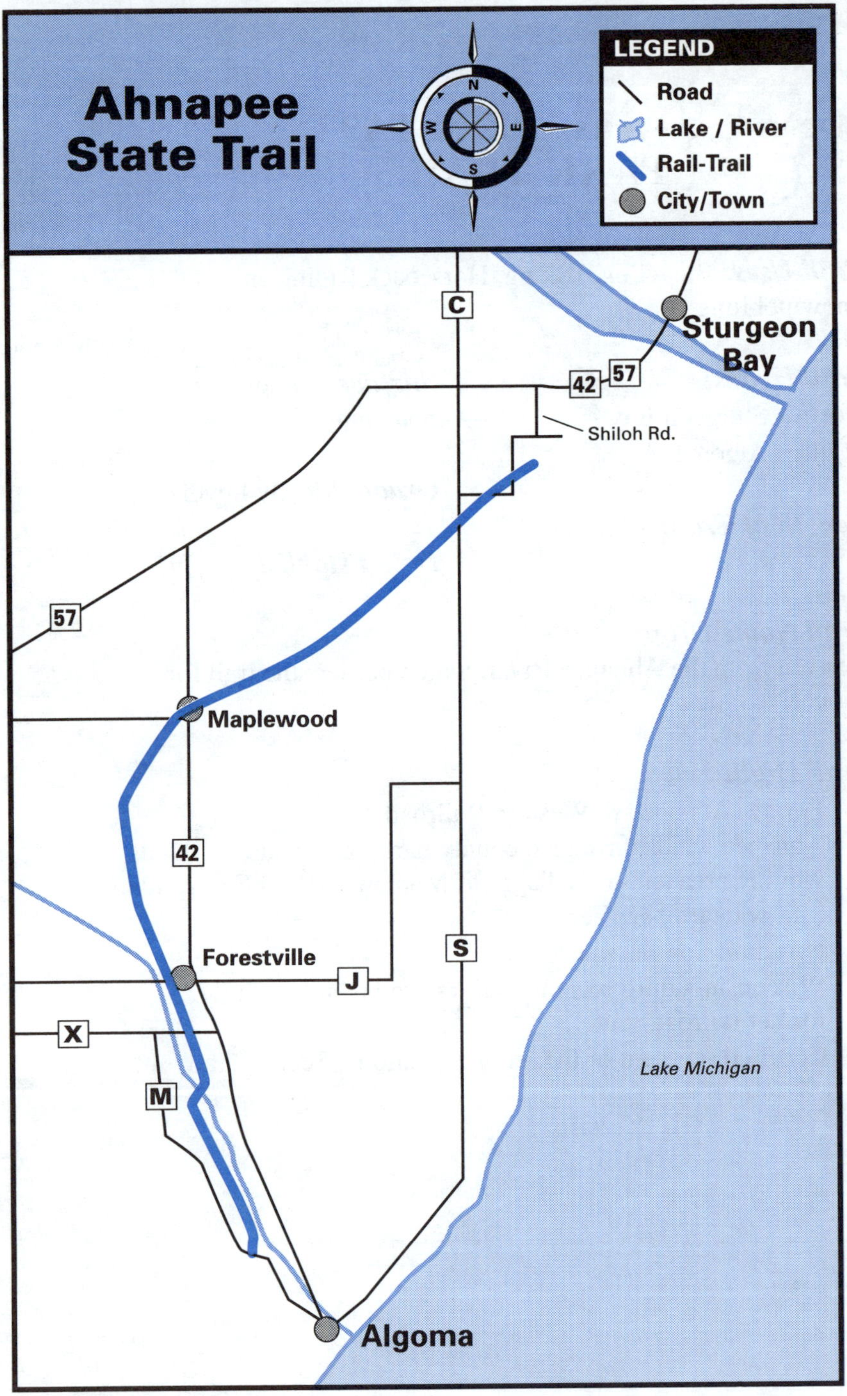
Ahnapee
State Trail
N
E
S
W
LEGEND
Road
Lake / River
Rail-Trail
City/Town
C
Sturgeon
Bay
57
42
Shiloh Rd.
57
Maplewood
42
Forestville
J
S
X
M
Lake Michigan
Algoma

Ahnapee State Park Trail

Suggested Auto Routes

Madison to Algoma

Road	Direction	Miles
US151 to ST26	NE	57.8
ST26 to US41	NE	20.8
US41 to Rte 172	NE	50.5
ST172 to ST57	E	3.2
ST57 to ST54	E	9.9
ST54	E	23.4
Total: 165.6 miles; 3 hours, 37 minutes		

Milwaukee to Algoma

Road	Direction	Miles
I-43 to US151	N	77.5
US151 to ST42	N	3.9
ST42	N	41.1
Total: 122.5 miles; 2 hours, 31 minutes		

Additional information sources:
Arnie Lindauer
Ahnapee State Park Trail
c/o Potawatomi State Park
3740 Park Drive
Sturgeon Bay, WI 54235
(414) 746-2890

Carol Wiese, Executive Director
Algoma Area Chamber of Commerce
1226 Lake Street
Algoma, WI 54201
(414) 487-2041
(414) 487-5519 FAX

#3 BEARSKIN STATE PARK TRAIL

Trail Uses: Bicycling, Hiking and Snowmobiling

Trail Heads:
North - Minocqua
South - County Highway K, NE of Heafford Junction

Surface: Compacted Granite

Grade: 2% to 3%

Length of Trail: 18 miles

Date Established: 1973

Trail Name Origin:
Derived from the Bearskin Creek, a tributary of the Tomahawk River it traverses.

Trail Highlights:
- Former Chicago, Milwaukee & St. Paul and Wisconsin Valley Railroad lines.
- Bearskin provides users with scenic views over bluffs of numerous springs and spring fed ponds, lakes, abundant with wildlife and flowers. Trail crosses Bearskin Creek 10 times and Rocky Run Creek 2 times.
- Near the Chequamegon National Forest.
- Trail admission fees applicable to bikers' age 16 or older.

137

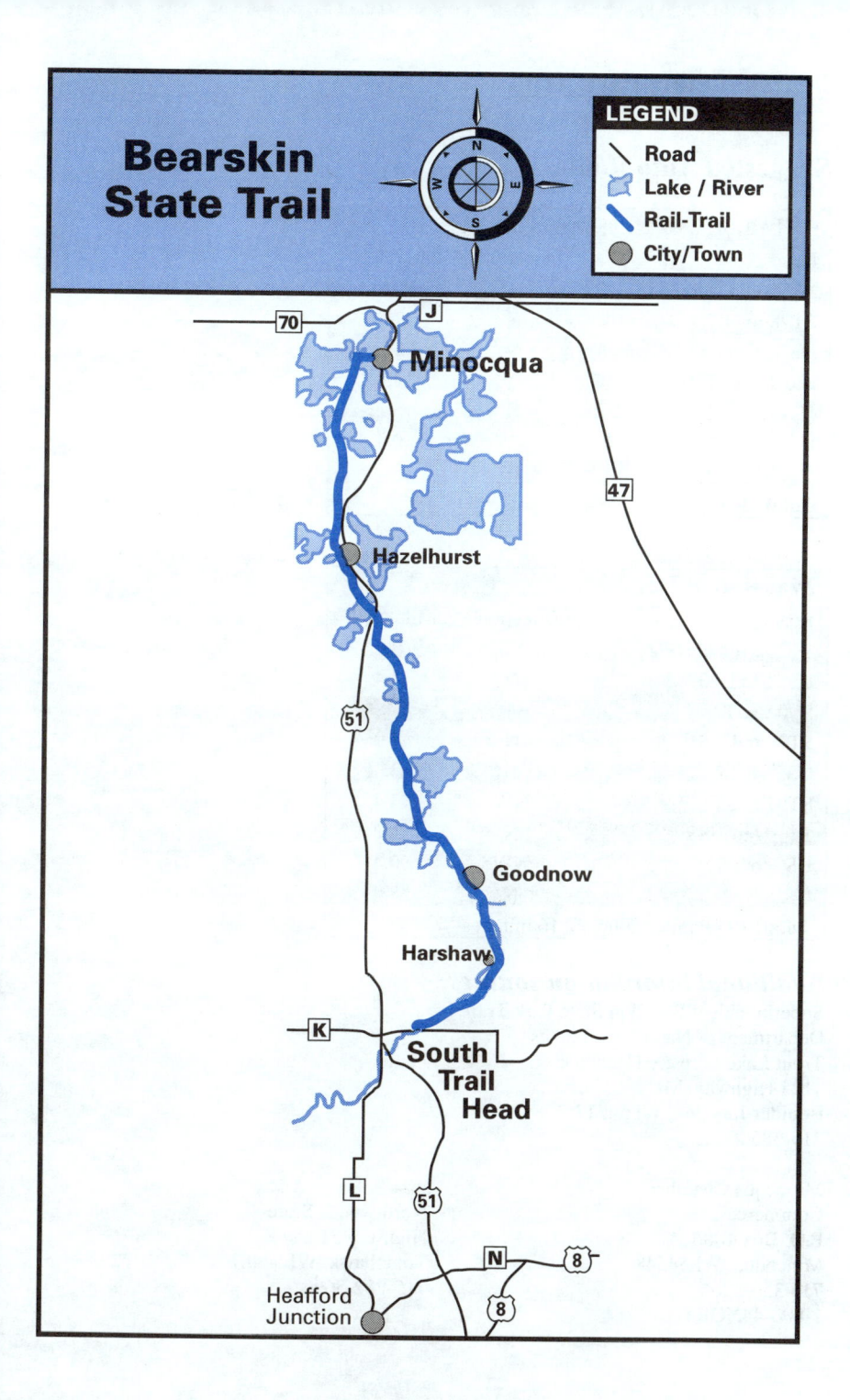

Bearskin State Park Trail

Suggested Auto Routes

Milwaukee to Harshaw		
Road	Direction	Miles
I-94 to ST78	W	101.6
ST78 to US51	N	7.9
US51 to ST91	N	135.6
Rte 91 to ST107	NW	3.4
ST107 to US8	N	5.2
US8 to US51	NW	0.4
US51	N	8.4
Total: 265 miles; 4 hours, 25 minutes		

Madison to Harshaw		
Road	Direction	Miles
US151 to US51	NE	3.8
US51 to I-90	N	3.4
I-90 to ST78	NW	24.3
ST78 to US51	N	7.9
US51 to ST91	N	135.6
ST91 to ST107	NW	3.4
ST107 to US8	N	5.2
US8 to US51	NW	0.4
US51	N	8.4
Total: 194.9 miles; 3 hours, 16 minutes		

Additional information sources:
Superintendent Bearskin State Park Trail
Department of Natural Resources
Trout Lake Forestry Headquarters
4125 Highway. M
Boulder Junction, WI 54512
715-385 2727

Minocqua Chamber of
Commerce
P.O. Box 1006
Mincoqua, WI 54548
715 356-5266
1-800-44NORTH

Northwoods Store
Highway 51 and K
Tomahawk, WI 54487
715-282-5696

#4 CHEESE COUNTRY RECREATION TRAIL

Trail Uses: Biking, Hiking, Horseback Riding, Cross-country Skiing and Snowmobiling

Trail Heads:
West - Mineral Point
East - Monroe

Length of Trail: 47 miles

Surface: Limestone Screenings

Grade: Flat

Date Established: 1988

Trail Name Origin:
Derived from trail's location in the most intense foreign type cheese industry anywhere in the country.

Trail Highlights:
- Former Milwaukee Road Railroad line.
- Cheese Country Parallels the Pecatanica River – a 440-ft. Bridge spans the river west of Brownstone.
- Trail users will experience nature at its best as only seen by railroad employees and landowners – prairie grass, wildflowers, bald eagle and many species of wildlife. Cheese Country traverses through six quaint towns each offers trail users a unique opportunity to enhance their trail experience.
- Depot museum located in Parlington brings to life the history of the Milwaukee Road rail route taken by the trail.
- 30 cheese factories produce large quantities of Swiss, Muenster, Limburger and a number of Italian varieties of cheese are located within a few miles of trail.
- Trail is located six miles from the Illinois border and forty miles from the Iowa border.
- Links to the Pecatonica State Park Trail.

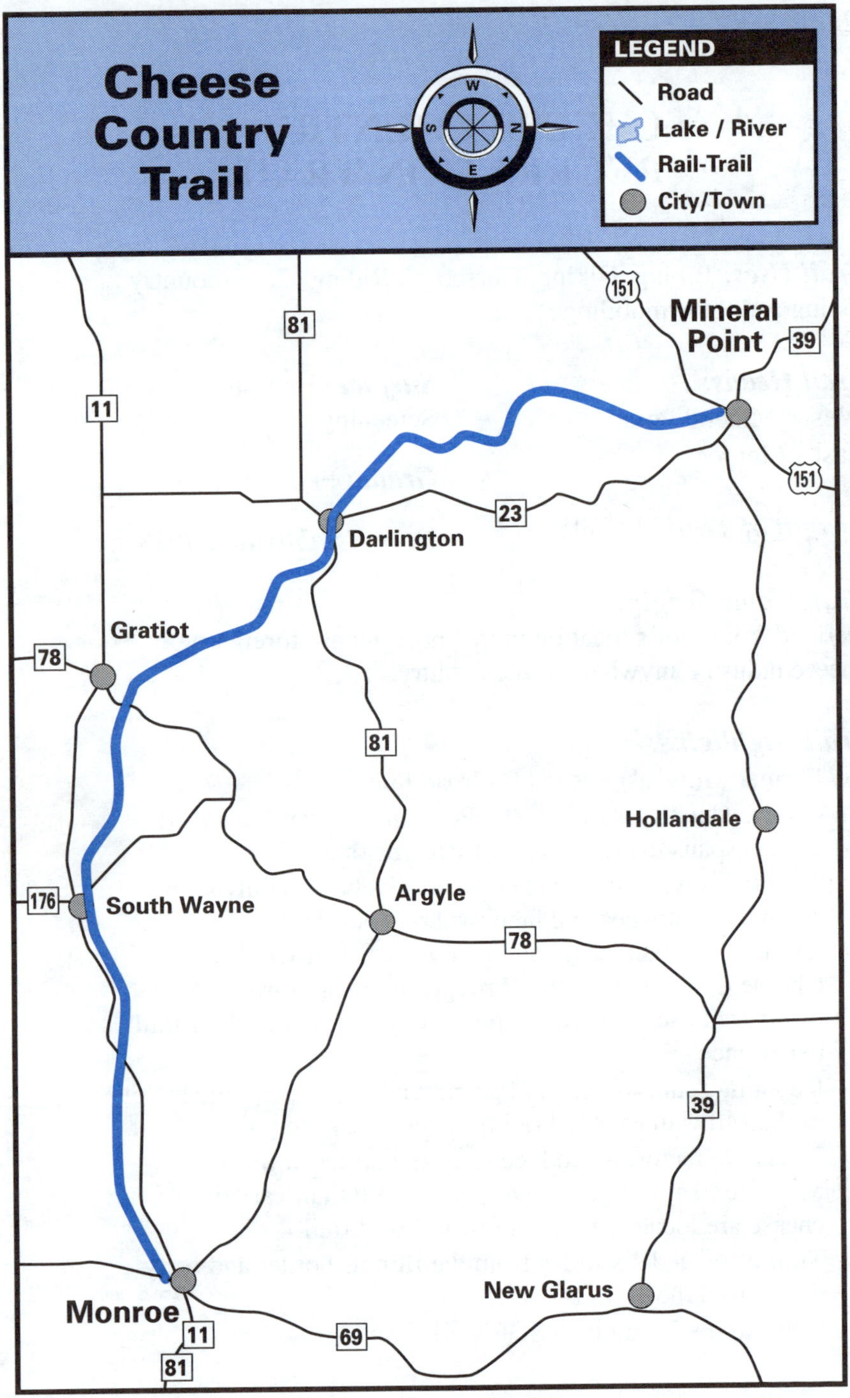
Cheese
Country
Trail
W
S
N
E
LEGEND
Road
Lake / River
Rail-Trail
City/Town
151
Mineral
Point
39
81
11
151
23
Darlington
Gratiot
78
81
Hollandale
176
South Wayne
Argyle
78
39
New Glarus
Monroe
11
69
81

Cheese Country Recreation Trail

Suggested Auto Routes

Madison to Monroe		
Road	Direction	Miles
US151 to US12	S	2
US12 to US18	W	3.4
US18 to ST69	SW	5.9
ST69 to X MON	S	35.3
X MON	S	2
Total: 48.6 miles; 1 hour, 7 minutes		

Milwaukee to Monroe		
Road	Direction	Miles
I-94 to I-894	S	5.1
I-894 to US45	W	4.8
US45 to I-43	SW	1.1
I-43 to ST81	W	62.8
ST81 to X MON	W	30
X MON	W	3
Total: 106.8 miles; 2 hours, 9 minutes		

Additional information sources:
Stephen Hubner, Trail Coordinator
Tri-County Trail Commission
627 Washington Street
Darlington, WI 53530
(608) 776-4830

Mineral Point Chamber of Commerce
P.O. Box 78
Mineral Point, WI 53565
(608) 987-3201

Monroe Area Chamber of Commerce
1516 11th Street
Monroe, WI 53566-1747
(608) 325-7648
(608) 325-7710 FAX

#5 CHIPPEWA RIVER STATE TRAIL

Trail Uses: Bicycling, Hiking, In-line Skating, Cross-country Skiing and Snowmobiling (in designated areas)

Trail Heads:
East - Eau Claire
West - Caryville

Surface: Asphalt

Grade: Relatively Level

Length of Trail: 23 miles

Date Established: 1985

Trail Name Origin:
Named after the Chippewa River, which parallels the trail.

Trail Highlights:
- Former Chicago, Milwaukee & St. Paul Railroad lines.
- Chippewa River Trail traverses through the city of Eau Claire, passing commercial districts, park, UW Eau Claire and a Fine Arts Center.
- 860 feet trestle spanning the Chippewa River.
- Links with Red Cedar State Park Trail.

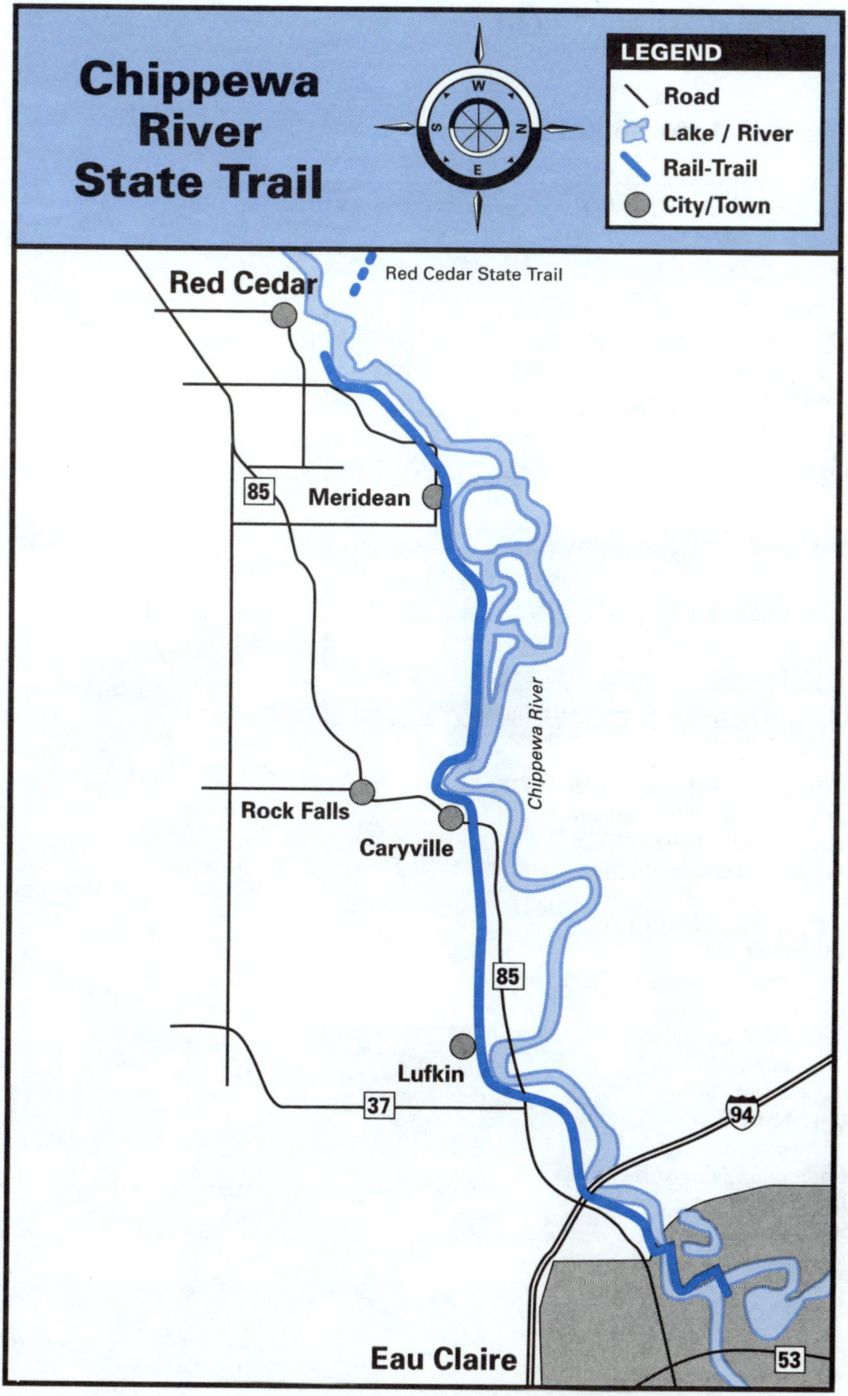

Chippewa River State Trail
LEGEND
Road
Lake / River
Rail-Trail
City/Town
W
S
N
E
Red Cedar
Red Cedar State Trail
85
Meridean
Chippewa River
Rock Falls
Caryville
85
Lufkin
37
94
Eau Claire
53

Chippewa River State Trail

Suggested Auto Routes

Madison to Eau Claire

Road	Direction	Miles
US151 to US51	NE	3.8
US51 to I-90	N	3.4
I-90 to I-94	NW	86.7
I-94 to US53	NW	77.2
US53 to US12	NW	2.8
US12	W	2.1

Total: 176 miles; 2 hours, 47 minutes

Milwaukee to Eau Claire

Road	Direction	Miles
I-94 to US53	NW	241.2
US53 to US12	NW	2.8
US12	W	2.1

Total: 246.1 miles; 3 hours, 46 minutes

Additional information sources:

Jean Rygiel, Trails Coordinator
Western District Headquarters
1300 West Clairmont Avenue
P.O. Box 4001
Eau Claire, WI 54701-6127
(715) 839-1607
TTY (715) 839-2786 Eau Claire

Eau Claire Visitors Center
3625 Gateway Drive
Eau Claire, WI 54701
(800) 344-FUNN

Greater Eau Claire Area Chamber of Commerce
505 Dewey Street
Eau Claire, WI
(715) 834-1956

#6 ELROY-SPARTA STATE PARK TRAIL

Trail Uses: Biking, Hiking, Cross-country Skiing and Snowmobiling

Trail Heads:
East - Elroy
West - Sparta

Length of Trail: 32 miles

Surface: Limestone Screenings

Grade: Less than 3%

Date Established: 1965

Trail Name Origin:
Named for the communities at the east and west borders of the trail.

Trail Highlights:
- Former Chicago & Northwestern Railroad line.
- Trail users will experience a unique visit to railroad history via historic museums, train depots, preserved train tunnels and bridges.
- "Sparta" is known as "The Bicycle Capital of America."
- Elroy-Sparta is Wisconsin's oldest recreation trail.
- Train depot at Kendall is listed on the National Register of Historical Places.
- Elroy is the birthplace and home of Governor Tommy Thompson.
- 3 Railroad tunnels (built in 1873 by the Chicago & Northwestern Railroad – 3/4 mile: Norwalk and two 1/4 mile long: Kendall and Wilton).
- Note! Take along a rain jacket and flashlight for tunnel travel.
- Links with La Crosse River State Park Trail in Sparta, "400" and Omaha Trails in Elroy.

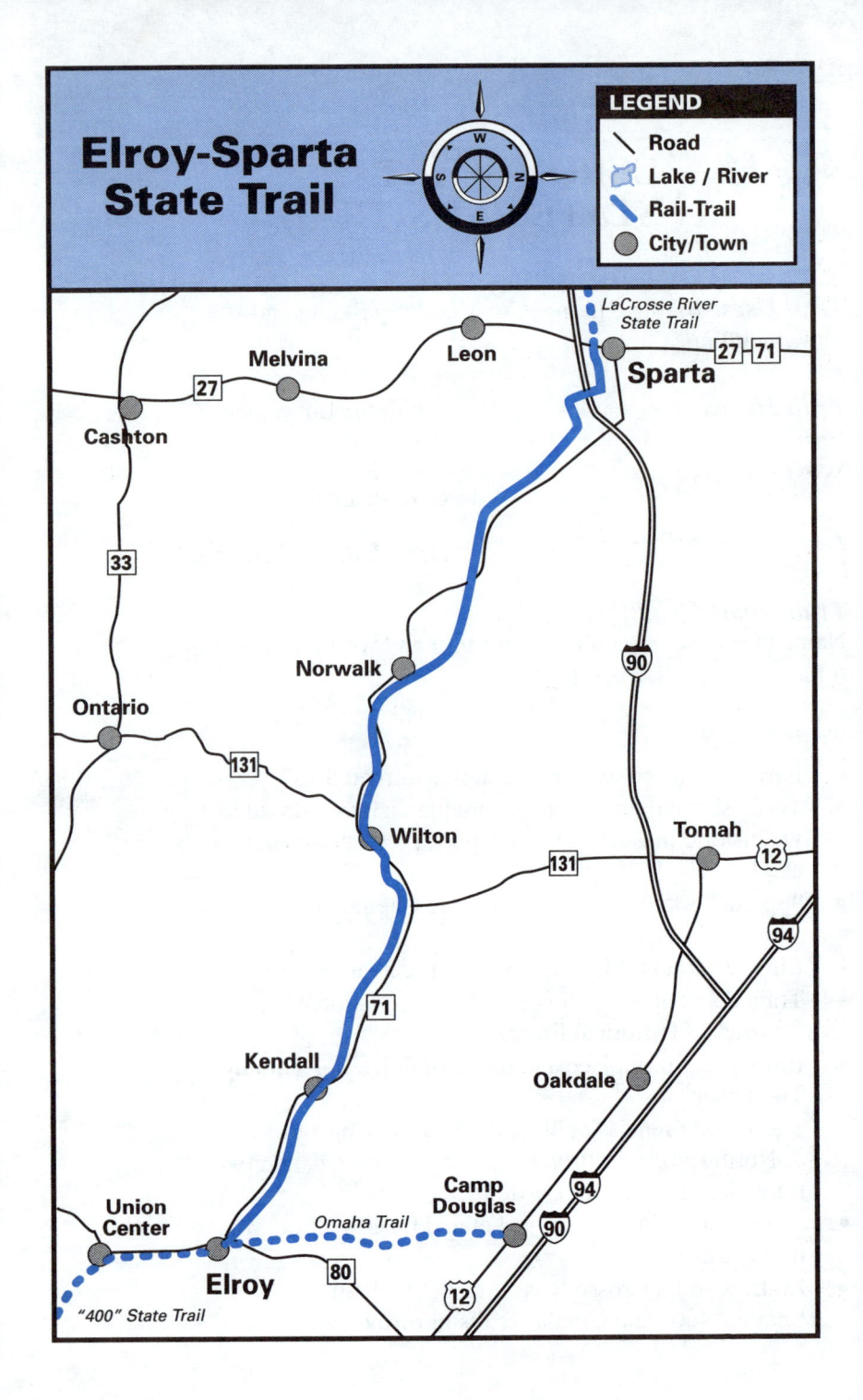

Elroy-Sparta State Trail

Elroy-Sparta State Park Trail

Suggested Auto Routes

Madison to Elroy		
Road	Direction	Miles
US151 to US51	NE	3.8
US51 to I-90	N	3.4
I-90 to ST82	NW	62.5
ST82	W	14.1
Total: 83.8 miles; 1 hour, 34 minutes		

Milwaukee to Elroy		
Road	Direction	Miles
I-94 to ST82	W	139.8
ST82	W	14.1
Total: 153.9 miles; 2 hours, 33 minutes		

Auto Shuttle/Bicycle Rental:
Car shuttles and bicycle rentals are available at Kendall Depot. This service is available for cyclists wishing to ride the trail one way. A driver will transport cyclists to desired starting area and drive vehicle to a requested finish destination. Contact the trail headquarters at (608) 463-7109 for additional information and shuttle reservations.

Additional information sources:
Elroy-Sparta State Headquarters
P.O. Box 297
Kendall, WI 54638
(608) 463-7109

Sparta Depot/Chamber of Commerce
111 Milwaukee St.
Sparta, WI 54656
(608) 269-4123 (800) 354-BIKE

Elroy Commons Trail Shop
303 Railroad Street
Elroy, WI 53929
(608) GO2-BIKE

#7 GANDY DANCER TRAIL

Trail Uses: Bicycling, Hiking, Horseback Riding and Snowmobiling

Trail Heads:
South - St. Croix Falls
North - Danbury

Length of Trail: 98 miles

Surface: Crushed Limestone & Original Ballast

Grade: Level

Date Established: 1991

Trail Name Origin:
Named to commemorate the "Gandy Dancer Crews" who built the railroad.

Trail Highlights:
- Former Soo Line/Wisconsin Central Railroad line.
- Gandy Dancer crosses four bridge trestles offering scenic vistas of lakes, rivers, forests and abundant wildlife. Trail crosses the St. Croix River via a 520-foot trestle bridge more than 75 feet above the river – a trail highlight.

Suggested Auto Routes

Milwaukee to St Croix Falls		
Road	Direction	Miles
I-94 to US53	NW	241.2
US53 to US8	NW	50.1
US8	W	39.5
Total: 330.8 miles; 5 hours, 36 minutes		

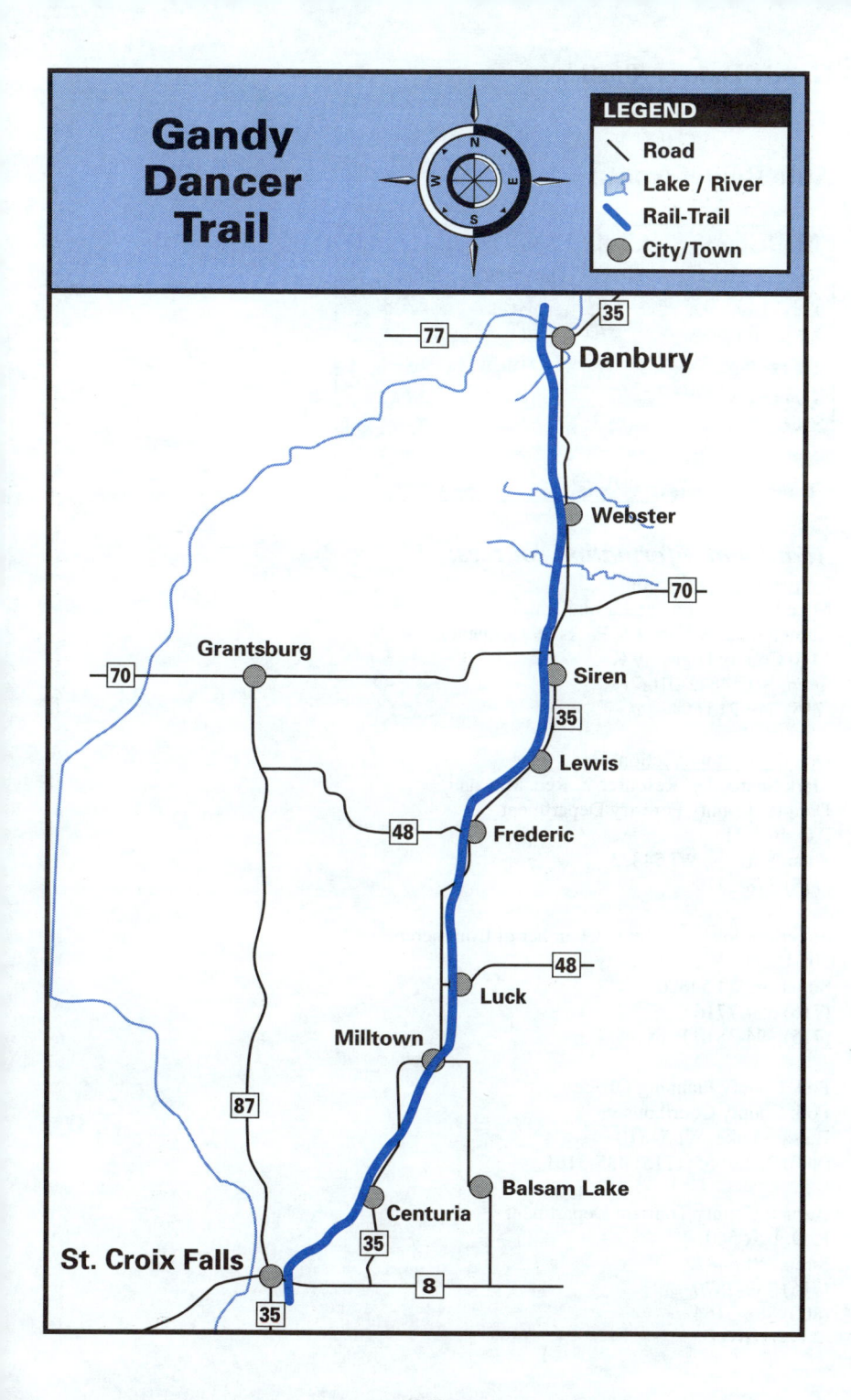

Gandy Dancer Trail

Gandy Dancer Trail

Auto Routes (cont.)

Madison to St. Croix Falls		
Road	Direction	Miles
US151 to US51	NE	3.8
US51 to I-90	N	3.4
I-90 to I-94	NW	86.7
I-94 to US53	NW	77.2
US53 to US8	NW	50.1
US8	W	39.5
Total: 260.7 miles; 4 hours; 27 minutes		

Additional information sources:
Burnett County Section
Mike Luedeke, Forest Administrator
Burnett County Forest & Parks Department
7410 County Highway K
Siren, WI 54872-0106
(715) 349-2157

Douglas County Section
Mark Schroeder, Resource & Rec. Manager
Douglas County Forestry Department
P.O. Box 211
Solan Springs, WI 54873
(715) 378-2219

Superior/Douglas County Chamber of Commerce
305 Harbor View Parkway
Superior, WI 54880
(715) 394-7716
(715) 394-3810 FAX

Polk County Planning Office
Polk County Courthouse
Balsam Lake, WI 54810
(800) 222-7655; (715) 485-3161

Burnett County Tourism Department
P. O. Box 560
Siren, WI 54872
(715) 349-7570
(800) 788-3164

#8 GLACIAL DRUMLIN STATE PARK TRAIL

Trail Uses: Biking, Hiking, Cross-country Skiing and Snowmobiling

Trail Heads:
East - Waukesha
West - Cottage Grove

Length of Trail: 47.2 miles

Surface: Crushed Limestone

Grade: 3%

Date Established: 1986

Trail Name Origin:
Derived from the hills (drumlins) that remained from the glaciers.

Trail Highlights:
- Former Chicago & Northwestern Railroad line.
- Glacial Drumlin provides trail users with scenic views of wetlands, prairies, farmlands and elongated hills formed by glaciers (drumlins). Trail passes through nine villages.
- Near the Aztalen State Park and Kettle Moraine State Forest.
- Trail crosses the Rock and Crawfish Rivers.

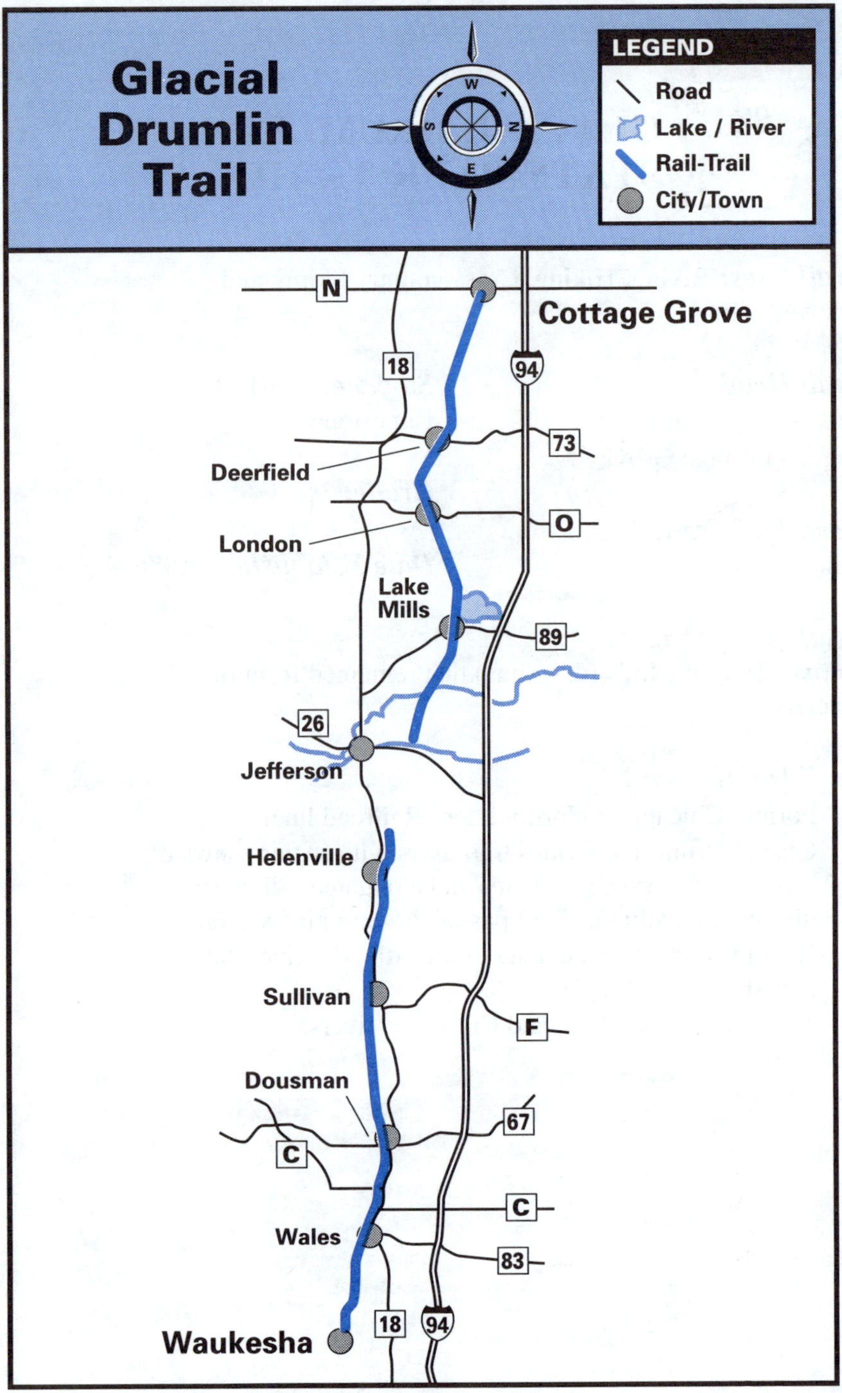
Glacial Drumlin Trail
W
S
N
E
LEGEND
Road
Lake / River
Rail-Trail
City/Town
N
Cottage Grove
18
94
73
Deerfield
London
O
Lake Mills
89
26
Jefferson
Helenville
Sullivan
F
Dousman
67
C
C
Wales
83
18
94
Waukesha

Glacial Drumlin State Park Trail

Suggested Auto Routes

Madison to Cottage Grove

Road	Direction	Miles
US151 to ST30	NE	2.7
ST30 to I-94	E	2.9
I-94	E	5.1
Total: 13 miles; 17 minutes		

Milwaukee to Waukesha

Road	Direction	Miles
I-94 to US18	W	12.6
US18	W	4.1
Total: 16.7 miles; 18 minutes		

Additional information sources:

Eastern Section
Paul Sandgren, Park Manager
Glacial Drumlin State Park Trail
N846 W329/DNR-Lapham Peak
Unit-KMSF CTH Co. "C"
Delafield, WI 53018
(414) 646-3025

West Section
Dana White, Park Manager
Glacial Drumlin State Park Trail
Wisconsin Department of Natural Resources
1213 S. Main Street
Lake Mills, WI 53551-1818
(414) 648-8774

Nancy Koeniguer, Sr. Financial Analyst
Waukesha Area Chamber of Commerce
223 Wisconsin Avenue
Waukesha, WI 53186
(414) 542-4241
chamber@Wauknet.com: e-mail

#9 GREAT RIVER STATE PARK TRAIL

Trail Uses: Bicycling, Hiking, Cross-country Skiing and Snowmobiling

Trail Heads:
South - Onalaska
North - Marshland

Length of Trail: 24 miles

Surface: Finely Crushed Limestone

Grade: 3%

Date Established: 1988

Trail Name Origin:
Trail shadows the Mississippi River.

Trail Highlights:
- Former Chicago & Northwestern Railroad line built in the late 1800's.
- Great River traverses through prairies and river bottomland providing users with tranquil views of glacial remnants, prairie plants, waterways and wildlife.
- Trail borders Trempealeau Mountain and 500-ft. bluffs of Perrot Park offers breathtaking views of the Mississippi River.
- 18 Bridges cross over Black River, Shingle Creek, Tank Creek and Halfway Creek.
- Links to La Crosse River State Park Trail.

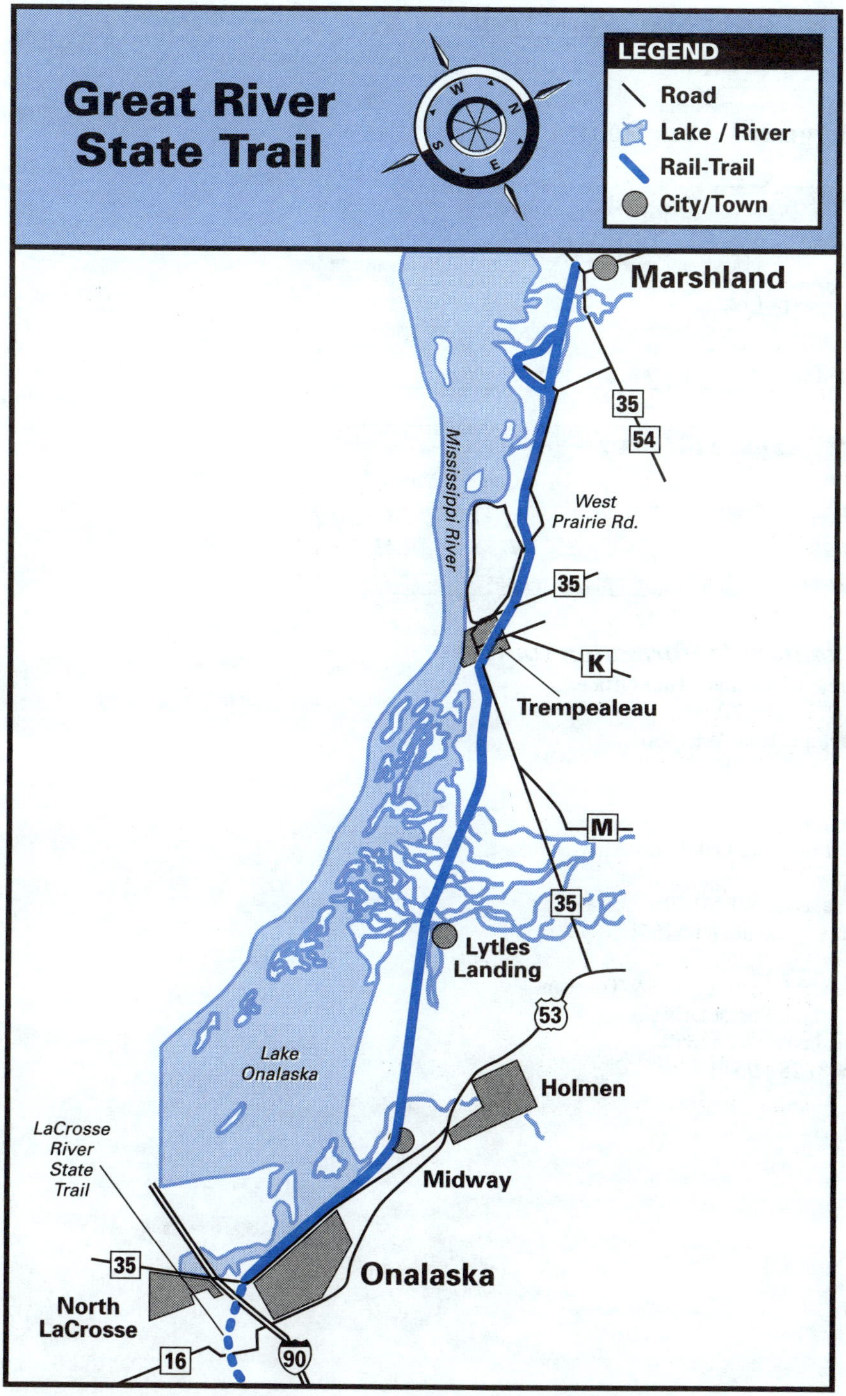
Great River
State Trail
W
N
S
E
LEGEND
Road
Lake / River
Rail-Trail
City/Town
Marshland
35
54
Mississippi River
West
Prairie Rd.
35
K
Trempealeau
M
35
Lytles
Landing
53
Lake
Onalaska
Holmen
Midway
LaCrosse
River
State
Trail
35
Onalaska
North
LaCrosse
16
90

Great River State Park Trail

Suggested Auto Routes

Madison to Onalaska

Road	Direction	Miles
US151 to US51	NE	3.8
US51 to I-90	N	3.4
I-90	W	129.7

Total: 136.9 miles; 2 hours, 12 minutes

Milwaukee to Onalaska

Road	Direction	Miles
I-94 to I-90	W	164
I-90	W	43

Total: 207 miles; 3 hours; 15 minutes

Additional information sources:
Great River State Trail Office
P.O. Box 407B
Trempealeau, WI 54661
(608) 534 6409

Trailhead
Hilltopper & Oak Forest Drive
Hwy 35
Onalaska, WI 54650
Trempealeau, WI 54661

Center for Commerce & Tourism
800 Oak Forest Drive
Onalaska, WI 54650
(608) 781-9570

#10 LA CROSSE RIVER STATE PARK TRAIL

Trail Uses: Bicycling, Hiking, Cross-country Skiing and Snowmobiling

Trail Heads:
East - Sparta
West - Medary Junction

Length of Trail: 21.5 miles

Surface: Packed Limestone Screenings

Grade: Less than 2%

Date Established: 1978

Trail Name Origin:
Derived from the La Crosse River that parallels the trail.

Trail Highlights:
- Former Chicago & Northwestern Railroad line.
- La Cross River Trail offers scenic views of prairie remnants, trout streams, wooded hillsides and farmland.
- Links to Elroy-Sparta and Great River State Trails.

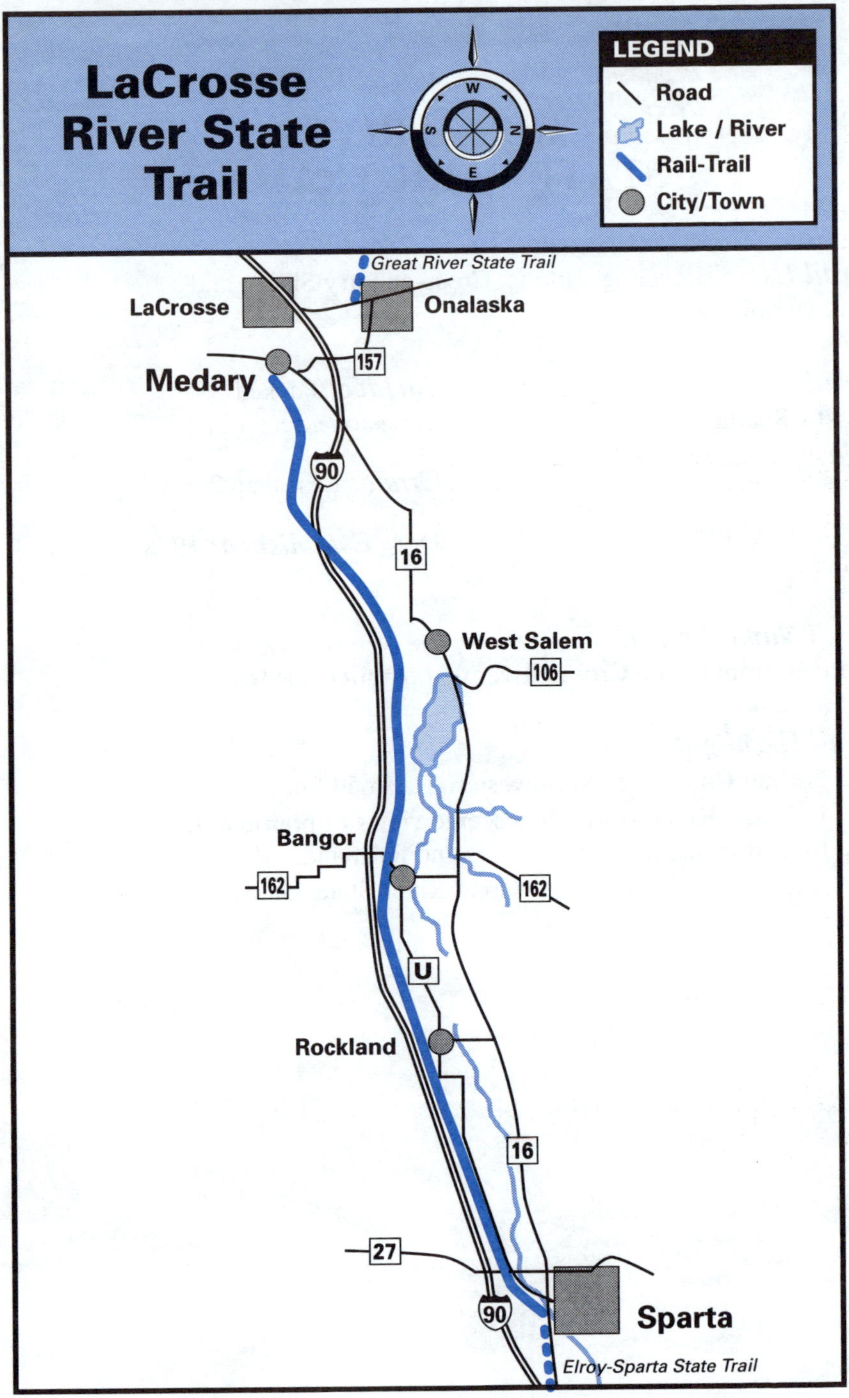
LaCrosse
River State
Trail
W
S
N
E
LEGEND
Road
Lake / River
Rail-Trail
City/Town
Great River State Trail
LaCrosse
Onalaska
157
Medary
90
16
West Salem
106
Bangor
162
162
U
Rockland
16
27
90
Sparta
Elroy-Sparta State Trail

La Crosse River State Park Trail

Suggested Auto Routes

Madison to Sparta		
Road	Direction	Miles
US151 to US51	NE	3.8
US51 to I-90	N	3.4
I-90 ST16	NW	104.1
ST16	W	2.8
Total: 114.1 miles; 1 hour, 51 minutes		

Milwaukee to Sparta		
Road	Direction	Miles
I-94 to I-90	W	164
I-90 to ST16	W	17.4
ST16	W	2.8
Total: 184.2 miles; 2 hours, 55 minutes		

Additional information sources:
Ronald E. Nelson, Park Superintendent
Wildcat Work Unit
P.O. Box 99
Ontario, WI 54651-0099
(608) 337-4775

La Crosse Convention & Visitors Bureau
Riverside Park
Box 1895
La Crosse, WI 54602-1895
(608) 782-2366

Sparta Depot/Sparta Chamber of Commerce
111 Milwaukee Street
Sparta, WI 54656
(608) 269-4123

#11 MILITARY RIDGE STATE PARK TRAIL

Trail Uses: Bicycling, Hiking, Cross-country Skiing and Snowmobiling

Trail Heads:
East - Verona
West - Dodgeville

Length of Trail: 39.6 miles

Surface: Packed Limestone

Grade: 2% to 5%

Date Established: 1981

Trail Name Origin:
Trail traverses along Military Ridge, which is the crest above the historic "Military Road" established by President Zachary Taylor.

Trail Highlights:
- Former Chicago & Northwestern Railroad line built in 1835.
- Military Ridge crosses 48 bridges providing scenic views of glacial moraines, limestone spring quarries, wetlands wooded areas, farms and small cities.

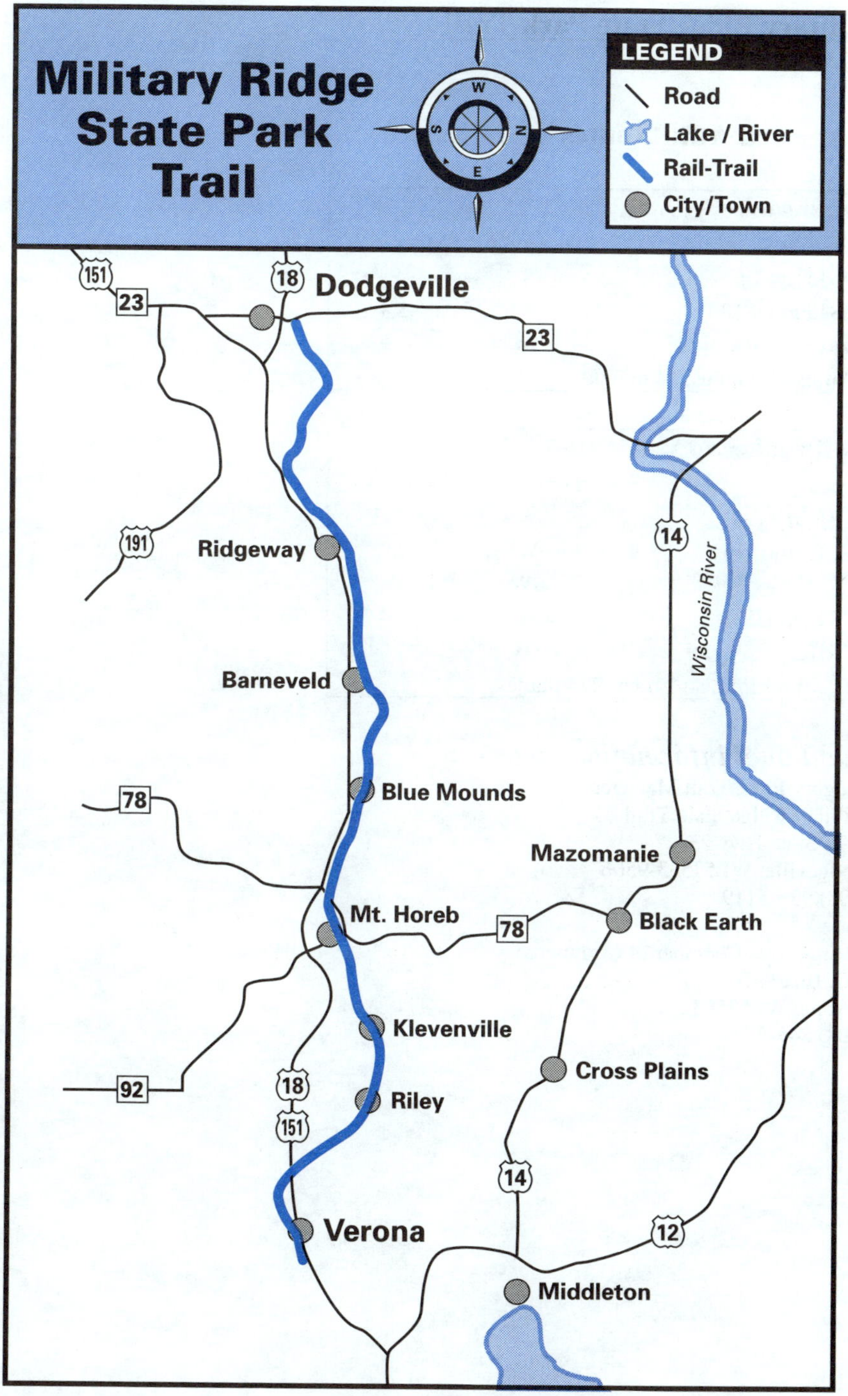
Military Ridge State Park Trail
W
S
N
E
LEGEND
Road
Lake / River
Rail-Trail
City/Town
151
18
Dodgeville
23
23
191
Ridgeway
14
Wisconsin River
Barneveld
78
Blue Mounds
Mazomanie
Mt. Horeb
78
Black Earth
Klevenville
Cross Plains
92
18
Riley
151
14
Verona
12
Middleton

Military Ridge State Park Trail

Suggested Auto Routes

Madison to Verona

Road	Direction	Miles
US151 to US12	S	2
US12 to US18	W	3.4
US18	SW	5.9
Total: 11.3 miles; 14 minutes		

Milwaukee to Verona

Road	Direction	Miles
I-94/ to ST30	W	72.2
ST30 to US151	W	2.9
US151 to US12	SW	4.7
US12 to US18	W	3.4
US18	SW	5.9
Total: 89.1 miles; 1 hour, 27 minutes		

Additional information sources:

Gregory Pittz, Trail Manager
Military Ridge State Trail
4175 State Hwy 23
Dodgeville, WI 53533-9506
(608) 935-5119

Verona Area Chamber of Commerce
P.O. Box 930003
Verona, WI 53593
(608) 845-5777

#12 MOUNTAIN-BAY TRAIL

Trail Uses: Bicycling, Hiking, Cross-country Skiing and Snowmobiling (in designated areas)

Trail Heads:
South - Howard
North - Weston

Surface: Crushed Granite

Grade: Flat

Length of Trail: 83 miles

Date Established: 1995

Trail Name Origin:
Countywide contest was held to select name.

Trail Highlights:
- Former Chicago & Northwestern Railroad line.
- Mountain-Bay crosses six bridges providing scenic views of creeks, rivers and wetlands.
- Longest recreational trail in state of Wisconsin.

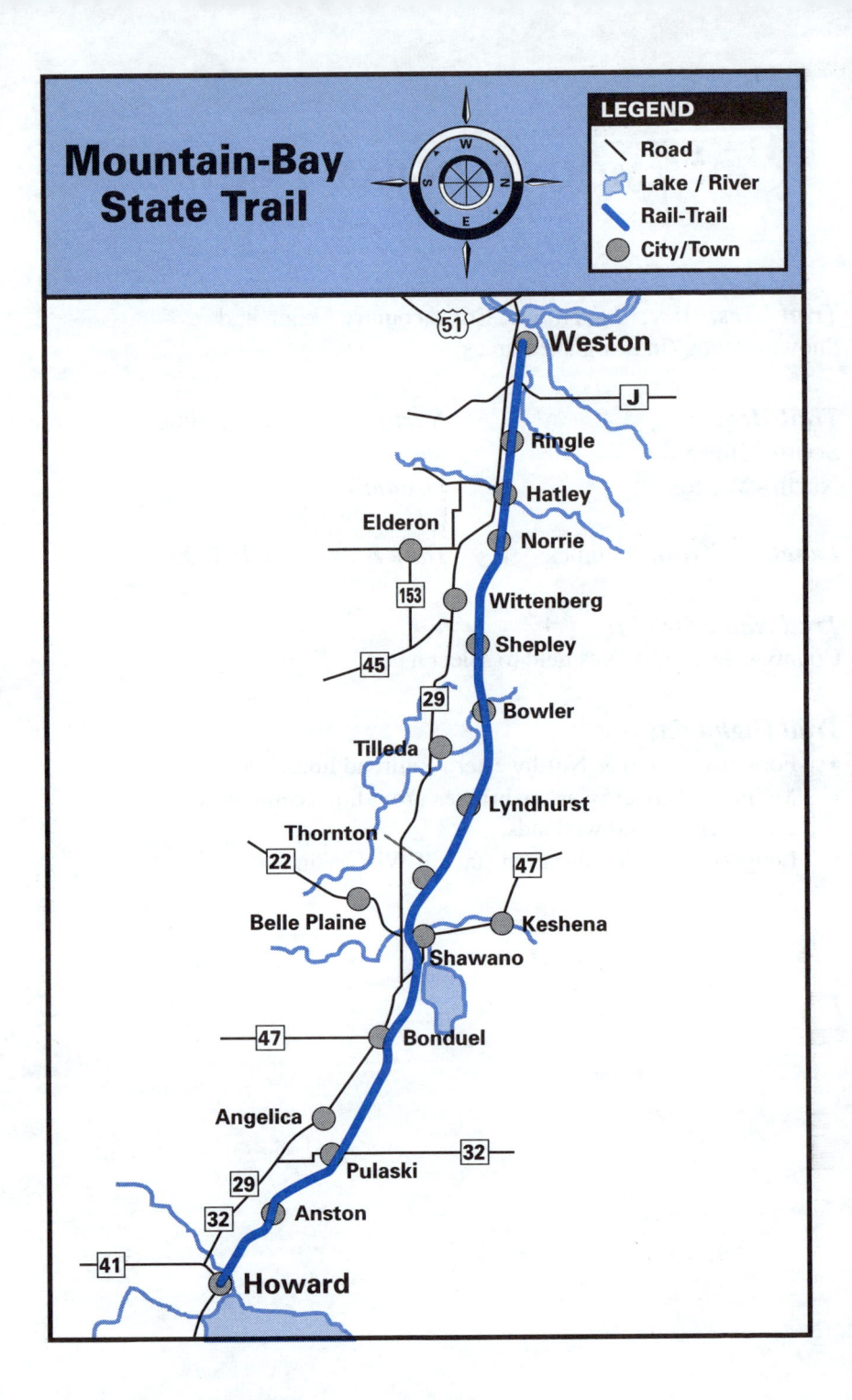

Mountain-Bay State Trail

LEGEND
- Road
- Lake / River
- Rail-Trail
- City/Town

Mountain-Bay Trail

Suggested Auto Routes

Milwaukee to Howard

Road	Direction	Miles
I-43 to ST172	N	109.3
ST172 to US41	W	6.2
US41	N	3.7
Total: 119.2 miles 2 hours, 17 minutes		

Madison to Weston

Road	Direction	Miles
US151 to US51	NE	3.8
US51 to I-90	N	3.4
I-90 to ST78	NW	24.3
ST78 to US51	N	7.9
US51 to ST29	N	97.2
ST29	E	4.1
Total: 140.7 miles 2 hours, 55 minutes		

Additional information sources:
Brown County Park Department
305 East Walnut Street
Green Bay, WI 54301
(920) 448-4466

Shawano County Park/Planning Department
311 North Main Street
Shawano, WI 54166
(715) 524-5165

Marathon County Park Department
500 Forest Street
Wausau, WI 54403
(715) 847-5235

#13 OMAHA TRAIL

Trail Uses: Bicycling, Hiking, Cross-county Skiing and Snowmobiling

Trail Heads:
West - Camp Douglas
East - Elroy

Surface: Asphalt & Gravel

Grade: Level

Length of Trail: 12.5 miles

Date Established: 1992

Trail Name Origin:
Contest was held to name trail.

Trail Highlights:
- Former Chicago & Northwestern Railroad line.
- Sandstone bluffs, rural communities and several small towns, surround Omaha.
- Links with Elroy-Sparta Trail via an 875 ft. tunnel and The "400" Trail.

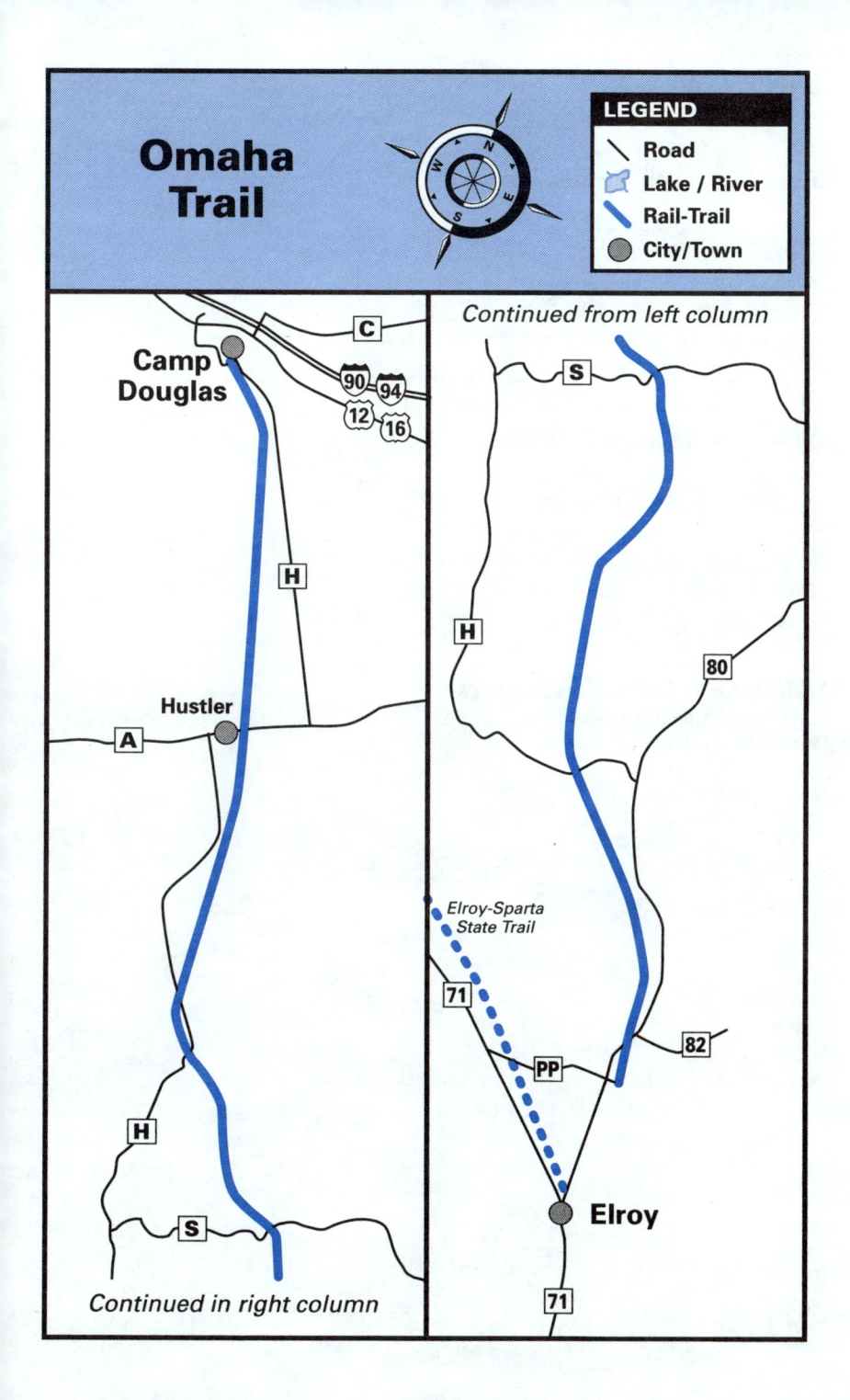

Omaha Trail

LEGEND
- Road
- Lake / River
- Rail-Trail
- City/Town

Camp Douglas

90 94 12 16 C H

Hustler

A

H
S

Continued in right column

Continued from left column

S H 80

Elroy-Sparta State Trail

71 PP 82

Elroy

71

167

Omaha Trail

Suggested Auto Routes

Madison to Elroy

Road	Direction	Miles
US151 to US51	NE	3.8
US51 to I-90	N	3.4
I-90 to ST80	NW	62.5
ST82	W	14.1
Total: 83.8 miles 1 hour 34 minutes		

Milwaukee to Elroy

Road	Direction	Miles
I-94 to ST82	W	139.8
ST82	W	14.1
Total: 153.9 miles; 2 hours, 33 minutes		

Additional information sources:
Dale Dorow, Administrator
250 Oak Street
Mauston, WI 53948
(608) 847-9389

#14 PINE LINE

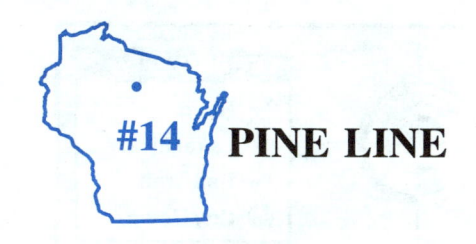

Trail Uses: Bicycling, Hiking, Horseback Riding and Snowmobiling

Trail Heads:
North - Prentice
South - Medford

Length of Trail: 28 miles
Parallel Equestrian trail

Surface: Limestone Screening & Crushed Gravel

Grade: Flat

Date Established: 1989

Trail Name Origin:
Named for the huge quantities of eastern white pines shipped by the Wisconsin Central Railroad on the route between 1876 and 1988 and for the beautiful stand of pine which presently clothe the trail.

Trail Highlights:
- Former Wisconsin Central Railroad line.
- Pine Line traverses through terminal moraine, hardwood forests, cedar swamps, bogs and wetlands.
- No trail admission fee.
- Three miles from the Ice Age National Scenic Trail.

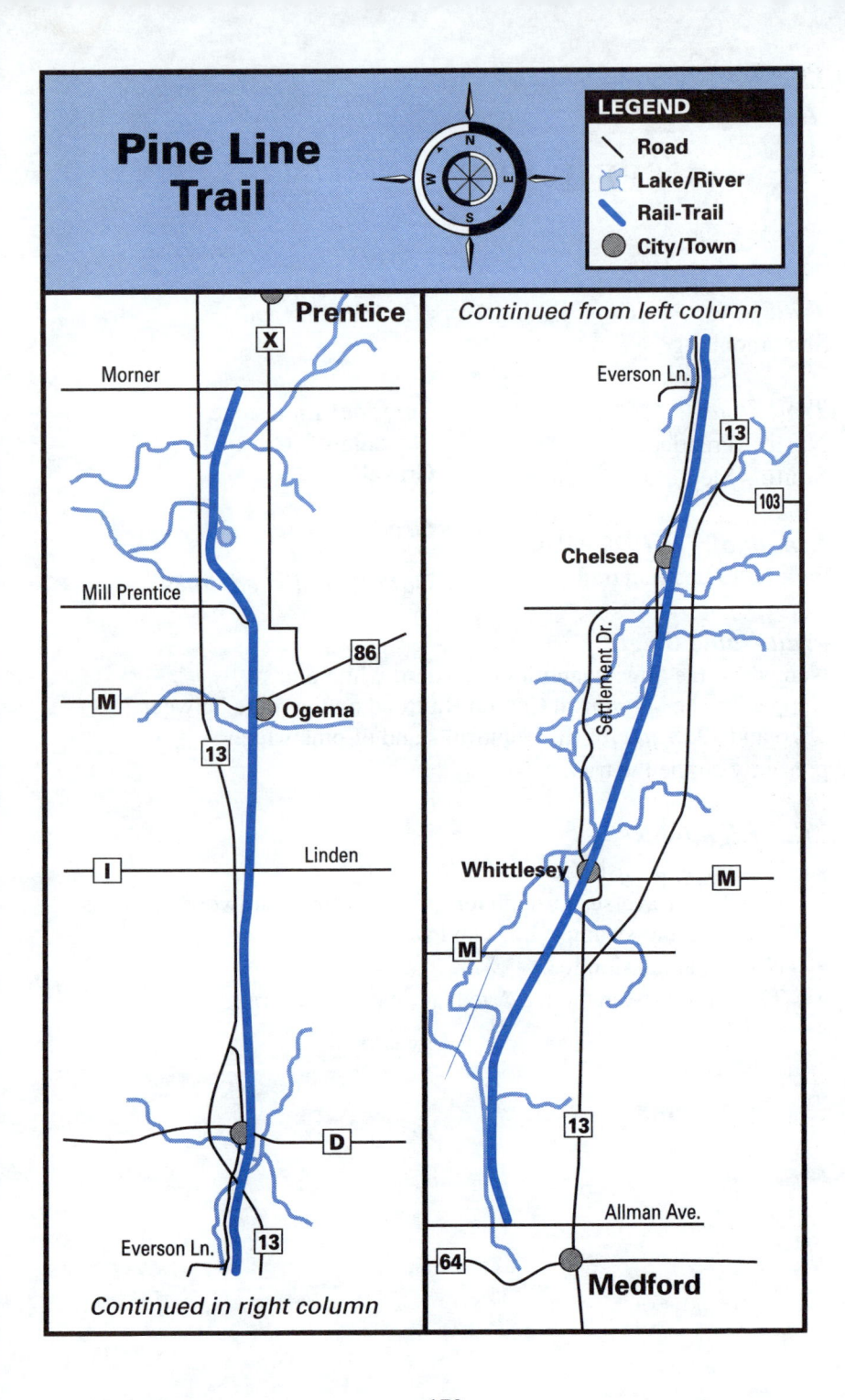

Pine Line Trail

LEGEND
- Road
- Lake/River
- Rail-Trail
- City/Town

Prentice
Morner
Mill Prentice
[M]
[13]
86
Ogema
Linden
[I]
[D]
Everson Ln.
[13]

Continued in right column

Continued from left column

Everson Ln.
[13]
103
Chelsea
Settlement Dr.
Whittlesey
[M]
[M]
[13]
Allman Ave.
[64]
Medford

170

Pine Line

Suggested Auto Routes

Madison to Medford		
Road	Direction	Miles
US151 to US51	NE	3.8
US51 to I-90	N	3.4
I-90 to ST80	NW	69.3
ST80 to ST13	N	42.3
ST13	N	52.9
Total: 171.7 miles; 3 hours 15 minutes		

Milwaukee to Medford		
Road	Direction	Miles
I-94 to ST80	W	146.6
ST80 to ST13	N	42.3
ST13	N	52.9
Total: 241.8 miles; 4 hours, 40 minutes		

Additional information sources:
Price County Section
Price County Tourism Office
126 Cherry Street Phillips
WI 54555
(800) 269-4505
(715) 339-4505

Taylor County Section
Taylor County Tourism Council
224 South Second Street
Medford, WI 54451
(800) 257-4729
(715) 748-4729

Medford Area Chamber of Commerce
P.O. Box 172
Medford, WI 54451
(715) 748-4729
(715) 748-6899 FAX

#15 RED CEDAR STATE TRAIL

Trail Uses: Bicycling, Hiking, Cross-country Skiing and Snowmobiling (Dunnville to Chippewa River)

Trail Heads:
North - Menomonie
South - Dunnville Wildlife Area

Length of Trail: 14.5 miles

Surface: Crushed Stone

Grade: 2% to 3%

Date Established: 1973

Trail Name Origin:
Derived from the Red Cedar River, which parallels the trail.

Trail Highlights:
- Former Chicago & Milwaukee, St. Paul & Pacific Railroad lines.
- Red Cedar provides breathtaking views of the Chippewa River, farmlands, wooded sandstone, bluffs, prairies and wetlands. Trail crosses the Chippewa River via an 800-ft. railroad trestle. Opportunities to view many varieties of wildlife including bald eagle and osprey.
- Visitor information center is located in an original Railroad freight depot building in Menomonie.
- Link to Chippewa River State Trail.

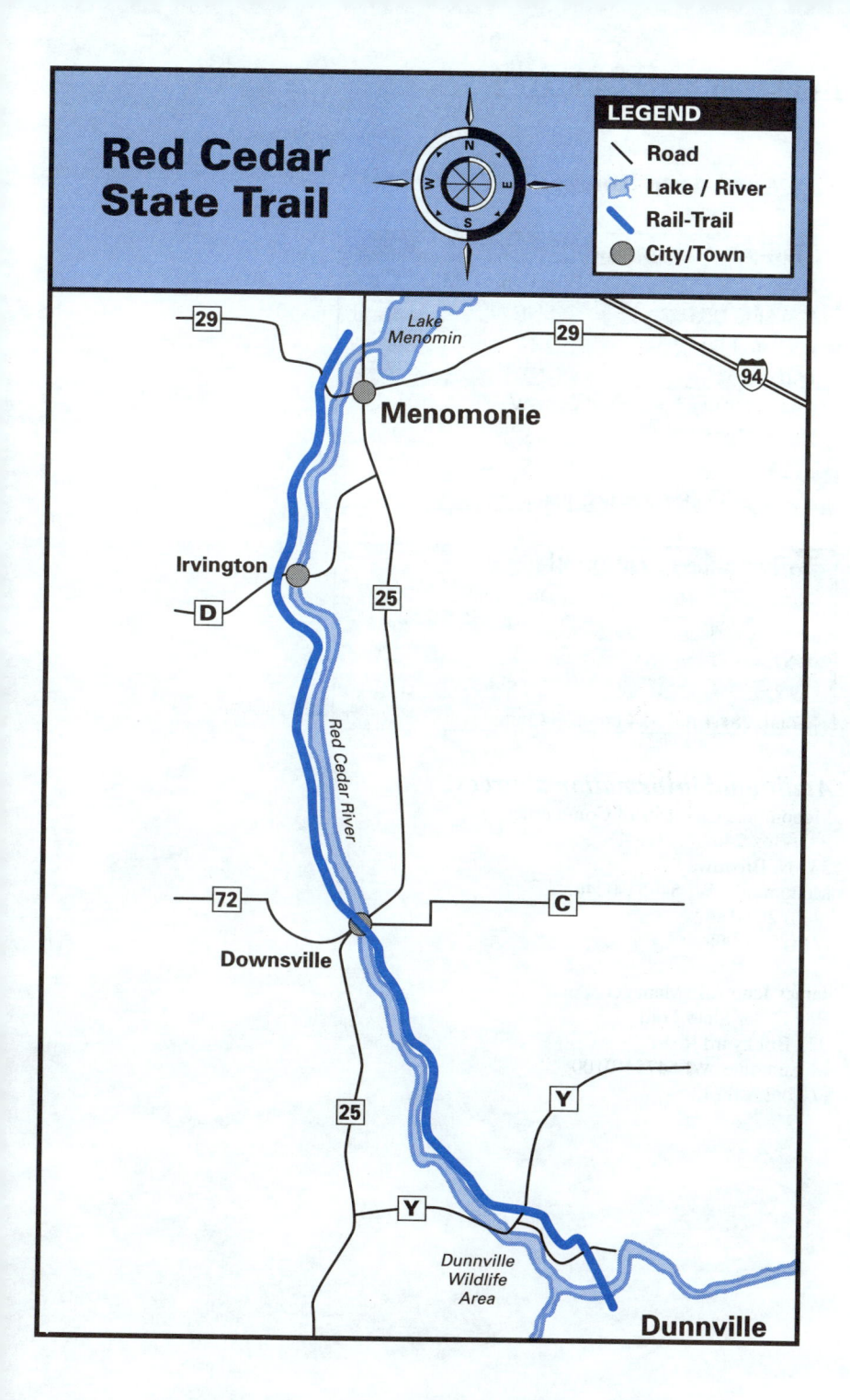

Red Cedar State Trail

Red Cedar State Park Trail

Suggested Auto Routes

Madison to Dunnville

Road	Direction	Miles
US151 to US51	NE	3.8
US51 to I-90	N	3.4
I-90 to I-94	NW	86.7
I-94 to US12	NW	104.6
US12 to ST25	S	2.2
ST25	S	11.5

Total: 214 miles; 3 hours, 40 minutes

Milwaukee to Dunnville

Road	Direction	Miles
I-94 to US12	NW	268.6
US12 to ST25	S	2.2
ST25	S	11.5

Total: 284.1 miles, 4 hours, 44 minutes

Additional information sources:

Menomonie Chamber of Commerce
P.O. Box 246
533 N. Broadway
Menomonie, WI 54751-0246
(800) 283-1862
(715) 235-9087

James Janowak, Manager
Red Cedar State Trail
921 Brickyard Road
Menomonie, WI 54751-9100
(715) 232-1242

#16 SUGAR RIVER STATE PARK TRAIL

Trail Uses: Bicycling, Hiking, Cross-country Skiing and Snowmobiling

Trail Heads:
North - New Glarus
South - Brodhead

Length of Trail: 23.5 miles

Surface: Crushed Limestone

Grade: Less than 1%

Date Established: 1972

Trail Name Origin:
Derived from the Sugar River, which parallels portions of the trail.

Trail Highlights:
- Former Chicago, Milwaukee & S. Paul Railroad line.
- New Glarus is known as "Little Switzerland" a quaint town boasting "Chalet like" architecture and Swiss heritage.
- Trail offers picturesque views of rolling hills, meadows, rushing streams, state wildlife refuge, trestle and covered bridges.
- Trail headquarter resides in the New Glarus Historical Railroad Depot.
- Part of the 1,000 mile Ice-Age National Scenic Trail and a National Recreation trail.

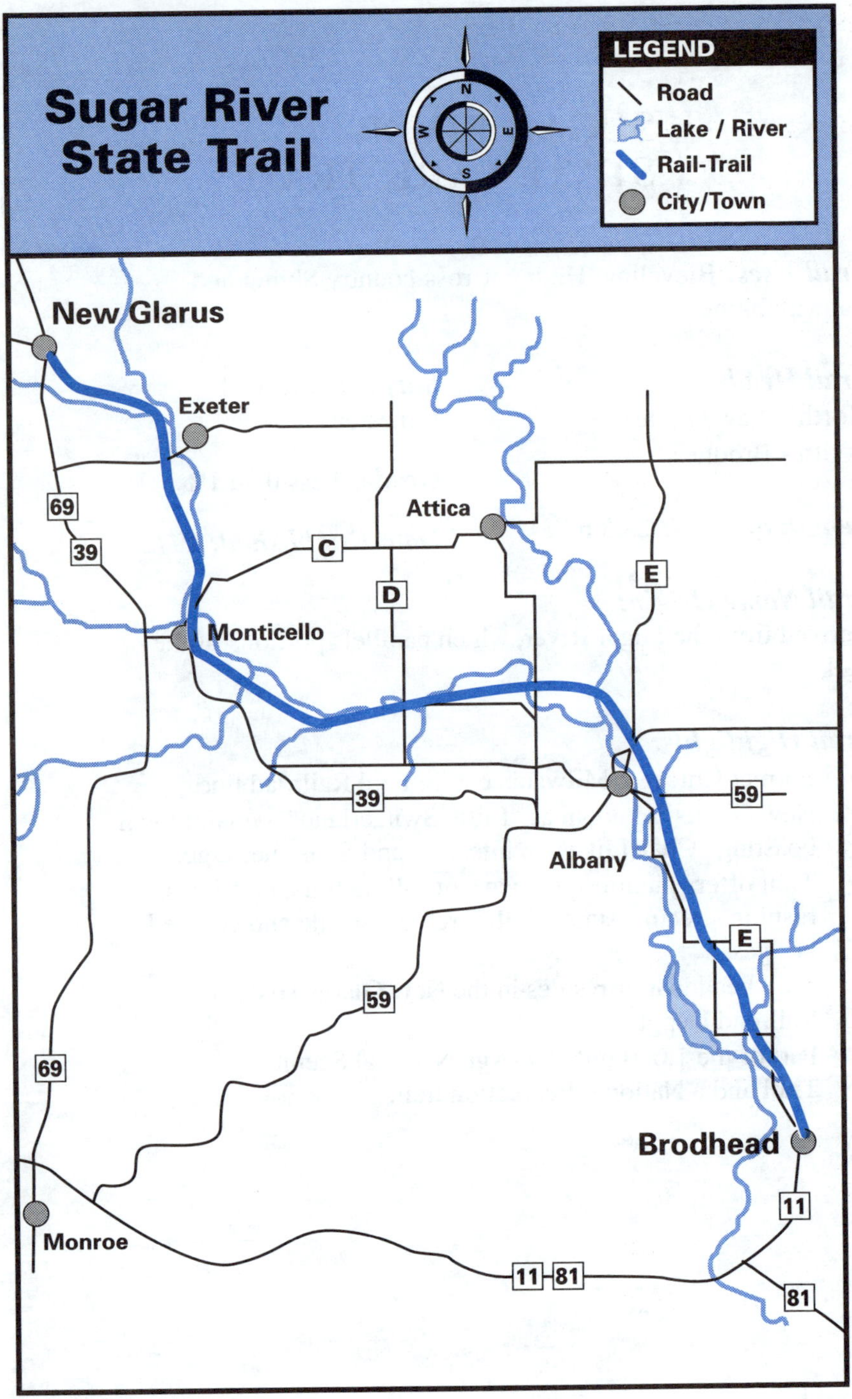

Sugar River State Trail
N
E
S
W
LEGEND
Road
Lake / River
Rail-Trail
City/Town
New Glarus
Exeter
69
39
C
Attica
D
E
Monticello
39
59
Albany
E
59
69
Brodhead
11
Monroe
11
81
81

Sugar River State Park Trail

Suggested Auto Routes

Madison to New Glarus

Road	Direction	Miles
US151 to US12	S	2
US12 to US18	W	3.4
US18 to ST69	SW	5.9
ST69	S	17.3
Total: 28.6 miles; 40 minutes		

Milwaukee to Brodhead

Road	Direction	Miles
I-94 to I-894	S	5.1
I-894 to US45	W	4.8
US45 to I-43	SW	1.1
I-43 to ST81	W	62.8
ST81 to ST213	W	1
ST213 to ST11	NW	14
ST11	W	6
Total: 94.8 miles; 1 hour, 51 minutes		

Auto Shuttle Available
For further information call or write:
Sugar River Trail
P. O. Box 781
New Glarus, WI 53574
(608) 527-2334

Additional information sources:
Reynold Zeller, Superintendent
Sugar River State Park Trail
P.O. Box 781
New Glarus, WI 53574-0781
(608) 527-2334

New Glarus Chamber of Commerce
P.O. Box 713
New Glarus, WI 53574-0713
(800) 527-6838

#17 TUSCOBIA STATE TRAIL

Trail Uses: Hiking, Mountain Bicycling, Cross-country Skiing and Snowmobiling

Trail Heads:
West - Rice Lake
East - Park Falls

Length of Trail: 74 miles
(portions undeveloped)

Surface: Gravel, Original Ballast & Grass

Grade: Flat

Date Established: 1966

Trail Name Origin:
Tuscobia is an old Indian word meaning "very level place."

Trail Highlights:
- Former Chippewa Valley & Northwestern, Chicago St. Paul Minneapolis & Omaha Railroad lines.
- Tuscobia provides users with scenic views of lakes, streams, rolling hills, abundant wildlife and northwoods.
- Part of the Ice Age National Scenic Trail.

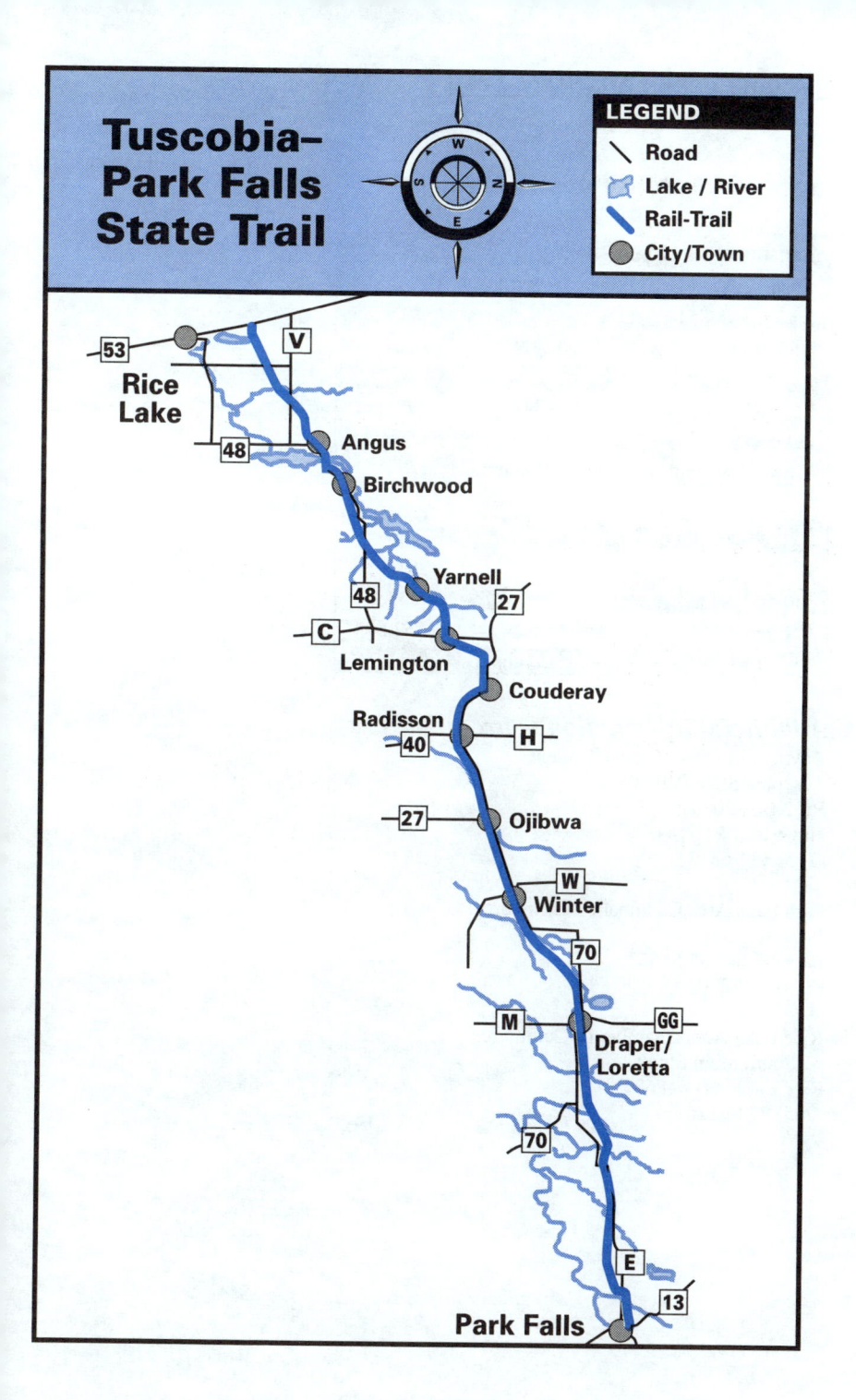

Tuscobia–Park Falls State Trail

Tuscobia Park Falls State Trail

Suggested Auto Routes

Madison to Rice Lake

Road	Direction	Miles
US151 to US51	NE	3.8
US51 to I-90	N	3.4
I-90 to I-94	NW	86.7
I-94 to US53	NW	77.2
US53	NW	57.6
Total: 228.7 miles; 3 hours, 40 minutes		

Milwaukee to Rice Lake

Road	Direction	Miles
I-94 to US53	NW	241.2
US53	NW	57.6
Total: 298.8 miles; 4 hours, 45 minutes		

Additional information sources:

Raymond Larsen, Superintendent
Tuscobia State Park Trail
Rt. 2 Box 2003
Hayward, WI 54843
(715) 634-6513

Park Falls Area Chamber of Commerce
P.O. Box 246
Parks Falls, WI 54552
(715) 762-2703

Rice Lake Area Chamber of Commerce
37 South Main Street
Rice Lake, WI 54868
(715) 234-2126

#18 WILD GOOSE STATE TRAIL

Trail Uses: Bicycling, Hiking, Cross-country Skiing and Snowmobiling

Trail Heads:
North - Fond du Lac
South - Clyman Junction

Length of Trail: 34 miles
3.5 mile Equestrian trail

Surface: Limestone Screenings

Grade: Less than 4%

Date Established: 1986

Trail Name Origin:
Trail passes through Horicon Marsh Wildlife Area and National Wildlife Refuge. Trail name was derived from the geese found in Horicon Marsh.

Trail Highlights:
- Former Chicago & Northwestern Railroad line.
- Wild Goose provides trail users with a mix of picturesque scenery including farms, forests, glacial end moraines, prairie plants wildflowers and wildlife. Two wildlife refuges are located along trail.

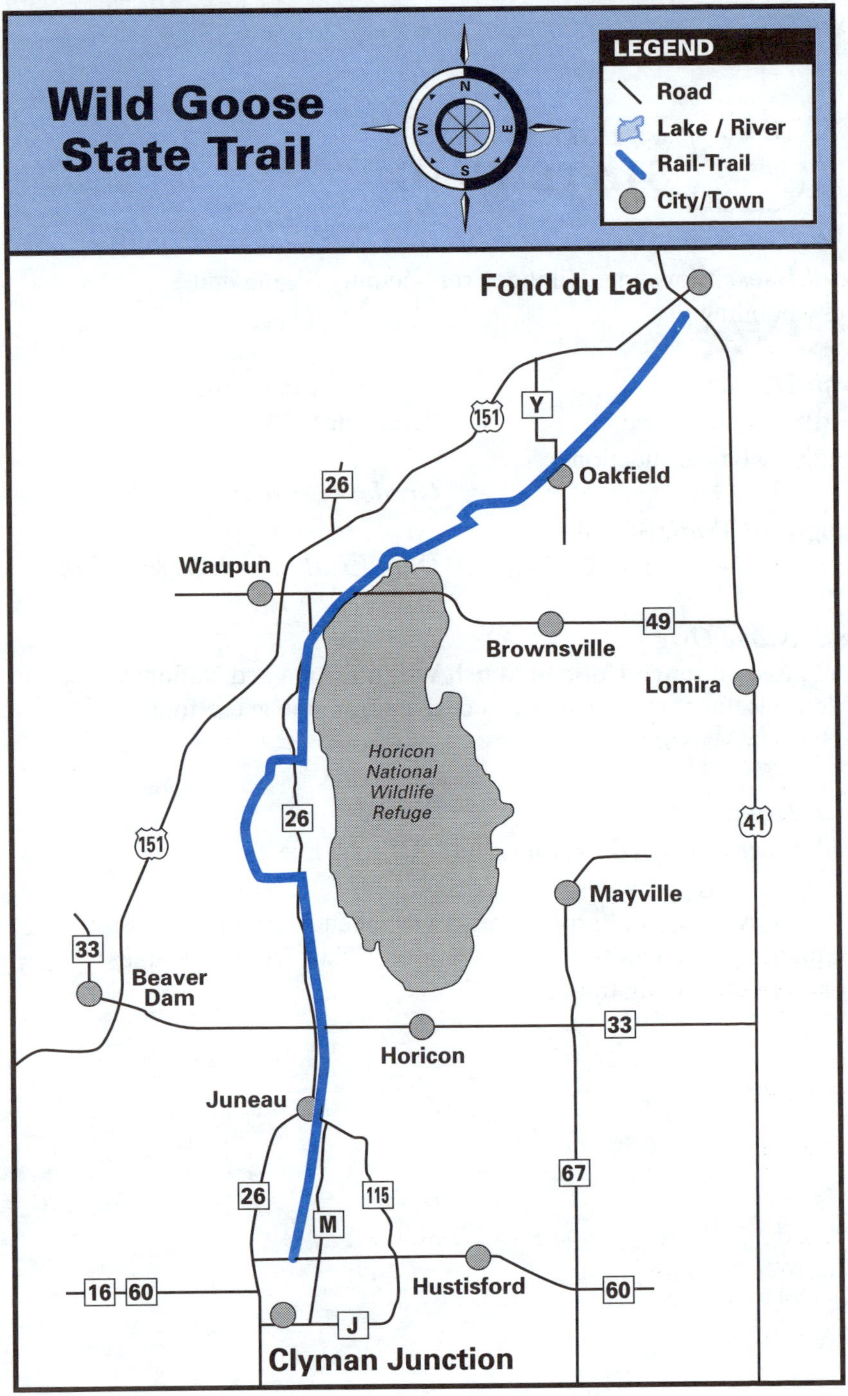
Wild Goose
State Trail
N
E
S
W
LEGEND
Road
Lake / River
Rail-Trail
City/Town
Fond du Lac
151
Y
Oakfield
26
Waupun
49
Brownsville
Lomira
Horicon
National
Wildlife
Refuge
26
151
41
Mayville
33
Beaver
Dam
33
Horicon
Juneau
67
26
115
M
16
60
Hustisford
60
J
Clyman Junction

Wild Goose State Trail

Suggested Auto Routes

Madison to Clyman Junction

Road	Direction	Miles
US151 to ST73	NE	24.9
ST73 to ST16	NE	1.5
ST16	E	14.7

Total: 41.1 miles; 55 minutes

Milwaukee to Clyman Junction

Road	Direction	Miles
I-94 to ST67	W	29.1
ST67 to ST16	NW	3.8
ST16	NW	22.6

Total: 55.5 miles; 1 hour 13 minutes

Additional information sources:

Dodge County Section
David Carpenter, Executive Director
Dodge County Planning & Development
Administration Building
Juneau, WI 53039
(414) 386-3700

Fond du Lac County Section
Wayne Rollin or Sam Tobias
Fond du Lac County Planning & Parks Dept.
160 S. Macy Street
Fond du Lac, WI 54935-4241
(414) 929-3135

Friends of the Recreation Trail (F.O.R.T.)
Virginia Seaholm, Co-President
P. O. Box 72
Juneau, WI 53039
(414) 485-2917

Waukesha County Parks & Planning Department
500 Riverview Avenue
Waukesha, WI 51388
(414) 548-7801

OTHER TRAILS

The following trails are also developed Rail-Trails. Most are open for bicycling, hiking, horseback riding, cross-country skiing, and snowmobiling.

For additional information on trail uses speak to the trail manager listed.

ILLINOIS

DELYTE MORRIS BIKEWAY
Trail Heads: Edwardsville
Counties: Madison
Length: 2.6 miles
Surface: Crushed stone
Uses: Bicycling & Hiking
Manager: Anna Schonlau, Assistant Recreation Director Southern Illinois University at Edwardsville Recreation Department
P. O. Box 1057
Edwardsville, IL 62026
(618) 692-3235

~~~~~

EL PASO TRAIL
Trail Heads: El Paso
Counties: Woodford
Length: 2.7 miles
Surface: Crushed stone
Uses: Bicycling & Hiking
Manager: Ted Gresham, Administrator
Town of El Paso City Hall
52 North Elm
El Paso, IL 61738-1545
(309) 527-4005

~~~~~

GREAT RIVER TRAIL
Trail Heads: Rock Island to Savanna
Counties: Carroll, Rock Island & Whiteside
Length: 62 miles (portions may be undeveloped)
Surface: Asphalt & crushed stone
Uses: Bicycling, Hiking, In-line Skating & Cross-country Skiing
Manager: Patrick Marsh, Bikeway Coordinator
Bi-State Regional Commission
1504 Third Avenue
Rock Island, IL 61201
(309) 793-6300

~~~~~

GREAT WESTERN TRAIL (DU PAGE PARKWAY SECTION)
Trail Heads: Villa Park
Counties: Du Page
Length: 12 miles
Surface: Crushed stone
Uses: Bicycling, Hiking, Horseback Riding & Cross-country Skiing
Manager: Charles Tokarski, County Engineer
Du Page County DOT
130 North County Farm Road
Wheaton, IL 60189
(630) 682-7318

~~~~~

ILLINOIS

GREEN BAY TRAIL
Trail Heads: Highland Park to Wilmette
Counties: Cook & Lake
Length: 9.5 miles
Surface: Asphalt & crushed stone
Uses: Bicycling, Hiking & Cross-country Skiing
Manager:
Glencoe Section
John Houde, Community Development Head
Village of Glencoe
675 Village Court
Glencoe, IL 60022-1639
(847) 835-4111

Highland Park Section
Larry King, Superintendent
Highland Park Forestry Department
1150 Half Day Road
Highland Park, IL 60035
(847) 432-0800

Wilmette Section
Bill Lambrecht
Wilmete Park District
1200 Wilmete Avenue
Wilmette, IL 60091-2793
(847) 256-6100

Winnetka Section
Dan Newport, Director
Winnetka Park District
520 Glendale Road, Suite 200
Winnetka, IL 60093-2552
(847) 501-2040

~~~~~

HEARTLAND PATHWAYS
Trail Heads: Seymour to Clinton & Cisco
Counties: Champaign, DeWitt & Platt
Length: 40 miles (portions may be undeveloped)
Surface: Original ballast
Uses: Hiking, Horseback Riding, Mountain Bicycling, Cross-country Skiing & Snowmobiling
Manager: David Monk, President Heartland Pathways
115 North Market Street
Champaign, IL 61820-4004
(217) 351-1911

~~~~~

LIBERTYVILLE TRAIL
Trail Heads: Libertyville
Counties: Lake
Length: 3 miles
Surface: Crushed stone
Uses: Bicycling, Hiking & Cross-country Skiing
Manager: Steve Magnusen, Director of Public Works
200 East Cook Avenue
Libertyville, IL 60048-2090
(847) 362-2430

~~~~~

LOWELL PARKWAY BICYCLE PATH
Trail Heads: Dixon
Counties: Lee
Length: 3.1 miles
Surface: Asphalt
Uses: Bicycling, Hiking, Cross-country Skiing & Snowmobiling
Manager: Dave Zinnen, Director of Administration & Recreation
Dixon Park District
804 Palmyra Avenue
Dixon, IL 61021-1960
(815) 284-3306

~~~~~

ILLINOIS

PECATONICA PRAIRIE PATH
Trail Heads: Freeport to Rockford
Counties: Stephenson & Winnebago
Length 20 miles
Surface: Original ballast
Uses: Bicycling, Hiking, Horseback Riding & Cross-country skiing
Manager: Rick Strader, Manager of Planning & Development
Rockford Park District
1401 North Second Street
Rockford, IL 61107
(815) 987-8856

PIMITEOUI BIKE TRAIL
Trail Heads: Peoria
Counties: Peoria
Length: 4.2 miles (portions may be undeveloped)
Surface: Asphalt
Uses: Bicycling, Hiking & Cross-country Skiing
Manager: Peoria Parks District
2218 North Prospect Road
Peoria, IL 61603
(309) 682-1200

PIONEER PARKWAY
Trail Heads: Peoria to Alta
Counties: Peoria
Length: 2.5 miles
Surface: Crushed stone
Uses: Bicycling, Hiking, Cross-country Skiing
Manager: Peoria Parks District
2218 North Prospect Road
Peoria, IL 61603
(309) 682-1200

ROCK ISLAND TRAIL STATE PARK
Trail Heads: Alta to Toulon
Counties: Peoria & Stark
Length: 28.3 miles
Surface: Crushed stone
Uses: Bicycling, Hiking & Cross-country Skiing
Manager: Paul Oltman, Trail Ranger
Rock Island Trail State Park
P. O. Box 64
Wyoming, IL 61491-0064
(309) 695-2228

ROCK RIVER RECREATION PATH
Trail Heads: Rockford to Love's Park
Counties: Winnebago
Length: 3.3 miles
Surface: Asphalt
Uses: Bicycling, Hiking, In-line Skating & Cross-country Skiing
Manager: Vance Barrie, Marketing Coordinator
Rockford Park District
1401 North Second Street
Rockford, IL 61107
(815) 987-8694

ILLINOIS

RONALD J. FOSTER HERITAGE TRAIL
Trail Heads: Glen Carbon
Counties: Madison
Length: 3.2 miles
Surface: Asphalt
Uses: Bicycling, Hiking & Cross-country Skiing
Manager: Glen Carbon Village Hall
P. O. Box 757
151 North Main Street
Glen Carbon, IL 62034
(618) 288-1200

SAM VADALABENE GREAT RIVER ROAD BIKE TRAIL
Trail Heads: Alton to Grafton
Counties: Jersey & Madison
Length: 14 miles
Surface: Asphalt
Uses: Bicycling, Hiking & In-line Skating
Manager: Ronald Tedesco, District Bikeway Coordinator
Illinois Department of Transportation
1100 Eastport Plaza Drive
P. O. Box 988
Collinsville, IL 62234
(618) 346-3100

VADALABENE NATURE TRAIL
Trail Heads: Edwardsville to Long Lake
Counties: Madison
Length: 10.3 miles (portions may be undeveloped)
Surface: Original ballast
Uses: Hiking, Horseback Riding, Mountain Bicycling, Cross-country Skiing & Snowmobiling
Manager: George Arnold
Madison County Trail Volunteers
1306 St. Louis Street
Edwardsville, IL 62025-1310
(618) 656-7195

IOWA

BROOKFIELD WILDLIFE REFUGE TRAIL
Trail Heads: Brookfield Wildlife Refuge Trail
Counties: Clinton
Length: 2 miles
Surface: Grass & dirt
Uses: Hiking
Manager: Al Griffith, Director
Clinton County Conservation Board
P. O. Box 161
Grand Mound, IA 52751
(319) 847-7202

~~~~~

CINDER PATH
Trail Heads: Chariton to Lucas-Wayne County line
Counties: Lucas & Wayne
Length: 13.5 miles
Surface: Original ballast
Uses: Hiking, Mountain Bicycling, Cross-country Skiing, Snowmobiling
Manager: Dwayne Clanin, Supervisor
P. O. Box 78
Chariton, IA 50049-0078
(515) 774-2314

~~~~~

FORT DODGE NATURE TRAIL
Trail Heads: Fort Dodge
Counties: Webster
Length: 3 miles
Surface: Crushed stone & gravel
Uses: Hiking, Mountain Bicycling & Cross-country Skiing,

Manager: Michael Norris, City Forester Department of Parks, Recreation & Forestry
813 First Avenue South
Fort Dodge, IA 50501-4725
(515) 573-5791

~~~~~

HARRY COOK NATURE TAIL
Trail Heads: Osage to Spring Park
Counties: Mitchell
Length: 2 miles
Surface: Crushed stone & gravel
Uses: Hiking, Horseback Riding, Mountain Bicycling & Cross-country Skiing
Manager: Ted Funk, Director Parks & Recreation
114 South 7th Street
City Hall
Osage, IA 50461
(515) 732-3709

~~~~~

JACKSON COUNTY TRAIL
Trail Heads: Spragueville
Counties: Jackson
Length: 3.8 miles
Surface: Crushed stone
Uses: Bicycling, Hiking & Cross-country Skiing
Manager: Ann Burns
Jackson County Conservation Board
201 West Platt Road
Maquoketa, IA 52060
(319) 652-3783

~~~~~

IOWA

MAPLE LEAF PATHWAY
Trail Heads: Diagonal
Counties: Ringgold
Length: 2.5 miles
Surface: Crushed stone & grass
Uses: Bicycling & Hiking
Manager: Rick Hawkins, Director Ringgold County Conservation Board
P. O. Box 834, RR 1
Mount Ayr, IA 50854
(515) 464-2787

~~~~~

PERRY TO RIPPEY TRAIL
Trail Heads: Perry to Rippey
Counties: Boone, Dallas, & Greene
Length: 9 miles
Surface: Original ballast
Uses: Hiking, Horseback Riding, Mountain Bicycling & Cross-country Skiing
Manager:
Boone County Section
Tom Foster, Director
Boone County Conservation Board
610 H Avenue
Ogden, IA 50212
(515) 353-4237

Dallas County Section
Jeff Logsdon, Director
Dallas County Conservation Board
1477 K Avenue
Perry, IA 50220
(515) 465-3577

Greene County Section
Dan Towers, Director
Greene County Conservation Board
Courthouse
Jefferson, IA 50129
(515) 386-4629

~~~~~

PIONEER TRAIL
Trail Heads: Reinbeck to Holland
Counties: Grundy
Length: 12 miles
Surface: Crushed stone, Parallel grass treadway
Uses: Bicycling, Hiking, Horseback Riding & Cross-country Skiing
Manager: Kevin Williams, Director Grundy County Conservation Board
P. O. Box 36
Morrison, IA 50657
(319) 345-2688

~~~~~

PONY HOLLOW TRAIL
Trail Heads: Elkader
Counties: Clayton
Length: 4 miles
Surface: Crushed stone
Uses: Hiking, Horseback Riding, Mountain Bicycling & Cross-country Skiing, Snowmobiling
Manager: Don Menken, Director Clayton County Conservation Board
RR 2 Box 65A
Elkader, IA 52043-9524
(319) 245-1516

~~~~~

IOWA

PRAERI RAIL TRAIL
Trail Heads: Roland to Zearing
Counties: Story
Length: 10.5 miles
Surface: Crushed stone, gravel & dirt
Uses: Hiking, Horseback Riding, Mountain Bicycling, Cross-country Skiing & Snowmobiling
Manager: Steven Lekwa, Deputy Director
McFarland Park
RR 2, Box 272 E
Ames, IA 50010-9651
(515) 232-2516

~~~~~

PUDDLE JUMPER TRAIL
Trail Heads: Orange City to Alton
Counties: Sioux
Length: 2 miles
Surface: Crushed stone
Uses: Bicycling, Hiking, Horseback Riding & Cross-country Skiing
Manager: Mel D. Elsberry, Director Orange City Parks & Recreation Department
City Hall
Orange City, IA 51041
(712) 737-4885

~~~~~

RINGGOLD TRAILWAY
Trail Heads: Mount Ayr
Counties: Ringgold
Length: 2 miles
Surface: Original ballast
Uses: Hiking, Horseback Riding, Mountain Bicycling, Cross-country Skiing & Snowmobiling
Manager: Rick Hawkins, Director Ringgold County Conservation Board
P. O. Box 83A, RR 1
Mount Ayr, IA 50854
(515) 464-2787

~~~~~

RUSSELL WHITE NATURE TRAIL
Trail Heads: Lanesboro
Counties: Carroll
Length: 3.8 miles
Surface: Original ballast
Uses: Hiking, Horseback Riding, Mountain Bicycling, Cross-country Skiing & Snowmobiling
Manager: David Olson, Director Carroll Country Conservation Board
RR 1, Box 240A
Carroll, IA 51401-9801
(712) 792-4614

~~~~~

SHELL ROCK RIVER TRAIL
Trail Heads: Clarksville to Shell Rock
Counties: Butler
Length: 5.5 miles
Surface: Crushed stone
Uses: Hiking, Mountain Bicycling & Cross-country Skiing
Manager: Steve Brunsma, Director Butler County Conservation Board
28727 Timber Road
Clarksville, IA 50619
(319) 278-4237

~~~~~

IOWA

SHIMEK FOREST TRAIL
Trail Heads: Shimek State Forest
Counties: Lee & Van Buren
Length: 6 miles (portions may be undeveloped)
Surface: Original ballast, grass & dirt
Uses: Hiking, Mountain Bicycling, Cross-country Skiing & Snowmobiling
Manager: Wayne Fuhlbrugge, Area Forester Shimek State Forest
RR 1, Box 95
Farmington, IA 52626
(319) 878-3811

~~~~~

UPPER NISH HABITAT TRAIL
Trail Heads: Irwin
Counties: Shelby
Length: 4 miles
Surface: Original ballast & dirt
Uses: Hiking & Mountain Bicycling,
Manager: Darby Danders, Director Shelby County Conservation Board
514 Maple Road
Harlan, IA 51537
(712) 755-2628

~~~~~

WAPSI-GREAT WESTERN TRAIL
Trail Heads: Riceville
Counties: Mitchell
Length: 10.5 miles (portions may be undeveloped)
Surface: Crushed stone
Uses: Bicycling, Hiking, Horseback Riding, Cross-country Skiing & Snowmobiling (were designated)
Manager: Elaine Govern, Chairman Wapsi-Great Western Line Committee
P. O. Box 116
Riceville, IA 50466-016
(515) 985-4030

~~~~~

WINKEL MEMORIAL TRAIL
Trail Heads: Sibley to Allendorf with spur to Willow Creek Recreation Area
Counties: Osceola
Length: 10 miles
Surface: Gravel
Uses: Hiking, Horseback Riding, Mountain Bicycling Cross-country Skiing & Snowmobiling
Manager: Ron Spengler, Director Osceola County Conservation Board
5945 Highway 9
Ocheyedan, IA 51354
(712) 758-3709

~~~~~

IOWA

WINNEBAGO RIVER TRAIL
***Trail Heads*:** Forest City
Counties: Winnebago
Length: 6 miles (portions may be undeveloped)
Surface: Crushed stone, original ballast, & wood chips
Uses: Hiking, Mountain Bicycling & Cross-country Skiing
Manager: Robert Schwartz, Executive Director Winnebago County Conservation Board
33496 110th Avenue
Forest City, IA 50436-9205
(515) 565-3390

WINNESHIEK COUNTY TRAIL
***Trail Heads*:** Calmar to Winneshiek County line
Counties: Winneshiek
Length: 18 miles
Surface: Crushed stone
Uses: Bicycling, Hiking, Cross-country Skiing & Snowmobiling (on designated areas)
Manager: David Oestmann, Director Winneshiek County Conservation Board
2546 Lake Meyer Road
Fort Atkinson, IA 52144
(319) 534-7145

MICHIGAN

BAW BEESE TRAIL
Trail Heads: Hillsdale
Counties: Hillsdale
Length: 6 miles (portions may be undeveloped)
Surface: Original ballast
Uses: Hiking, Mountain Bicycling & Cross-country Skiing
Manager: Mark Reynolds, Director Hillsdale Recreation Department
43 McCollum Street
Hillsdale, MI 49242-1630
(517) 437-3579

~~~~~

BAY HAMPTON RAIL TRAIL
Trail Heads: Bay City to Hampton Township
Counties: Bay
Length: 6 miles
Surface: Asphalt
Uses: Bicycling, Hiking, In-line Skating & Cross-country Skiing
Manager:
Bay City Section
Al McFayden
City of Bay City
301 Washington Street
Bay City, MI 48708
(517) 894-8154

Hampton Section
Peg Vansummeran
Hampton Township
P. O. Box 187
Bay City, MI 48707
(517) 893-7541

~~~~~

CASS CITY WALKING TRAIL
Trail Heads: Cass City
Counties: Tuscola
Length: 1.4 miles
Surface: Gravel & original ballast
Uses: Hiking, Cross-country Skiing & Snowmobiling
Manager: Lou LaPonsie, Village Manager
6737 Church Street
P. O. Box 123
Cass City, MI 48726
(517) 872-2911

~~~~~

COALWOOD TRAIL
Trail Heads: Shingleton to Chatham
Counties: Alger & Schoolcraft
Length: 24 miles
Surface: Original ballast
Uses: Hiking, Horseback Riding, Mountain Bicycling, Cross-country Skiing & Snowmobiling,
Manager: Dick Anderson, Assistant Ranger
Hiawatha National Forest
Munising Ranger District
400 East Munising, RR #2
Box 400
Munising, MI 49862
(906) 387-2512

Bruce Veneberg, Area Forest Manager
Lake Superior State Forest
Shigleton Forest Area
M-28, P. O. Box 57
Shingleton, MI 49884
(906) 452-6227

~~~~~

MICHIGAN

FELCH GRADE TRAIL
Trail Heads: Narenta to Felch
Counties: Delta, Dickinson & Menominee
Length: 45 miles
Surface: Gravel & dirt
Uses: Hiking, Horseback Riding, Mountain Bicycling & Snowmobiling
Manager: Russ MacDonald, Assistant Area Forest Manager
Escanaba Forest Area
Escanaba River State Forest
6833 US 2
Gladstone, MI 49870
(906) 786-2354

~~~~~

FRANK N. ANDERSON TRAIL
Trail Heads: Bay City State Park
Counties: Bay
Length: 1.4 miles
Surface: Asphalt
Uses: Bicycling, Hiking, In-line Skating & Cross-country Skiing
Manager: Karen Gillispie
Bay City State Park
3582 State Park Drive
Bay City, MI 48706-1157
(517) 684-3020

~~~~~

FREDA TRAIL
Trail Heads: Freda to Bill Nichols Trail
Counties: Houghton
Length: 11.2 miles
Surface: Original ballast
Uses: Bicycling, Hiking, Horseback Riding, Cross-country Skiing & Snowmobiling
Manager: Martin Nelson or Dave Tuovila
Copper Country State Forest
P. O. Box 400
Baraga, MI 49908
(906) 353-6651

~~~~~

GALLUP TRAIL
Trail Heads: Ann Arbor
Counties: Washtenaw
Length: 3 miles
Surface: Asphalt
Uses: Bicycling, Hiking, In-line Skating & Cross-country Skiing
Manager: Tom Raynes, Manager
Ann Arbor Department of Parks & Recreation
P. O. Box 8647
Ann Arbor, MI 48107
(313) 994-2780

~~~~~

GAY TRAIL
Trail Heads: Gay to Mohawk
Counties: Houghton & Keweenaw
Length: 27 miles
Surface: Original ballast
Uses: Snowmobiling
Manager: Martin Nelson, Area Forrest Manager
Copper Country State Forest
P. O. Box 400
Baraga, MI 49908-0400
(906) 353-6651

~~~~~

MICHIGAN

GRAND MARAIS TRAIL
Trail Heads: Shingleton to Grand Marais
Counties: Alger & Schoolcraft
Length: 41.7 miles
Surface: Sand
Uses: Hiking, Horseback Riding, Mountain Bicycling Cross-country Skiing & Snowmobiling
Manager: Bruce Veneberg, Area Forest Manager
Lake Superior State Forest
Shingleton Forest Area M-28
Shingleton, MI 49884
(906) 452-6227

~~~~~

GRASS RIVER NATURAL AREA NATURE TRAIL
Trail Heads: Bellaire
Counties: Antrim
Length: 4 miles
Surface: Crushed stone, original ballast & dirt
Uses: Bicycling, Hiking & Cross-country Skiing
Manager: Mark Randolph
Grass River Natural Area
P. O. Box 231
Bellaire, MI 49615-0231
(616) 533-8314

~~~~~

HAYWIRE TRAIL
Trail Heads: Manistique to Shingleton
Counties: Alger & Schoolcraft
Length: 33 miles
Surface: Original ballast & cinder
Uses: Hiking, Horseback Riding, Mountain Bicycling, Cross-country Skiing & Snowmobiling
Manager: Dick Anderson, Assistant Ranger
Hiawatha National Forest
Munising Ranger District
400 East Munising,
RR #2 Box 400
Munising, MI 49862
(906) 387-2512

~~~~~

HOUGHTON WATERFRONT TRAIL
Trail Heads: Houghton
Counties: Houghton
Length: 4.5 miles
Surface: Asphalt
Uses: Bicycling, Hiking, In-line Skating, Cross-country Skiing & Snowmobiling
Manager: Scott MacInnes, Assistant City Manager
City of Houghton
P. O. Box 406
Houghton, MI 49931-0406
(906) 482-1700

~~~~~

HURON FOREST SNOWMOBILIE TRAILS
Trail Heads: Huron National Forest to Barton City
Counties: Alcona & Oscoda
Length: 95 miles
Surface: Dirt
Uses: Hiking, Horseback Riding, Mountain Bicycling & Snowmobiling
Manager: Nick Schmelter, Assistant Ranger
Huron National Forest
Huron Shores Ranger District
5761 Skeel Avenue
Oscoda, MI 48750
(517) 739-0728

~~~~~

MICHIGAN

IRON RANGE TRAILS
Trail Heads: Crystal Falls to Iron River
Counties: Iron
Length: 25 miles
Surface: Original ballast
Uses: Hiking, Horseback Riding, Mountain Bicycling Cross-country Skiing & Snowmobiling,
Manager: Dave Tuovila, District Fire & Recreation Specialist
Copper Country State Forest
P. O. Box 440
Baraga, MI 49908
(906) 353-6651

~~~~~

IRON'S AREA TOURIST ASSOCIATION SNOWMOBILE TRAIL
Trail Heads: Manistee National Forest
Counties: Lake, Manistee & Wexford
Length: 22 miles
Surface: Original ballast
Uses: Hiking, Horseback Riding, Mountain Bicycling, Cross-country Skiing & Snowmobiling
Manager: John Hojnowski, Assistant Ranger
Manistee Ranger District
1658 Manistee Highway
Manistee, MI 49660
(616) 723-2211

~~~~~

JORDAN VALLEY SNOWMOBILE TRAIL
Trail Heads: Jordan Valley
Counties: Antrim & Charlevoix
Length: 33 miles
Surface: Original ballast
Uses: Snowmobiling
Manager: Duane Hoffman, District Fire & Recreation Specialist
Mackinaw State Forest
P. O. Box 667
Gaylord, MI 49735-0667
(517) 732-3541

~~~~~

KENT TRAILS
Trail Heads: Grand Rapids
Counties: Kent
Length: 15 miles
Surface: Asphalt
Uses: Bicycling, Hiking, In-line Skating & Cross-country Skiing
Manager: Roger Sabine, Assistant Director of Planning
Kent County Road & Park Commission
1500 Scribner NW
Grand Rapids, MI 49504
(616) 242-6948

~~~~~

KEWEENAW TRAIL
Trail Heads: Houghton to Calumet
Counties: Houghton & Keweenaw
Length: 58 miles
Surface: Grass & dirt
Uses: Snowmobiling
Manager: Martin Nelson or Dave Tuovila
Copper Country State Forest
P. O. Box 400
Baraga. MI 49908
(906) 353-6651

~~~~~

MICHIGAN

KIWANIS TRAIL
Trail Heads: Adrian to Tecumseh
Counties: Lenawee
Length: 8 miles
Surface: Asphalt & original ballast
Uses: Hiking, Horseback Riding, Mountain Bicycling, In-line Skating & Cross-country Skiing
Manager: Mark Gasche, Director Community Services
Adrian City Hall
100 East Church Street
Adrian, MI 49221
(517) 263-2161

~~~~~

L'ANSE TO BIG BAY TRAIL
Trail Heads: L'Anse to Big Bay
Counties: Baraga & Marquette
Length: 54 miles
Surface: Dirt
Uses: Snowmobiling
Manager: Martin Nelson, Area Forest Manager
Copper Country State Forest
P. O. Box 400
Baraga, MI 49908-0400
(906) 353-6651

~~~~~

LAKELANDS TRAIL STATE PARK
Trail Heads: Pinckney to Stockbridge
Counties: Ingham, Jackson, Livingston & Oakland
Length: 36 miles (portions may be undeveloped)
Surface: Crushed stone & parallel gravel treadway
Uses: Bicycling, Hiking, Horseback Riding & Cross-country Skiing
Manager: Jon LaBossiere
Pinckney Recreation Area
8555 Silver Hill
Pinckney, MI 48169-8901
(313) 426-4913

~~~~~

LAKESIDE TRAIL
Trail Heads: Spring Lake
Counties: Ottawa
Length: 1.8 miles
Surface: Asphalt
Uses: Bicycling, Hiking, In-line Skating, & Cross-country Skiing
Manager: Andy Lukasik, Administrative Assistant
Village of Spring Lake
102 West Savidge Street
Spring Lake, MI 49456
(616) 842-1393

~~~~~

LITTLE FALLS TRAIL
Trail Heads: Ottawa National Forest
Counties: Gogebic & Ontonagon
Length: 6.5 miles
Surface: Original ballast & grass
Uses: Hiking, Horseback Riding, Mountain Bicycling & Snowmobiling
Manager: Wayne Petterson, Forestry Technician
Ottawa National Forest
P. O. Box 276
Watersmeet, MI 49969-0276
(906) 358-4551

~~~~~

MICHIGAN

MACKINAW/ALANSON TRAIL
Trail Heads: Mackinaw to Alanson
Counties: Emmet
Length: 24 miles
Surface: Grass, gravel & dirt
Uses: Hiking, Horseback Riding, Mountain Bicycling, Cross-country Skiing & Snowmobiling
Manager: Duane Hoffman, District Fire & Recreation Management Specialist
Mackinaw State Forest
P. O. Box 667
Gaylord, MI 49735
(517) 732-3541

~~~~~

MICHIGAN SHORE TO SHORE RIDING-HIKING TRAIL
Trail Heads: Cadillac & Empire to Sheck's Place
Counties: Benzie, Grand, Traverse, Missaukee & Wexford
Length: 75 miles – 2 separate sections: Cadillac Spur & Scheck's Place
Surface: Sand
Uses: Hiking, Horseback Riding & Mountain Bicycling,
Manager: Steve Cross, Forest Management Specialist
Forest Management Division
8015 Mackinaw Trail
Cadillac, MI 49601-9746
(616) 775-9727

~~~~~

NAHMA GRADE TRAIL
Trail Heads: Rapid River to Alger County line
Counties: Delta
Length: 32 miles
Surface: Dirt
Uses: Hiking, Horseback Riding, Mountain Bicycling, Cross-country Skiing & Snowmobiling,
Manager: Anne Okonek, Assistant District Ranger
Hiawatha National Forest
Rapid River Ranger District
8181 U. S. Highway 2
Rapid River, MI 49878-9501
(906) 474-6442

~~~~~

OLD GRADE NATURE TRAIL
Trail Heads: Glen Lake
Counties: Leelanau
Length: 1 mile
Surface: Grass
Uses: Hiking & Cross-country Skiing
Manager: William Herd, Park Ranger
Sleeping Bear Dunes National Lakeshore
9922 Front Street
Empire, MI 49630-0277
(616) 326-5134

~~~~~

MICHIGAN

PERE-MARQUETTE STATE TRAIL
Trail Heads: Baldwin to Clare
Counties: Clare, Lake & Osceola
Length: 54 miles
Surface: Original ballast
Uses: Hiking, Horseback Riding, Mountain Bicycling, Cross-country Skiing & Snowmobiling
Manager: Philip Wells,
Trailways Program Leader
Michigan Department of Natural Resources
Forest Management Division
P. O. Box 30452
Lansing, MI 48909
(517) 335-3038

~~~~~

PESHEKEE TO CLOWRY ORV TRAIL
Trail Heads: Champion
Counties: Marquette
Length: 6.1 miles
Surface: Gravel, original ballast & dirt
Uses: Hiking, Horseback Riding, Mountain Bicycling & Snowmobiling
Manager: Dennis Nezich, Area Forest Manager
Ishpeming Forest Area
Escanaba River State Forest
1985 US-41
Ishpeming, MI 49849
(906) 485-1031

~~~~~

RAILROAD TRAIL
Trail Heads: Frederick to Gaylord
Counties: Crawford
Length: 22 miles
Surface: Dirt
Uses: Snowmobiling

Manager: Phil Silverio-Mazzela, Director Alpine Snowmobile Trails, Inc.
2583 Old 27
Gaylord, MI 49735
(517) 732-7171

~~~~~

REPUBLIC-CHAMPION GRADE TRAIL
Trail Heads: Champion to Republic
Counties: Marquette
Length: 8.1 miles
Surface: Original ballast
Uses: Hiking, Horseback Riding, Mountain Bicycling & Snowmobiling,
Manager: Dennis Nezich, Area Forest Manager
Ishpeming Forest Area
Escanaba River State Forest
1985 US-41
Ishpeming, MI 49849
(906) 485-1031

~~~~~

RIVERTRAIL PARK
Trail Heads: Portland
Counties: Ionia
Length: 3.7 miles
Surface: Asphalt
Uses: Bicycling, Hiking, In-line Skating, & Cross-country Skiing
Manager: Mary Scheurer
City of Portland Parks & Recreation Department
259 Kent Street
Portland, MI 48875-1458
(517) 647-7985

~~~~~

MICHIGAN

SOO/STRONGS TRAIL
Trail Heads: Sault Ste. Marie to Strongs
Counties: Chippewa
Length: 32 miles
Surface: Original ballast & dirt
Uses: Hiking, Horseback Riding, Mountain Bicycling, Cross-country Skiing & Snowmobiling
Manager:
Raco to Strongs Section
William Rhoe, District Ranger
Hiawatha National Forest
Sault Ste. Marie Ranger District
4000 I-75, Business Spur
Sault St. Marie, MI 49783
(906) 635-5511

Sault Ste. Marie to Raco Section
Mike Renner, Area Manager
Sault St. Marie Forest Area
Lake Superior State Forest
P. O. Box 798
Sault St. Marie, MI 49783
(906) 635-5281

SOUTH LYON RAIL-TRAIL
Trail Heads: South Lyon
Counties: Oakland
Length: 2.7 miles
Surface: Asphalt
Uses: Bicycling, Hiking, In-line Skating & Cross-country Skiing
Manager: Rodney Cook, City Manager
City of South Lyon
214 West Lake Street
South Lyon, MI 48178-1377
(810) 437-1735

ST. IGNACE TO TROUT LAKE TRAIL
Trail Heads: St. Ignace to Trout Lake
Counties: Mackinac
Length: 26 miles
Surface: Crushed stone
Uses: Bicycling, Hiking, Horseback Riding & Snowmobiling
Manager: Joe Hart, Assistant District Manager
Hiawatha National Forest
1498 West US-2
St. Ignace, MI 49781
(906) 643-7900

TAHQUAMENON FALLS STATE PARK TRAILS
Trail Heads: Tahquamenon Falls State Park
Counties: Chippewa & Luce
Length: 35.9 miles
Surface: Dirt & grass
Uses: Hiking & Cross-country Skiing
Manager: Jon Spiels, Park Interpreter
Tahquamenon Falls State Park
Route 48, Box 225
Paradise, MI 49768
(906) 492-3415

MICHIGAN

TRAVERSE AREA RECREATION TRAIL (TART)
Trail Heads: Traverse City to Acme
Counties: Grand Traverse
Length: 7.8 miles (portions may be undeveloped)
Surface: Asphalt
Uses: Bicycling, Hiking, In-line Skating & Cross-country Skiing
Manager: Mike Dillenbeck, Manager Grand Traverse County Road Commission
3949 Silver Lake Road
Traverse City, MI 49684
(616) 922-4848

WATERSMEET/LAND O'LAKES TRAIL
Trail Heads: Watersmeet to Land O'Lakes
Counties: Gogebic
Length: 8.8 miles
Surface: Original ballast
Uses: Hiking, Horseback Riding, Mountain Bicycling & Snowmobiling
Manager: Wayne Petterson, Forestry Technician
Ottawa National Forest
P. O. Box 276
Watersmeet, MI 49969-0276
(906) 358-4551

WELLSTON AREA TOURIST ASSOCIATION SNOWMOBILE TRAIL
Trail Heads: Manistee National Forest
Counties: Lake & Manistee
Length: 51.5 miles
Surface: Original ballast
Uses: Snowmobiling
Manager: Greg Peterson, Forester Manistee Ranger District
1658 Manistee Highway
Manistee, MI 49660
(616) 723-2211

WEST BLOOMFIELD TRAIL NETWORK
Trail Heads: West Bloomfield Township
Counties: Oakland
Length: 5.3 miles
Surface: Crushed stone
Uses: Bicycling, Hiking & Cross-country Skiing
Manager: Sally Slater-Pierce or Joey Spano
West Bloomfield Parks & Recreation Commission
4640 Walnut Lake Road
West Bloomfield, MI 48323
(810) 334-5660

MICHIGAN

WEST CAMPUS BICYCLE PATH
Trail Heads: Eastern Michigan University
Counties: Washtenaw
Length: 1 mile
Surface: Asphalt
Uses: Bicycling, Hiking & In-line Skating
Manager: Dan Klenczar
Eastern Michigan University
Physical Plant
Ypsilanti, MI 48197
(313) 487-4194

WHITE PINE STATE PARK
Trail Heads: White Pine State Park
Counties: Kent Mecosta, Montcalm, Osceola, & Wexford
Length: 92 miles
Surface: Original ballast
Uses: Hiking, Horseback Riding, Mountain Bicycling, Cross-country Skiing & Snowmobiling
Manager: Paul Yauk
Michigan Department of Natural Resources Parks & Recreation Division
P. O. Box 30257
Lansing, MI 48909
(517) 335-4824

MINNESOTA

AFTON TO LAKELAND
Trail Heads: Afton to Lakeland
Counties: Washington
Length: 3.4 miles
Surface: Asphalt
Uses: Bicycling, Hiking, In-line Skating & Cross-country Skiing
Manager: Jerry Skelton
P. O. Box 2050
St. Paul, MN 55109
(612) 770-2311

~~~~~

ARROWHEAD STATE TRAIL
Trail Heads: Kabetogama State Forest
Counties: Koochiching & St. Louis
Length: 143 miles
Surface: Original ballast
Uses: Hiking, Horseback Riding, Mountain Bicycling Cross-country Skiing & Snowmobiling
Manager: Ron Porter, Area Supervisor
Minnesota DNR Trails & Waterways Unit
P. O. Box 388
406 Main Street
Tower, MN 55790
(218) 753-6256

~~~~~

BLUE OX TRAIL
Trail Heads: Bemidji to International Falls
Counties: Beltrami, Itasca & Koochiching
Length: 107.3 miles
Surface: Original ballast
Uses: Hiking, Horseback Riding, Mountain Bicycling & Snowmobiling
Manager: Ardon Belcher
Minnesota DNR Trails & Waterways Unit
2115 Birchmont Beach Road, NE
Bemidji, MN 56601
(612) 296-6048

~~~~~

GANDY DANCER
Trail Heads: St. Croix State Forest to Nemadji State Forest
Counties: Carlton & Pine
Length: 31 miles
Surface: Original ballast
Uses: Hiking, Horseback Riding Cross-country Skiing & Snowmobiling
Manager: Kevin Arends, Area Supervisor
Minnesota DNR Trails & Waterways Unit
Route 2, 701 South Kenwood
Moose Lake, MN 55767
(218) 485-5410

~~~~~

MINNESOTA

GATEWAY SEGMENT OF THE WILLARD MUNGAR TRAIL
Trail Heads: St. Paul to Pine Point Regional Park
Counties: Ramsey & Washington
Length: 20 miles (portions may be undeveloped)
Surface: Asphalt & parallel gravel treadway
Uses: Bicycling, Hiking, Horseback Riding In-line Skating & Cross-country Skiing,
Manager: Larry Killien, Area Supervisor
Minnesota DNR Trails & Waterways Unit
1200 Warner Road
St. Paul, MN 55106-6793
(612) 772-7935

~~~~~

LAKEWALK TRAIL
Trail Heads: Canal Park Museum to Leif Erikson Park
Counties: St. Louis
Length: 3.2 miles
Surface: Asphalt & wood planks
Uses: Bicycling, Hiking, In-line Skating, Cross-country Skiing & Snowmobiling
Manager: Sue Moyer, Director
Duluth Parks & Recreation Department
City Hall, Room 330
411 West First Street
Duluth, MN 55802-1102
(218) 723-3337

~~~~~

MINNEHAHA TRAIL
Trail Heads: Fort Snelling State Park to Minneapolis
Counties: Hennepin
Length: 5 miles
Surface: Asphalt
Uses: Bicycling, Hiking, In-line Skating & Cross-country Skiing
Manager: Bob Piotrowski, Assistant Park Manager
Fort Snelling State Park
Highway 5 & Post Road
St. Paul, MN 55111
(612) 725-2390

~~~~~

MINNETONKA LOOP
Trail Heads: Minnetonka
Counties: Carver & Hennepin
Length: 24 miles
Surface: Crushed stone
Uses: Bicycling & Hiking
Manager: Robert Hill, Loop Trail Coordinator
City of Minnetonka
14600 Minnetonka Blvd
Minnetonka, MN 55345
(619) 938-7245

~~~~~

MINNEWASKA SNOWMOBILE TRAIL
Trail Heads: Starbuck to Villard
Counties: Pope
Length: 25 miles
Surface: Gravel & dirt
Uses: Snowmobiling
Manager: William Anderson, Trail Manager
Douglas Area Trails Association
P. O. Box 112
Alexandria, MN 56332
(612) 834-2033

~~~~~

MINNESOTA

RICHMOND TO WILLMAR
***Trail Heads*:** Richmond to Willmar
Counties: Kandiyohi & Stearns
Length: 36 miles (portions may be undeveloped)
Surface: Asphalt & crushed stone Parallel grass trail
Uses: Bicycling, Hiking, Horseback Riding, In-line Skating, Cross-country Skiing & Snowmobiling
Manager: Jeff Brown, Trail Manager Minnesota DNR
P. O. Box 508
New London, MN 56273
(612) 354-4940

Gregg Soupir
Minnesota DNR Trails & Waterways Unit
P. O. Box 457
Spicer, MN 56288-0457
(612) 796-6281

~~~~~

TACONITE STATE TRAIL
***Trail Heads*:** Ely to Grand Rapids
Counties: St. Louis
Length: 176 miles
Surface: Original ballast
Uses: Hiking, Horseback Riding, Mountain Bicycling, Cross-country Skiing & Snowmobiling
Manager: Ron Porter, Area Supervisor Minnesota DNR Trails & Waterways Unit
P. O. Box 388
406 Main Street
Tower, MN 55790
(218) 753-6256

WEST RIVER PARKWAY
***Trail Heads*:** Minneapolis
Counties: Hennepin
Length: 5.5 miles (potions may be undeveloped)
Surface: Asphalt & concrete
Uses: Bicycling, Hiking, In-line Skating & Cross-country Skiing
Manager: Bob Mattson, Park & Recreation Planner
Minneapolis Park & Recreation Board
200 Grain Exchange
400 South Fourth Street
Minneapolis, MN 55415
(612) 661-4824

~~~~~~~~~~~~~~~~~~~~

WISCONSIN

BANNERMAN TRAIL
Trail Heads: Red Granite to 5 miles south of Wautoma
Counties: Waushara
Length: 7 miles
Surface: Grass & dirt
Uses: Bicycling, Hiking, Horseback Riding & Snowmobiling
Manager: Scott Schuman
Parks Superintendent
Waushara County Parks
Wautoma, WI 54982
(414) 787-7037

~~~~~

BUFFALO RIVER STATE PARK TRAIL
Trail Heads: Fairfield (or Fairchild) to Mondovi
Counties: Buffalo, Eau Claire, Jackson, & Trempealeau
Length: 36.4 miles
Surface: Original ballast & dirt
Uses, Hiking, Horseback Riding, Mountain Bicycling Cross-country Skiing & Snowmobiling,
Manager: Jean Rygiel,
Trails Coordinator
Wisconsin Department of Natural Resources
Western Division
1300 West Clairmont Avenue
P. O. Box 4001
Eau Claire, WI 54701-6127
(715) 839-1607

~~~~~

BUGLINE TRAIL
Trail Heads: Menomonee Falls to Merton
Counties: Waukesha
Length: 13 miles
Surface: Crushed Stone & Parallel dirt treadway
Uses: Bicycling, Hiking, Horseback Riding & Snowmobiling
Manager: David Burch, Senior Landscape Architect
Waukesha County Parks & Planning Commission
1320 Pewaukee Road
Waukesha, WI 53188
(414) 548-7790

~~~~~

BURLINGTON TRAIL
Trail Heads: Burlington to Rochester
Counties: Racine
Length: 4 miles
Surface: Crushed Stone & Gravel
Uses: Bicycling, Hiking & Cross-country Skiing
Manager: Tom Statz, Director
Park Planning & Program
Racine County Public Works Department
14200 Washington Avenue
Sturtevant, WI 53177-1253
(414) 886-8440

~~~~~

WISCONSIN

CAT TAIL TRAIL
Trail Heads: Almena to Amery
Counties: Barron & Polk
Length: 28.9 miles (portions may be undeveloped)
Surface: Gravel
Uses: Hiking, Horseback Riding, Mountain Bicycling & Snowmobiling
Manager: Polk County Information Center
710 Highway 35 South
ST. Croix Falls, WI 54024
(800) 222-7655

~~~~~

CLOVER CREEK TRAIL
Trail Heads: Chequamegon National Forest
Counties: Price
Length: 15.8 miles
Surface: Grass & dirt
Uses: Hiking, Horseback Riding, Mountain Bicycling & Snowmobiling
Manager: Victor W. Peterson, Forestry Technician
Chequamegon National Forest
1170 South 4th Avenue
Park Falls, WI 54552
(715) 762-2461

~~~~~

FLORENCE COUNTY SNOWMOBILE TRAIL
Trail Heads: Nicolet National Forest
Counties: Florence
Length: 32.4 miles
Surface: Gravel & dirt
Uses: Hiking, Horseback Riding, Mountain Bicycling & Snowmobiling
Manager: Dave Poquette, Assistant Ranger
Nicolet National Forest
USFS-Florence Ranger District
HC 1, Box 83
Florence, WI 54121
(715) 528-4464

~~~~~

FORT ATKINSON KOSHKONONG TRAIL
Trail Heads: Fort Atkinson to Koshkonong
Counties: Jefferson
Length: 4 miles
Surface: Asphalt & crushed stone
Uses: Bicycling, Hiking & Cross-county Skiing
Manager: Joe Nehmer, Director
Jefferson County Parks Department Courthouse
320 South Main Street
Jefferson, WI 53549
(414) 674-7260

~~~~~

HIAWATHA TRAIL
Trail Heads: Tomahawk to Sara Park
Counties: Lincoln
Length: 10.6 mile (portions may be undeveloped)
Surface: Crushed stone
Uses: Bicycling, Hiking & Snowmobiling
Manager: William Wengeler, County Forestry Administrator
Lincoln County Forestry Land & Parks
Courthouse Building
Merril, WI 54452
(715) 536-0327

~~~~~

WISCONSIN

HILLSBORO TRAIL
Trail Heads: Hillsboro to Union Center
Counties: Juneau
Length: 4.3 miles
Surface: Crushed stone
Uses: Bicycling, Hiking & Snowmobiling
Manager: Dale Darrow, Administrator
Juneau County Forest & Parks Department
250 Oak Street
Mauston, WI 53948
(608) 847-9390

~~~~~

ICE AGE TRAIL
Trail Heads: Langlade County Forest
Counties: Langlade
Length: 18.4 miles
Surface: Gravel & original ballast
Uses: Hiking, Horseback Riding, Mountain Bicycling, Cross-country Skiing & Snowmobiling
Manager: Michael Sohasky, County Forest Administrator
Langlade County Forestry Department
P. O. Box 460
Antigo, WI 54409-0460
(715) 627-6236

~~~~~

IRON HORSE TRAIL
Trail Heads: Manitowish to Frontier Campground
Counties: Iron
Length: 55 miles
Surface: Gravel
Uses: Hiking, Mountain Bicycling & Snowmobiling
Manager: Tom Salzmann, Administrator
Iron County Forestry Office
603 Third Avenue
Hurley, WI 54537
(715) 561-2697

~~~~~

KENOSHA COUNTY BIKE TRAIL
Trail Heads: Racine County line to Illinois state line
Counties: Kenosha
Length: 14.2 miles
Surface: Asphalt & crushed stone
Uses: Bicycling, Hiking & Cross-country Skiing
Manager: Ric Ladine, Director of Parks
Kenosha County Parks
P. O. Box 549
Kenosha, WI 53104-0549
(414) 857-1862

~~~~~

KIMBALL CREEK TRAIL
Trail Heads: Nicolet National Forest
Counties: Forest
Length: 12 miles
Surface: Original ballast & parallel dirt treadway
Uses: Hiking, Horseback Riding, Mountain Bicycling & Snowmobiling
Manager: Bill Reardon, Forestry Technician
Nicolet National Forest
Eagle River Ranger District
P. O. Box 1809
Eagle River, WI 54521
(715) 479-2827

~~~~~

WISCONSIN

LAKE COUNTY TRAIL
Trail Heads: Delafield to Waukesha
Counties: Waukesha
Length: 8 miles
Surface: Asphalt & crushed stone
Uses: Bicycling & Hiking
Manager: David Burch, Senior Landscape Architect
Waukesha County Parks & Planning Commission
1320 Pewaukee Road
Waukesha, WI 53188
(414) 548-7790

MRK TRAIL
Trail Heads: Racine to Caledonia
Counties: Racine
Length: 5 miles
Surface: Crushed stone, gravel & original ballast
Uses: Bicycling, Hiking & Cross-country Skiing
Manager: Tom Statz, Director Park Planning & Program
Racine County Public Works Department
14200 Washington Avenue
Sturtevant, WI 53177-1253
(414) 886-8440

NEW BERLIN TRAIL
Trail Heads: Waukesha to West Allis
Counties: Waukesha
Length: 6 miles
Surface: Crushed stone
Uses: Bicycling & Hiking

Manager: David Burch, Senior Landscape Architect
Waukesha County Parks & Planning Commission
1320 Pewaukee Road
Waukesha, WI 53188
(414) 548-7790

NORTH SHORE TRAIL
Trail Heads: Racine to Kenosha County line
Counties: Racine
Length: 8 miles (portions may be undeveloped)
Surface: Crushed stone & gravel
Uses: Bicycling, Hiking & Cross-country Skiing
Manager: Tom Statz, Director Park Planning & Programs
Racine County Public Works Department
14200 Washington Avenue
Sturtevant, WI 53177-1253
(414) 886-8440

OLD ABE TRAIL
Trail Heads: Chippewa Falls to Cornell
Counties: Chippewa
Length: 17 miles
Surface: Original ballast
Uses: Snowmobiling
Manager: Jean Rygiel, Trails Coordinator
Wisconsin DNR Western Division
1300 West Clairmont Avenue
P. O. Box 4001
Eau Claire, WI 54701-6127
(715) 839-1607

WISCONSIN

OLIVER-WRENSHALL TRAIL
Trail Heads: Oliver to Wrenshall
Counties: Douglas
Length: 12 miles
Surface: Grass & dirt
Uses: Hiking, Horseback Riding, Mountain Bicycling, Cross-country Skiing & Snowmobiling,
Manager: David Epperly or Mark Schroeder
Douglas County Forestry Department
P. O. Box 211
Solan Springs, WI 54873
(715) 378-2219

PECATONICA STATE PARK TRAIL
Trail Heads: Calamine to Belmont
Counties: Grant & Lafayette
Length: 18 miles (portions may be undeveloped)
Surface: Crushed stone
Uses: Bicycling, Hiking, Horseback Riding, Cross-country Skiing & Snowmobiling
Manager: Stephen Hubner, Trail Coordinator Tri-County Trail Commission
627 Washington Street
Darlington, WI 53530
(608) 776-4830

RILEY LAKE SNOWMOBILE TRAIL
Trail Heads: Chequamegon National Forest
Counties: Price
Length: 23 miles
Surface: Dirt & grass
Uses: Hiking, Horseback Riding, Mountain Bicycling, Cross-county Skiing & Snowmobiling
Manager: Victor Peterson, Forestry Technician
Chequamegon National Forest
1170 Fourth Avenue South
Park Falls, WI 54552
(715) 762-2461

RUSH LAKE TRAIL
Trail Heads: Berlin to Ripon
Counties: Winnebago
Length: 5.3 miles
Surface: Original ballast
Uses: Hiking, Horseback Riding & Mountain Bicycling
Manager: Jeffrey A. Christensen, Parks Director
Winnebago County Parks
500 East County Road Y
Oshkosh, WI 54901
(414) 424-0042

TRI-COUNTY CORRIDOR
Trail Heads: Ashland to Superior
Counties: Ashland, Bayfield & Douglas
Length: 61.8 miles
Surface: Asphalt & original ballast
Uses: Hiking, Mountain Bicycling & Snowmobiling
Manager: Richard Mackey
P. O. Box 503
Ashland, WI 54806
(715) 682-5299

WISCONSIN

WATERFORD-WIND LAKE TRAIL
Trail Heads: Waterford to Wind Lake
Counties: Racine
Length: 5 miles
Surface: Crushed stone & gravel
Uses: Hiking, Mountain Bicycling & Cross-country Skiing
Manager: Tom Statz, Director Park Planning & Program
Racine County Public Works Department
14200 Washington Avenue
Sturtevant, WI 53177-1253
(414) 886-8440

WAUKESHA BIKE TRAILS
Trail Heads: Waukesha
Counties: Waukesha
Length: 2.5 miles
Surface: Asphalt & crushed stone
Uses: Bicycling, Hiking & In-line Skating
Manager: David Kopp, City Planner Waukesha City Planning Room 200
201 Delafield Street
Waukesha, WI 53188-3690
(414) 524-3752

WIOUWASH TRAIL
Trail Heads: Hortonville to Oshkosh
Counties: Outagamie & Winnebago
Length: 20.3 miles
Surface: Crushed stone & original ballast
Uses: Hiking, Horseback Riding, Mountain Bicycling & Snowmobiling
Manager:
Outagamie County Section
Christopher Brandt, Director
Outagamie County Parks
1375 East Broadway Drive
Appleton, WI 54915
(414) 832-4790

Winnebago County Section
Jeffrey Christensen, Director
Winnebago County
Department of Parks
500 East County Road
Oshkosh, WI 54901
(414) 424-0042

WOODVILLE TRAIL
Trail Heads: Woodville to St Croix County line
Counties: St. Croix
Length: 7 miles
Surface: Gravel & dirt
Uses: Hiking, Horseback Riding, Mountain Bicycling & Snowmobiling
Manager: Sue Nelson, County Clerk
Government Center
1101 Carmichael Road
Hudson, WI 54016
(715) 386-4600

Allen Stene, Chairman Woodville Trail Committee
210 South Main Street
P. O. Box 302
Woodville, WI 54028-9546
(715) 698-2401

| **GENEVA PUBLISHERS, INC.** | **ORDER INFORMATION** |

To order additional copies of this travel guide
Send check or money order for $15.95 plus $4.00
shipping and handling Payable to:

Geneva Publishers, Inc.
P.O. Box 926
Williams Bay, WI 53191

Please write or e-mail Geneva Publishers, Inc.

- To receive update notifications on forthcoming United States Rail-Trail Travel Guides. Information is available on the following travel guides: **Mid-Atlantic, Northeast, Northwest, Southeast, Southwest** and **West.**
- To be placed on our mailing list.
- Send us a note — Geneva Publishers, Inc is interested in your comments and/or suggestions about our Rail-Trail travel guide series.

genevapb@genevaonline.com   (414) 245-0848 phone & FAX